RESALE PRICE MAINTENANCE
IN PRACTICE

RESALE PRICE MAINTENANCE IN PRACTICE

J. F. PICKERING

University of Sussex

London

GEORGE ALLEN & UNWIN LTD

RUSKIN HOUSE   MUSEUM STREET

PRINTED IN GREAT BRITAIN
in 11 point Georgian type by
THE BLACKFRIARS PRESS LTD
LEICESTER

PREFACE

The history of resale price maintenance in this country dates back at least to the end of the last century and its influence has, until recently, spread over an increasingly wide range of products. This has given rise to a certain amount of public concern and several committees of inquiry have investigated the practice. The Restrictive Trade Practices Act, 1956, banned the worst features of the system of enforcement of r.p.m. while strengthening the hands of the individual manufacturer who wished to continue to insist on the maintenance of a prescribed resale price on his products.

The Resale Prices Act, 1964, has now cast a greater cloud over r.p.m. by making it necessary for suppliers who wish to continue to enforce a minimum resale price to justify their claim before the Restrictive Practices Court. It seems that in many of the trades where r.p.m. has traditionally been important suppliers will attempt to obtain permanent exemption for their goods from the general prohibition. Even if the Court does find the continuance of r.p.m. on most goods not to be in the public interest it will be some years before all the applications for exemption are disposed of.

In this book I have tried to provide an objective examination of the way in which r.p.m. has operated in the consumer goods sector of the British economy in recent years, especially in the light of the changes made by the Restrictive Trade Practices Act. During the course of my research it has become increasingly clear that the possibility of benefit accruing to the consumer from the abolition of r.p.m. depends very much on the structure of the distributive channels handling the products concerned. It is, therefore, my hope that this book will not only serve as a record of developments in the field of resale price maintenance since 1956 but will also help shed some light on the British retail trades.

The information on which much of this study is based was collected by means of extensive field work carried out between 1962 and 1964 while I was a research student in the Department of Political Economy at University College, London. Many people co-operated in my work. I had the opportunity of personally consulting more than 100 people including fellow academics, lawyers, editorial staff of trade journals, trade association officials and members of manufacturing and distributive organisations. Additional information was collected by means of mail questionnaires. One questionnaire was sent to a stratified sample of 700 manufacturers of consumer goods, 44% of whom replied. The results from this survey are referred to in various places in the text. In addition, the major price survey discussed in Chapter X was conducted by means of a mail questionnaire. To all who have helped by placing information at my disposal I offer my thanks. This book could not have been written without their assistance.

Financial aid for my research was provided by the University of London in the form of a University Postgraduate Studentship, supplemented by grants from the Irwin and Central Research Funds. A grant from the Staff Travel Fund of the University of Durham has recently made it possible for me to investigate the Register of applications for exemption from the general ban on r.p.m. provided for in the Resale Prices Act.

Professor G. C. Allen supervised my work which was submitted in an earlier form as a doctor's thesis to the University of London. To his kindly encouragement and advice I owe a great deal. I wish also to express my gratitude to Professor B. S. Yamey and Mr Henry Smith who commented upon earlier drafts of the manuscript, to Mrs V. L. Korah for helpful advice on Chapters V and VI and to Mr W. J. Corlett for guidance in the presentation of results contained in Chapter X. They have all helped clarify and improve the presentation of the material. Needless to say, I alone bear full responsibility for the facts and opinions which this book contains.

Some of the material included in Chapters V and VI first appeared in an article in *Public Law*, Autumn 1965, and is here reproduced by permission of the Editor.

Finally, I wish to pay tribute to the encouragement and

support of my parents without which the research for this book could not have been undertaken and to thank Miss Dorothy Pridie who has provided invaluable secretarial assistance in the preparation of successive drafts of the manuscript.

J.F.P.

University of Durham
December 1965

CONTENTS

CHAPTER I

THE HISTORICAL BACKGROUND

Resale price maintenance is the policy by which a supplier stipulates and enforces the price at which his product may be resold. This means that any article which is subject to such a condition is sold at the same price in all outlets. Whilst the distributor still has to sell the product by displaying it and providing, where necessary, service both before and after sale, he is therefore relieved by the supplier of the responsibility for fixing an appropriate price. Only when a product is branded by the manufacturer and so appears in each outlet as an easily identifiable, homogeneous, entity does the imposition of a fixed resale price condition of sale by suppliers become practicable.

Accordingly it was only near the end of the last century that price maintenance became significant and this coincided with the development of manufacturer branding and advertising. One of the first products on which r.p.m. was imposed was Alfred Marshall's *Principles of Economics* published in 1890. (Though we should note the information provided by Professor Arnold Plant that resale price maintenance had existed on books in the first half of the nineteenth century but had been abandoned in 1852.[1]) It is generally held that r.p.m. was adopted by manufacturers as a trading policy in response to pressure from retailers, a view which Professor B. S. Yamey has substantiated with factual data from the grocery, chemists' goods and cigarette and tobacco trades.[2] An alternative explanation that manufacturers adopted r.p.m. as a trading policy without external pressure being brought to bear on them has been put forward by the late

[1] A. Plant – 'The Distribution of Proprietary Articles', in Plant ed. *'Some Modern Business Problems'*. (London) 1937 p. 323.
[2] B. S. Yamey – 'The Origins of Resale Price Maintenance', *Economic Journal* vol. 62 (1952) p. 522 and *'The Economics of Resale Price Maintenance'*, (London) 1954.

Sir Henry Clay. His argument was that the development of r.p.m. and of branding and packaging,

'are the outcome of the tendency for producers to reach out towards the consumer and to endeavour to limit variations (both from one retailer to another and from one time to another) in type of product, price and terms of sale.[1]

Having started in the book trade the practice quickly spread to groceries, confectionery and cigarettes and tobacco and then to chemists' goods, stationery and after the First World War to some new trades such as photographic goods and electrical appliances. The first trade association to be formed for the enforcement of resale price maintenance is widely held to have been the Proprietary Articles Trade Association formed in 1896, followed by the Publishers Association founded in the same year and which introduced its first Net Book Agreement in 1900. However, the former secretary of the British Motor Trade Association has shown that in 1891 a Federation of Grocers' Associations of the United Kingdom was set up whose aim was a mutual agreement between their manufacturer, wholesaler and retailer members that price cutters would not be supplied with price controlled products.[2] This Federation then influenced and guided the founding of the P.A.T.A. five years later.

As resale price maintenance became more widespread, so too did the use of trade associations for collective enforcement on behalf of a number of manufacturers. In many cases they set up private enforcement systems to deal with price cutters by means of fines and even the Stop List for persistent offenders. There are two reasons why associations used private courts rather than normal legal processes. In the first place some associations were registered as trade unions and as such were affected by section 4 of the Trade Union Act, 1871, which provided that an agreement between members of a trade union concerning the conditions on which any members should or should not sell their goods could not be enforced in a court of law.[3] Secondly, the ordinary courts had refused to enforce fixed resale prices against a third party.

[1] Sir Henry Clay – 'Resale Price Maintenance', *Journal of Industrial Economics* vol. 3 (1954) p. 9.
[2] K. C. Johnson-Davies – '*Control in Retail Industry*'. (London) 1945. p. 2.
[3] Trade Union Act 1871 (34 & 35 Vict. c31) s. 4(1).

Thus a manufacturer could enforce his conditions against a wholesaler or retailer whom he supplied direct, but he had no remedy against a trader who acquired the goods via an intermediary. The two cases which determined the law on this point were, *Taddy* v. *Sterious* in 1904 and *Dunlop* v. *Selfridge* in 1915.[1] Patented articles were an exception to this since in a decision in 1911 it was held that the resale price condition could run with such goods and the manufacturer had a right of action against a third party.[2]

So, encouraged by force of circumstances, in a number of trades r.p.m. was enforced privately through the mechanism of the relevant trade association. As with many new practices, the enforcement of resale price maintenance was challenged at law. During the latter part of the nineteenth century the courts had been greatly exercised over the validity of restrictive trading agreements and from an earlier position of hostility to such agreements had, by 1900, become willing to uphold and enforce any agreement so long as it was –

(a) reasonable as between the parties

(b) neither a tortuous nor a criminal conspiracy, even where injury to another had been caused, so long as no malicious intention to injure existed and no illegal act committed.

Although we cannot dwell on the law relating to restraints on trade, we should note in passing that whilst many cases had at this time helped in the formation of the above principles, to three cases in particular has been accorded much of the significance of the court's support for restrictive agreements.[3] This triology of cases consists of the Mogul case,[4] *Allen* v. *Flood*[5] and *Quinn* v. *Leatham*.[6] They were all decided on appeal in the House of Lords and greatly contributed to a favourable legal climate towards restrictive practices which undoubtedly helped when resale price maintenance also became an issue before the courts at the turn of the century.

[1] [1904] 1Ch. 354 and [1915] A.C. 847.
[2] *National Phonograph Co. of Australia* v. *Menck* [1911] A.C. 336.
[3] cf. R. O. Wilberforce, A. Campbell & N. P. M. Elles. 'The Law of Restrictive Trade Practices and Monopolies' (London) 1957 para. 228.
[4] *Mogul Steamship Co. Ltd.* v. *McGregor, Gow & Co.* [1892] A.C. 25.
[5] *Allen* v. *Flood* [1898] A.C. 1.
[6] *Quinn* v. *Leatham* [1901] A.C. 495.

Both the enforcement of r.p.m. by individual manufacturers and the use of collective enforcement procedures became issues before the courts. Three cases heard between 1900 and 1930 established that an agreement between a supplier and a distributor to maintain fixed resale prices was enforceable at law,[1] though, as we have already observed, this did not apply to goods acquired for resale by third parties.

The use of collective enforcement procedures was also upheld in a number of actions brought to determine their legality. The first such decision was reached in 1921 in *Ware and de Freville* v. *Motor Trade Association*.[2] Here the judgment upheld the right of the association to place the plaintiff's name on a Stop List because he sold a car at a price above that fixed by the association. It was decided that to publish such a Stop List was in a *bona fide* protection of the trade interests of the members of the association (the plaintiffs were not members) and that the use of such a Stop List could not be held to be defamatory to those placed on it.

The development of the law was temporarily retarded in 1926 by the decision in *R.* v. *Denyer*[3] that to take a fine as an alternative to placing a person's name on a Stop List was a criminal offence. This was quickly altered by the Court of Appeal in *Hardie and Lane* v. *Chilton*[4] who concluded that where a trade association was justified in placing the name of a trader on a Stop List, it might instead lawfully adopt the more lenient course of asking the person to make, and for the association to accept, a money payment by way of compromise. This finding was confirmed by the House of Lords in 1937 in *Thorne* v. *Motor Trade Association*.[5] Here the imposition of a fine within reasonable limits in lieu of using a Stop List was held to be justifiable and not to be a demand of money with menaces and without reasonable cause within the meaning of section 29 (1) (i) of the Larceny Act, 1916,[6] as Thorne had claimed.

Thus, until 1956, a manufacturer could lawfully stop supplies from a price cutting trader, he could sue for an injunction and

---

[1] *Elliman* v. *Carrington* [1901] 2 Ch.275: *Dunlop* v. *New Garage* [1915] A.C.79: *Palmolive of England* v. *Freedman* [1927] 2 Ch.333; [1928] 1 Ch.264.
[2] [1921] 3 K.B.40.   [3] [1926] 2 K.B.258.   [4] [1928] 2 K.B.306.   [5] [1937] A.C.797.
[6] Larceny Act 1916 (6 & 7 Geo. 5, c.50).

damages where the goods were supplied direct, or groups of manufacturers could act collectively to penalize price cutting traders either by fining them or by placing their names on a Stop List.

The actual method of enforcement varied from trade to trade but in most trades there was at least a form of collective enforcement and resort to the courts by individual manufacturers for an injunction was virtually non-existent until 1956. By giving their support to collective enforcement schemes the courts had, unintentionally but indubitably, driven the enforcement of r.p.m. out of the normal courts of law into the private courts set up by trade associations.

The most elaborate collective enforcement system was that operated by the Price Protection Committee of the Motor Trade Association.[1] It dealt with both price cutting and price inflation and adopted, as far as possible, normal judicial procedures. The Chairman of the Committee was a retired colonial Judge. When the Committee found an accusation of price inflation or deflation proven the penalty was a fine which aimed to take away any profits the trader may have made by his 'illegal' exploits. The fine would therefore be between £50 and £200. Two safeguards existed. The aggrieved trader had a right of appeal to an appeal committee, again headed by an ex-colonial Judge and, secondly, the secretary of the M.T.A. could quash a decision if he felt that natural justice had been contravened. The Stop List was the ultimate sanction and was used only to deal with persistent price cutting. It was rarely needed and, apparently, no *bona fide* motor dealers were ever stop listed. In the inter-war years the M.T.A. court dealt with, on average, some 700 cases each year, but after 1945 the number dropped to about 120.

Although the courts found nothing wrong with either the individual or collective enforcement of r.p.m., public opinion was not so happy and (excluding the Monopolies and Restrictive Practices Commission) three committees of inquiry investigated the practice within thirty years or so from the end of the first world war.

At the end of the first world war the country suffered from a

[1] For a full description of this scheme see K. C. Johnson-Davies —'*The Practice of Price Maintenance*' (London) 1955.

scarcity of goods and this was reflected in a high level of prices. In the general range of investigations which were carried out between 1918 and 1921 into matters affecting the level of prices and profits, it is hardly surprising to find the practice of resale price maintenance called into question. The report was produced by a sub-committee of the Committee on Trusts and was generally favourable to the practice since it concluded that,

'Provided . . . the original price charged by the producer is a fair and reasonable one . . . the consumer . . . is not unfairly prejudiced by the system of fixed retail prices.'[1]

The reasons adduced for this conclusion were that fixed retail prices preserve the market for a product, exclude speculation by middlemen and ensure the continued existence of small retailers. The Committee recommended that where abuses of the practice were suspected they should be referred for investigation to the tribunal which the Committee on Trusts had already suggested should be set up.[2]

Economists today would hardly consider this reasoning adequate defence of resale price maintenance. The Committee overlooked completely the possibility that some traders might wish to cut prices. The reason for this is clearly to be found in the circumstances of the time. At a time of scarcity when demand is greater than supply there is little incentive to traders to cut prices and so this alternative issue did not arise. The history of British monopoly legislation and of the reports of committees of inquiry which have frequently preceded any new action, bears tribute to the influence of the economic conditions prevailing at the particular time in determining the action recommended or taken. It would in fact be surprising if this were not so.

The second inquiry into r.p.m. was initiated at a time of over-abundance of supplies and depression, during the period of office of the second Labour Government.[3] The Committee which made this report has become commonly known as the Greene Committee. The reference was –

[1] *Sub-Committee on Fixed Retail Prices* 1920 p. 5.
[2] *Report of the Committee on Trusts* 1919 Cd.9236. p. 11.
[3] *Report of the Committee on Restraint of Trade* 1931.

'To consider present trade practices which result in withholding from particular retail traders supplies of goods in which they wish to deal or which prevent the resale of such supplies except upon conditions imposed by the suppliers, and to report whether, in their opinion, all or any of such practices are detrimental to the public interest, and if so, what alterations in the existing law are necessary to prevent continuation of such practices.'

The main reason behind the creation of this Committee was the insistence of a number of manufacturers that the Co-operative dividend constituted a form of price cutting. These manufacturers either refused to supply the Co-operatives, or made them undertake not to give a dividend, or even in some cases made them add on to the retail price the value of the dividend. This treatment naturally upset the Co-operative Societies and with a Government favourable to their form of organization they were able to have the issue raised.

Unfortunately for the Co-operatives the Greene Committee was hardly sympathetic. In the first place it did not even reach a conclusion on the vital question whether the Co-operative dividend constituted a form of price cutting –

'We do not feel called upon to express any view as to the true nature of the Co-operative dividend.'[1]

Secondly, it came down in favour of resale price maintenance accepting that it prevents traders using a manufacturer's product as a loss leader thereby causing a detriment to the manufacturer since other traders refuse to handle the product. The case against price maintenance that it deflects competition between distributors away from price competition to competition on service was noted, but the Committee was not satisfied that any change in the law relating to r.p.m. would benefit the public. It decided that the right to freedom of contract should not normally be withdrawn ('without some compelling reason') and that to withhold supplies from some distributors was justifiable, though when it was suggested to the Committee that the law be eased to allow resale price conditions to run with the goods, it did not agree.

The only caveat in this report was the reference to the

[1] *Ibid.* p. 31.

importance of resale price maintenance and the use of boycotts in preserving the power of monopolies and trade associations and the Committee suggested that in a more general inquiry into monopolistic combinations and trusts 'the possibility of support being given by the price maintenance system and boycott . . . ought . . . not to be overlooked'.[1]

The Monopolies and Restrictive Practices Act, 1948, constituted the new inquiry into monopolistic combinations and trusts which the Greene Committee had anticipated and appropriately a new inquiry into resale price maintenance had already been initiated in 1947 and, under the chairmanship of Mr G. H. Lloyd Jacob, reported in 1949.[2] This report proved to be both informative and remarkably thorough with considerable effort having been made to investigate the actual working of resale price maintenance in particular industries.

The arguments for and against the practice were noted and fairly considered. The case for r.p.m. was that it ensures continuity of demand thereby making mass production techniques possible, it allows more distributors to remain in existence and the danger of loss leader selling is avoided, after sales service could continue to be given and the evidence of certain women's organizations suggested that consumers prefer fixed prices in the shops. The case against, was that high profits are allowed which leads to waste in providing unnecessary services, restriction on the freedom of distributors and the dissimilarity of distribution costs prevents manufacturers from fixing a margin which gives a fair return to all traders. The problem facing the Committee was how to avoid the potential evils of price cutting such as loss leading and quality deterioration whilst avoiding undesirable rigidity in distribution.

In reaching a conclusion the Committee made an important distinction between individual and collective enforcement of resale price maintenance. This distinction had not been made in either of the two earlier reports. In the trades which it investigated where collective action by means of a Stop List was the method of enforcement, the Committee found that its use had been taken too far since those trade associations using this

[1] *Ibid.* para. 73(f).
[2] *Report of the Committee on Resale Price Maintenance* 1949 Cmd.7696.

sanction –

'have turned price maintenance from a reasonable means of preventing damage to well-known high quality brands . . . to a comprehensive system for regulating and policing entire industries'.[1]

The Committee objected to the use of any sanction not applied through the due process of law[2] and recommended therefore that schemes for the collective enforcement of resale price maintenance should be made illegal.

So far as individual enforcement was concerned, the Committee recommended that 'no action should be taken which would deprive the individual producer of the power to prescribe and enforce resale prices for goods bearing his brand',[3] though it indicated that this was really to avoid the undesirable consequences of loss leader selling and said that r.p.m. should not be allowed to hinder the passing on to the public of the benefits of improvements in distribution. In an explanatory note, Mr Henry Smith stated that he supported the recommendations of the remainder of the Committee since they represented a marked advance from the present position. In his opinion, however, all forms of resale price maintenance were harmful. It was only because he did not think that legislation designed to limit the use of loss-leaders would be easy to frame or practicable to operate that he was prepared to support the recommendation that r.p.m. be allowed to continue in a restricted form.

Although the Committee did not suggest withdrawing the right of individual enforcement, it is significant that the report contained no suggestion that the difficulties of enforcing against third parties should be eased, even though the incongruity existing over this between patented goods and those which were not patented was recognized.

Between 1945 and 1951 the Labour Party formed the Government in this country and in June 1951 the then President of the Board of Trade, Sir Hartley Shawcross, introduced a White Paper on resale price maintenance.[4] In this the Government said that it would make illegal all collective agreements designed to ensure that goods were sold at or above specified retail prices and

[1] *Ibid.* para. 147.   [2] *Ibid.* para. 142.   [3] *Ibid.* para 163.
[4] *'A statement on Resale Price Maintenance'* 1951 Cmd.8274.

any indication, by a manufacturer or other supplier of goods, of a resale price for those goods unless that price was clearly stated to be a maximum. This meant that all forms of resale price maintenance would be declared illegal[1] other than the fixing of maximum prices and therefore went much further than the Lloyd Jacob Committee had recommended. However, in the election of 1951 the Labour Government was replaced by a Conservative one who did not, for another five years, act against resale price maintenance.

In 1948 the Monopolies and Restrictive Practices (Inquiry and Control) Act was passed.[2] This provided for the establishment of a permanent body to be known as the Monopolies and Restrictive Practices Commission. It was to report on the conditions existing and practices pursued in industries where one-third or more of a commodity was supplied in the United Kingdom or any substantial part of it, by or to any one person or group of persons acting in such a way as to restrict competition. In other words, where one firm or a group of firms connected by a restrictive trading agreement were responsible for the supply or purchase of one-third or more of the total supplies of a product the Commission could be asked to report. It was open to the Board of Trade to ask the Commission to give an opinion as to whether the practices it found were in the public interest and to suggest any action which the Commission thought should be taken to prevent or remedy undesirable consequences. In most references made to it, the Commission was asked to comment on the way in which the practices found affected the public interest.

To guide the Commission the Act enumerated certain desirable objectives in the light of which any restrictions ought to be judged. These were:

(a) efficiency in production and distribution;
(b) encouragement of new enterprise in industry and trade;
(c) the fullest use and best possible distribution of resources;
(d) to facilitate technical improvements and expansion of markets.

---

[1] With provision for exemptions in certain cases where a ban on r.p.m. would prove undesirable or unworkable. (para. 43.)
[2] 1948 (11 & 12 Geo. 6. c.66).

Provision was also made in the Act for the Commission to be asked to produce reports on the existence and working in industry generally of specific practices which it had found in its reports on particular industries.

In 1953, in answer to criticisms made by the Select Committee on Estimates[1] as a result of its inquiry into the slow progress made by the Commission, the Government introduced amending legislation[2] to speed up the work of the Commission by increasing the size of its membership and allowing it to divide into groups to make a report.

The Commission had completed eighteen reports by the time of the passing of the Restrictive Trade Practices Act in 1956 and a further three were signed in September 1956. In this study we can only concern ourselves with the opinions of the Commission regarding resale price maintenance and a separate chapter[3] is devoted later on to its findings on this practice. For convenience and for purposes of comparison, discussion of the opinions on r.p.m. expressed in the Commission's reports presented before 1956 are reserved until that later chapter. Very briefly, we may summarize the Commission's views by saying that where collective enforcement schemes or a collective agreement for the enforcement of r.p.m. were found, these were opposed, but where individual enforcement existed, the Commission did not raise any objection. In three cases, where individual enforcement was not at that time practised, the Commission said it would not favour its introduction. In one of these (*Report on the Supply and Export of Pneumatic Tyres* 1955) the reason given was that to allow individual enforcement but not collective enforcement would favour the large manufacturer at the expense of the small manufacturer and even here a minority of four strongly opposed the Commission's findings on this point. In the other two cases (*Report on the Supply of Linoleum* 1956 and *Report on the Supply and Export of Electrical and Allied Machinery and Plant* 1956) the Commission said it would not approve of individual enforcement if it did exist, but as we show in the later chapter, the opinions in these two cases are so unimportant and

[1] Sixth Report from the Select Committee on Estimates 1953.
[2] Monopolies and Restrictive Practices Commission Act 1953 (1 & 2 Eliz. 2, c.51).
[3] Chapter xiii.

unsupported by any form of justification as to be best ignored.

Thus we find that the views of the Commission on r.p.m. coincided very closely with those of the Lloyd Jacob Committee; collective enforcement was against the public interest but there was no objection to enforcement of r.p.m. by individual manufacturers. In other words, it is the method of enforcement to which objection was raised, not the practice of r.p.m. itself.

Before any general legislative action was taken to deal with r.p.m. collective enforcement was further condemned in the general report prepared by the Monopolies Commission on Collective Discrimination.[1] This was the first reference made to the Commission for a general report and is still the only one to have been completed (a second reference on common prices and level tendering was also made but was not proceeded with after the passing of the Restrictive Trade Practices Act).

The reference called on the Commission to investigate and report on all collective agreements or arrangements which required the parties to them to discriminate in their dealings with other persons. Agreements over the granting of aggregated rebates were also to be included. The enforcement of resale price maintenance as such was not therefore within the scope of the Commission report but in so far as collective action was used to enforce r.p.m. then this was within its purview. The Commission was not happy about this situation and during the course of the inquiry asked the Board of Trade whether it should not investigate r.p.m. as a whole. The Board of Trade refused to agree to this and in the course of its report the Commission emphasized that it had not been asked to pass judgment on the desirability or otherwise of resale price maintenance in general.

There were six practices which the Commission dealt with:

(a) collective discrimination by suppliers;

(b) collective discrimination by suppliers in return for exclusive buying;

(c) collective agreements to adopt conditions of sale, especially r.p.m.;

[1] Monopolies and Restrictive Practices Commission, *Collective Discrimination.* A Report on Exclusive Dealing, Collective Boycott, Aggregated Rebates and other Discriminatory Trade Practices 1955. Cmd.9504.

(d) collective agreements to enforce conditions of sale, especially r.p.m.;

(e) collective discrimination by buyers;

(f) aggregated rebates.

Each of these the Commission found to be generally contrary to the public interest, though it acknowledged that there could be instances where one or more of them might be beneficial. We are really concerned with practices (c) and (d) – collective agreements to adopt and to enforce resale price maintenance, and as such they normally exist together. They received the same condemnation as the other practices, though the Commission did observe that there might be instances where a common price yielded a benefit and the backing of a collective agreement to adopt and enforce r.p.m. was necessary to achieve this. (The Commission had reported on such a situation in its *Report on the Supply of Electric Lamps* 1951.) The Commission objected to collective enforcement of r.p.m. by means of fines, the withdrawal of trade terms and the use of the Stop List, on the grounds that this method gave too much power to trade associations and caused too great a rigidity of prices and an absence of competition between retailers which could lead to a waste of economic resources.

Although avoiding making any general comment on the desirability of resale price maintenance, the Commission declared itself opposed to collective enforcement although it acknowledged that enforcement of conditions of sale through the courts of law was difficult and expensive and that the traditional arguments against loss leader selling might be valid. A minority of four signed a note of dissent, stating that they would not favour the abolition of collective enforcement of resale price maintenance, one of the reasons given being that it was more effective than individual enforcement.

The members of the Commission were unable to reach unanimous agreement on the action to be taken to deal with these practices (those involving resale price maintenance were not here differentiated from the others). Two possible alternatives were set out. The first was the registration and investigation of all agreements to decide whether, in the light of certain predetermined criteria, the practices in each trade were in the public interest. Those found not to be in the public interest would be prohibited by Statutory Order. This was not a new recommendation - it had been suggested in the *Report of the Committee on Trusts* in 1919 but it had the apparent advantage of being less drastic than the alternative and therefore more likely to gain the support of industry and would, furthermore, provide a better understanding of the problems on which more general legislation could be based later. The alternative was to prohibit all those agreements covered by the reference for the Commission's general report with provision for granting exceptions in approved instances.

Although a minority of three favoured the former approach because they did not think that sufficient evidence had been forthcoming to justify such drastic legislative action as was proposed in the alternative, the majority of the Commission favoured the latter, more dogmatic, approach. A number of arguments were put forward for this method. It would be quicker, would avoid duplication of the work of the Commission and overall would probably mean that fewer investigations would have to be carried out.

The three members who wanted registration and case by case investigation were three of the four who also stated that they did not think that collective enforcement of r.p.m. was always contrary to the public interest. The fourth member of this group, whilst supporting the dogmatic approach of general prohibition of the agreements investigated, joined with the other three dissenters in suggesting that schemes for the collective enforcement of r.p.m. should be subject to registration and case by case investigation.

There is no doubt that this report was most influential and convinced the Government of the need to introduce legislative action to deal with restrictive practices in industry. So far as restrictive practices in general are concerned, the Government, in the Restrictive Trade Practices Act 1956, chose to adopt the more pragmatic approach of registration and case by case investigation advocated by the minority. It is arguable that it really had no practicable alternative. The Collective Discrimination Report covered six practices known to be used extensively in industry. The Commission's reports on particular industries had also dealt with other practices, some of which, such as common price fixing and quota fixing, occurred even more frequently than those investigated in the general inquiry. To introduce legislation banning just the six practices would have been piecemeal legislation. To ban also price and quota fixing without having much condemnatory evidence on these practices would have been unjustifiable. The Government might have waited for the second general report - on common prices and level tendering - before introducing the new Bill, although it is understood that a long wait for this report would have been necessary and even then all possible restrictive practices would still not have been covered. Thus, whilst the new Bill did not move as fast as the majority of the Commission would have liked, it was moving in the right direction in adopting the pragmatic approach outlined in the Collective Discrimination Report.

The only instance where the majority recommendation in the Collective Discrimination Report was adopted was in the case of collective enforcement of resale price maintenance. As we have seen in this chapter, although the courts had given legal backing to collective enforcement, various inquiries and public opinion had opposed the practice and the Government, as a result, decided to make illegal the methods used in this form of price maintenance.

CHAPTER II

THE RESTRICTIVE TRADE PRACTICES ACT, 1956[1]

In this study we are really only concerned with the way in which the Restrictive Trade Practices Act affected resale price maintenance. Primarily this involves Part II of the Act, though, as we shall discover, both the first and third parts of the Act have also had an important bearing on r.p.m. in particular trades. In this chapter we shall therefore merely summarize the provisions of the first and third parts of the Act but the provisions of Part II will be dealt with in a little more detail.

The preamble to the Act states clearly the intentions behind the legislation –

'the registration and judicial investigation of certain restrictive trading agreements, and for the prohibition of such agreements when found contrary to the public interest.

to prohibit the collective enforcement of conditions regulating the resale price of goods and to make further provisions for the individual enforcement of such conditions by legal proceedings.

to amend the Monopolies and Restrictive Practices Acts 1948 and 1953.'

The agreements which have had to be registered are those made between two or more persons carrying on business in the United Kingdom in the production or supply of goods or in the application to goods of any process of manufacture and which provide for the fixing of prices or discounts, allocation of quotas, market sharing, discrimination between purchasers or any agreement over the method of manufacture of a product.[2] Agreements relating to the construction of buildings and other work by contractors are also specifically included within the meaning of the

[1]Restrictive Trade Practices Act 1956 (4 & 5 Eliz. 2, c.68)
[2]Section 6(1)

28

Act and this includes therefore agreements for level tendering.[1] An agreement is defined as any agreement or arrangement whether or not it is intended to be enforceable at law, and also includes any negative obligation.[2] Agreements made by trade associations and recommendations from a trade association to its members are also registrable and are to be treated as if binding on all the members of the association concerned.[3]

A new post was created – Registrar of Restrictive Trading Agreements. The holder is responsible for compiling a register of all the agreements which the Act requires to be registered. It is also the responsibility of the Registrar to bring the agreements before the Restrictive Practices Court for investigation.[4]

Certain types of agreement are specifically exempt from registration. The most important are those between inter-connected bodies corporate or individuals carrying on business in partnership with each other; agreements authorized under the Iron and Steel Act 1953; agreements to maintain standards approved by the British Standards Institution and agreements concerning the supply of labour. Agreements relating to manufacture under patents or trade marks and agreements relating solely to exports or other activities where the goods are not imported into the United Kingdom are also not registrable.[5] Discretion is left to the Board of Trade acting on the advice of the Registrar to authorize the removal of any restrictions which are found to be of no substantial economic significance.[6]

The second stage in this method of dealing with restrictive practices is judicial investigation. Agreements are investigated by the Restrictive Practices Court – a superior court of record having the status of a branch of the High Court. It is unusual (though not unique in British legal institutions) that both lawyers and laymen sit as judges in the Court. A simple majority of those judges hearing a case determines the Court's decision and, as it is a civil court, judgment is given on the balance of the probabilities only. Either party may appeal to the Court of Appeal on a point of law but there is no appeal on a question of fact.

There is a general presumption in the Act that 'a restriction

---

[1] Section 36(2).   [2] Section 6(3).   [3] Section 6(6) and 6(7).
[4] Sections 1 and 20(2)(a).   [5] Sections 7 and 8.   [6] Section 12.

accepted in pursuance of any agreement shall be deemed to be contrary to the public interest'.[1] The function of the Court is therefore to apply this presumption and, in its adjudication on registered agreements referred to it, only to declare the restriction to be in the public interest if the parties to it have managed successfully to make out a case under one or more of the 'gateways' specified in section 21 and have then further convinced the court in the 'tailpiece' that the advantages of the restriction outweigh any detriments arising from its operation. Only then may the Court declare a restriction to be in the public interest. The 'gateways' under which the parties may seek to defend their restrictive arrangements can be summarized as follows:

(a) that the restriction is necessary to protect the public against injury.

(b) that removal of the restriction would deny to the public other specific and substantial benefits and advantages.

(c) that the restriction is necessary to counteract measures taken by any person, not a party to the agreement, to restrict competition.

(d) that the restriction is necessary to facilitate the negotiation of fair terms with a powerful buyer or seller.

(e) that removal of the restriction would cause serious and persistent unemployment in any area.

(f) that removal of the restriction would cause a substantial loss in either the volume of exports or in earnings from exports.

(g) that the restriction is necessary to maintain any other restriction between the parties which has been found to be not contrary to the public interest.

The 'tailpiece' requires the Court to be satisfied that 'The restriction is not unreasonable having regard to the balance between those circumstances and any detriment to the public or to persons not parties to the agreement . . . resulting or likely to result from the operation of the restriction'.[2]

Attention should here be drawn to the fact that the operative term is 'restriction' rather than 'agreement'. This acknowledges the fact that many agreements have more than one restriction

[1] Section 21(1).   [2] Section 21(1).

and so leaves the way clear for the Court to approve part of an agreement but to declare another part contrary to the public interest.

Where the Court finds a restriction to be contrary to the public interest, this automatically becomes void and the Registrar may also ask for an order to be made restraining 'all or any of the parties to the agreement who carry on business in the United Kingdom –

(a) from giving effect to, or enforcing or purporting to enforce, the agreement in respect of those restrictions;

(b) from making any other agreement (whether with the same party or with other parties) to the like effect'.[1]

Such orders may also be made against trade associations and parties to agreements which have been voluntarily determined or varied by the parties concerned after proceedings have commenced. It is in the Court's discretion to decide whether to make an Order or not and early cases have shown that the Court does not usually consider this to be necessary. Should there be a material change in the circumstances affecting the parties to an agreement which has been adjudicated upon by the Court, either the parties to the agreement or the Registrar may ask the Court to vary the declaration or Order, which had previously been made concerning the agreement.[2]

This, then, is the machinery which has been created for the investigation and control of restrictive trading agreements. It follows closely the recommendation made by the minority in the Monopolies Commission report on Collective Discrimination, though they did not anticipate that any such legislation would embody a general presumption that such agreements were *prima facie* contrary to the public interest unless proved otherwise.

Having made restrictive trading agreements subject to judicial investigation the Government had therefore taken away a large area of activity from the Monopolies Commission. In Part III of the Act the position of the Commission was amended to take account of this development. First of all the full title of the Commission was significantly changed from 'Monopolies and Restrictive Practices Commission' to 'Monopolies Commission'.[3]

[1] Section 20 (3).   [2] Section 22.   [3] Section 28(1).

The Commission was still to be responsible for investigating monopolies of scale and to make general reports when called upon to do so and it was now also to be responsible for investigating agreements relating solely to exports which the Act required to be registered with the Board of Trade.[1] Thus, whilst the Commission had removed from its sphere of activity those practices on which it spent the greater part of its time until 1956, it did still potentially retain considerable powers; but in fact the Board of Trade has not used them fully. Evidence that it was intended to reduce the future activities of the Commission was given in the Act when the maximum size of the Commission was reduced from twenty-five to ten and their previous right to exercise their functions in small groups was withdrawn.

The Act contained two major changes in the law relating to resale price maintenance. First, certain forms of collective action to deal with price cutting were prohibited. Secondly, an individual supplier, for the first time (other than on patented goods), was given the right to take legal action against a trader who was cutting the price of his products where the two were not in a direct contractual relationship with each other.

Section 24 made illegal agreements between two or more persons to discriminate against dealers selling goods at other than the fixed price by either withholding supplies from them or by agreeing to supply only on less favourable terms. The usual methods of collective enforcement action - the exaction of fines and other penalties and the conduct of domestic proceedings - were specifically mentioned in the section and prohibited. Similarly, distributors were not to agree to discriminate against, or refuse to handle the goods of, manufacturers who refused to enforce fixed resale price conditions on their products. Trade association activities were specifically included within the scope of this section.[2]

Two exceptions were allowed. Normal business contracts between a supplier and a single purchaser were not disturbed and they might still continue to give undertakings to each other over the goods involved in such a contract.[3] Thus a manufacturer who supplied a wholesaler could still obtain an agreement from the wholesaler that he would not supply a price cutting

[1] Section 31(1).   [2] Section 24(5).   [3] Section 24(3).

retailer, but an agreement to the same effect between two or more manufacturers or wholesalers would be illegal. Inter-connected bodies corporate were also excepted from this section.[1] Where two or more companies were members of the same group of companies (i.e. inter-connected bodies corporate), they could still agree amongst themselves to take collective action against price cutters. An interesting example of this could have arisen in the case of, say, the Unilever group of companies where Birds Eye Foods Ltd., Batchelors Foods Ltd., Van den Berghs Ltd., T. Wall and Sons Ltd., Lever Brothers Ltd., etc., could all lawfully have agreed to refuse to supply goods to a particular price cutting trader.

Where this section is contravened no criminal offence arises. The Crown or an individual may bring a civil action for an injunction or other appropriate relief. Chitty also argues that if a third party (e.g. a retailer) suffers injury as a result of a collective agreement for the enforcement of resale prices, he may also sue the participants to the agreement in conspiracy on the grounds that their agreement involves the use of unlawful means.[2]

This was the only instance in the Restrictive Trade Practices Act where the majority recommendation contained in the Collective Discrimination report was accepted by the Government as a basis for legislative action. In view of the hardening of opinion against collective enforcement on the part of such investigating committees as the Lloyd Jacob Committee and the Monopolies Commission itself, and indeed the growth of general public hostility towards this practice, especially after the publication of the Commission's report on Pneumatic Tyres in which the motor trade's system of private courts was described, it is not surprising that the Government decided it was justified in acting to make this practice illegal.

Whilst section 24 aimed at removing the worst features of the resale price maintenance system, the Act did not go as far as many opponents of r.p.m. would have liked and ban the practice altogether. Section 25 did in fact strengthen the power of the individual manufacturer in acting against a price cutter, by allowing him to take legal proceedings against any dealer not

[1] Section 26(2). [2] *Chitty on Contracts* Vol. II 22nd edition (London) 1961 p. 572.

C

in direct contractual relationship with the supplier. By giving this new legal power the Government helped the manufacturer to overcome his disability in the enforcement of r.p.m. that the decision in *Dunlop* v. *Selfridge* had shown up and which was also part cause for the establishment of the private trade courts which were now being prohibited. If r.p.m. was to remain as a viable system then it was only logical and proper that this right to act against third parties should be given to the manufacturer.

To succeed in an action brought under section 25 the manufacturer had to prove that the retailer had notice that the goods concerned were subject to a fixed price condition and then to prove that the prices of his products were being cut. Having proved his case satisfactorily the manufacturer might, at the court's discretion, be granted an injunction restraining the defendant from selling any of the plaintiff's goods in breach of the fixed price condition.[1] This is a better remedy than that which was available under the common law where such injunctions related solely to the product which had been price cut and not to all the other products of the same manufacturer. The grant of a general injunction in this way is important in that it saves the manufacturer the cost and effort involved in seeking a separate injunction in respect of each of his products against each price cutter. The grant of an injunction is also without prejudice to any other legitimate relief such as the award of damages or the right of the manufacturer to refuse to supply.

Section 26 included within the scope of this part of the Act any condition which a price maintaining supplier imposed against the giving of either an immediate or deferred discount. The giving of trading stamps and the Co-operative dividend could therefore be treated as breaches of an r.p.m. condition. Limitations on the size of part exchange allowances and hire purchase terms could also be treated as subject to r.p.m. within the terms of the Act. The inclusion of the Co-operative dividend as by implication a form of price cutting was a cause of concern to the Co-operative Union. Although manufacturers in a number of leading consumer goods industries had resolutely refused to supply the Co-operative Societies for many years on the grounds

[1] Section 25(4)

that their dividends constituted a form of price cutting, this was the first time that official support for this view had been forthcoming. Despite efforts by Co-operative M.P.s during the debates on the Bill to have this particular provision excluded or some safeguard written into the Act to exempt the Co-operative dividend from its terms, they proved unsuccessful.

Two questions need now to be asked about the sections dealing with r.p.m. Are sections 24 and 25 consistent with each other and with the rest of the Act, and secondly, what did the Government hope to achieve by these two sections? It may well be argued that a section strengthening a manufacturer's right to prevent price competition between distributors of his goods is rather incongruous in an Act whose general aim is to restore competition in industry wherever undesirable restrictions are found. Although there is, no doubt, justification for this point of view, we would argue that no alternative policy towards the individual enforcement of resale price maintenance would have been justified at that time. As has already been seen, no committee of inquiry had raised any objections to resale price maintenance as enforced by individual manufacturers which would have justified a general prohibition of the practice. The only articulate condemnation of all forms of r.p.m. had come from certain economists[1] and even then there were some who upheld the practice.[2] Certainly then, this did not constitute a satisfactory justification for Government action in banning the individual enforcement of resale price maintenance too. Having decided that there was no cause for such action, it would seem to be only logical that any difficulties found in enforcing r.p.m. in this way should be overcome. The main difficulty was that resale price conditions could not run with the goods so, in order to assist the manufacturer effectively to enforce his conditions of sale, the Government logically amended the law so that legal action could now be taken against price cutters who were strangers to the original contract.

Section 24 was, of course, in keeping with the spirit of the rest of the Act and was even complementary to it since the collective

[1] E.g. J. D. Kuipers 'Resale Price Maintenance' (Wageningen) 1950. B. S. Yamey 'The Economics of Resale Price Maintenance' (London) 1954.
[2] E.g. Sir Henry Clay op. cit.

action of manufacturers in enforcing r.p.m. was often part of a wider policy of collective price fixing and general restraint on competition between manufacturers. Conversely, the action of the Restrictive Practices Court in declaring void agreements between manufacturers providing for the limitation of quantity discount terms and adherence to lists of approved dealers, could in itself contribute to a weakening of resale price maintenance. Thus section 24 was complementary to the spirit and intentions of the rest of the Act and if section 25 was hardly that, at least it was the correct decision on the evidence available to the Government at the time and by making the conditions run with the goods and making them enforceable against less direct forms of price cutting, the Government were taking the only reasonable and logical step open to them.

What did the Government hope to achieve by this action? The opinion most commonly held, especially amongst those in the trades closely concerned with r.p.m., is that this was a *quid pro quo* - in return for manufacturers giving up the most undesirable features of the system - collective enforcement - the hand of the individual manufacturer would be strengthened and in fact industry was largely satisfied with the deal. The change in the law relating to enforcement through the courts was expected to help especially the smaller manufacturers who had hitherto relied heavily on collective enforcement and who therefore in theory at least stood to lose most from its abolition. In practice, however, it is suggested that since the evidence is that price cutting tends to be concentrated for promotional reasons on the leading brands in a trade, this was a protection the small manufacturer rarely needed to rely upon.

A further possible explanation is that whilst the Government was prepared to allow resale price maintenance to continue, it wanted to ensure that each manufacturer chose to adopt the practice as a matter of independent policy rather than being forced to do so as a result of collective pressure brought upon them as it was believed happened under the old system. There are those who interpret sections 24 and 25 as a political compromise, acting in response to the public outcry against the methods used in collective enforcement whilst pandering to the views of small shopkeepers (traditional Conservative voters) and others who thought they depended on the retention of r.p.m. for their livelihood. This may be a cynical view, it may even be right (!), but as we have shown, whatever the true explanation for the Government's action, there was no alternative really open to it.

During the Parliamentary debates on the Bill the Labour Party argued that all forms of r.p.m. should be made illegal. The Conservatives' case against this and in defence of section 25 makes interesting reading. For example, in the House of Commons, Mr Derek Walker-Smith M.P. stated that,

'On balance there is a proper place for individual resale price maintenance in our economic system.'[1]

whilst in the House of Lords, Lord Kilmuir admitted that the Government was seeking a *via media* in the matter of resale price maintenance, but claimed that the effects of the measures contained in the Bill would be to give –

'Some measure of stability in distribution from the manufacturers' point of view without causing stagnation or denying the public the benefits of new or cheaper methods.'[2]

It is difficult to see how in any one trade the policy on r.p.m. enumerated in the Act could be expected to achieve both stability and competition in distribution. Neither is there any guarantee that the distributive trades most needing stability would find it and those most needing competition would achieve this.

Whether there was a genuine belief on the part of the Government in the economic desirability of any form of resale price maintenance must be open to some doubt. Besides the apparent uncertainty in the two statements quoted above and the 'woolly thinking' in the latter, two other points need to be borne in mind. In the first place, Mr Peter Thorneycroft, who was then President of the Board of Trade, is widely believed to have favoured the abolition of all forms of r.p.m. Thus it was reliably reported to the present writer that the Government were hoping that the measures contained in the Act would bring to an end all forms of resale price maintenance. This was considered to be needed in order to reduce the cost of living and also to speed

[1] *Hansard* volume 551 (Commons) col. 2038.
[2] *Hansard* volume 198 (Lords) col. 1010.

up innovation in the distributive trades; the Collective Discrimination report had shown that self service was not developing as fast as it should and a newspaper article had claimed that in the years 1951-1954 there had been a 10% increase in the number of staff employed in distribution in order to deal with a 5% increase in sales volume.[1] There was at least some support for the view that banning collective enforcement would cause the complete breakdown of r.p.m. since in his study of the subject, J. D. Kuipers found –

> 'The history of British trading since the end of the nineteenth century has shown that, in most trades it is quite impracticable for individual producers to operate their own systems of resale price maintenance.'[2]

However, Kuipers does not make it clear whether this is because manufacturers did not have the right to act against third parties or whether without collective enforcement action no other means of enforcing r.p.m. could succeed.

Whilst the major developments relating to r.p.m. were to be expected from the operation of Part II of the Act, actions arising as a result of Parts I and III might also affect r.p.m.

First, resale price maintenance could come under the scrutiny of the Restrictive Practices Court.[3] Any group of manufacturers could agree to individually impose and/or legally enforce fixed resale price conditions on their products. This was not banned by section 24 but was a registrable agreement falling within Part I of the Act and referrable to the Court for defence under one or more of the 'gateways' specified in section 21. If the agreement was found to be in the public interest it could be retained, but what would happen if such an agreement were declared contrary to the public interest? Clearly it would become void but the question also arises – would the manufacturer lose the right to enforce his fixed price conditions under section 25? The relevant subsection in the Act reads –

> 'Nothing in this section shall be construed as enabling any person to enforce a condition imposed in pursuance of any restriction which is declared by an order of the Restrictive

---

[1] *Financial Times* August 18, 1955.
[2] Kuipers *op. cit.* p. 247.
[3] See below chapter xii.

Practices Court for the time being in force under Part I of the Act to be contrary to the public interest' (s.25(3)).

Wilberforce, discussing this point, says that,

'Such an agreement is registrable under section 6 and may be declared invalid under section 20. In that event the individual supplier (not withstanding section 25) could not enforce the term against persons acquiring his goods. In other words a defendant to proceedings brought under section 25 may set up as a defence that the supplier is party to an agreement which has been declared invalid under section 20. The supplier might of course reply that the condition would have been imposed in any event and that it was not imposed in pursuance of any agreement and it would be a question of fact whether this was so or not.'[1]

Another commentator also agrees that,

'Provided [a supplier] is in no way acting in pursuance of any agreement with other suppliers, he is entitled to impose resale price conditions when selling his goods and . . . he may enforce such conditions.'[2]

Thus an adverse judgment in the Restrictive Practices Court on an agreement to adopt or enforce resale price maintenance would not automatically deny a supplier the right to seek redress against price cutters under section 25. If a trader argued in his defence, where such a situation arose, that the manufacturer was taking enforcement action only because of this agreement then the manufacturer would not succeed under section 25, if the courts upheld the defence plea on this very delicate question of fact. If this were the case, failure of the manufacturer to obtain an injunction would be a very minor part of his worries, since such a successful defence would mean that the court accepted that although the agreement had been declared void under section 20 the parties were still giving effect to its provisions and this would constitute contempt of court which is punishable by fine or imprisonment! Thus it is likely that a finding by the Restrictive Practices Court under Part I of the 1956 Act that an agreement relating to resale price maintenance

1 Wilberforce, Campbell and Elles *op. cit.* para. 931.
2 Heathcote Williams, Roberts and Bernstein – '*The Law of Restrictive Trade Practices and Monopolies*'. (London) 1956 p. 87.

was contrary to the public interest would not deprive the individual manufacturer acting alone of his rights under section 25 of that Act.[1]

A potentially more serious conflict could arise between the provisions of Part II and Part III of the Act. During the course of its investigations the reconstituted Monopolies Commission might come across a situation where a manufacturer in a monopolistic position (as defined in the 1948 legislation) was enforcing fixed price conditions against his distributors. If, upon investigation, the Commission found that in this particular instance the practice was contrary to the public interest (as they have in fact done[2]) it would then still be open to Parliament to make an Order declaring such a practice by the particular firm under investigation to be unlawful[3] (an action which Parliament has not taken since 1956). In the event of such an Order being made, it would deny the organization concerned the right to the statutory powers provided for the individual enforcement of resale price maintenance under section 25 of the 1956 Act.

The effects which the Restrictive Trade Practices Act was likely to have on the enforcement of resale price maintenance seemed to depend upon three important factors. The first was the way in which the courts would interpret the wording of the relevant sections in answer to the legal arguments which plaintiffs and defendants could be expected to put forward; secondly, the extent to which manufacturers, separated from the moral support and protection of other suppliers enforcing the same policy, sufficiently believed in r.p.m. to be prepared to enforce it alone; and thirdly, the extent to which distributors were able to bring effective pressure to bear on manufacturers to cause them to drop the practice.

For those who wanted to see sudden and marked increases in competition as a result of the Act, 1956 was an unpropitious time to introduce the legislation since it was a period of rising demand

[1] A number of manufacturers who did not defend agreements which included provision for r.p.m. before the Restrictive Practices Court and therefore had their agreements declared contrary to the public interest have, in fact, continued successfully to obtain injunctions under section 25 to restrain price cutting traders.
[2] See below ch. xiii.
[3] Under the Monopolies and Restrictive Practices (Inquiry and Control) Act 1948 section 10(2).

and scarcity of supplies - a legacy of the war and immediate post-war period. This was especially true of the consumer goods trades and meant that any manufacturer or distributor who had products to sell could find a market without much difficulty. As supplies became more plentiful and were sufficient and even more than sufficient to meet demand, then the real challenge to resale price maintenance was to be expected.

CHAPTER III

THE IMPORTANCE OF R.P.M.
IN 1956

Resale price maintenance only becomes a live issue when there is a desire on the part of distributors of a particular product to cut the price of it. Any attempt to estimate the actual extent to which resale price maintenance is practised in an economy is therefore fraught with difficulties. On some products such as groceries, cigarettes and tobacco and chemists' goods there has been at various times a considerable amount of price cutting and so schemes have been organized to act against this. In other trades, however, there has been little or no attempt to cut prices with the result that it is hard to be certain whether resale price maintenance exists or not. Economic conditions directly affect this. Where demand for a product is in excess of supply there is no incentive to cut prices, indeed the problem here is preventing overcharging, as the motor trade discovered in the inter-war years. This also explains why there was little price cutting in general between 1939 and 1955. Only when the economic climate changes and supplies become plentiful and perhaps demand becomes depressed is there any incentive to cut prices and it is only then that a manufacturer's true policy over resale price maintenance becomes clear.

A further problem is that where a trader wishes to cut the price of an article he will almost always cut the prices of the products of the major manufacturers – the brand leaders. These are the lines on which his price cuts will have the greatest appeal to the greatest number of consumers. Such manufacturers, if they favour r.p.m., will have to take the appropriate steps to ensure that price cutters are dealt with, manufacturers of lesser brands will rarely be troubled by price cutting and there will therefore be less incentive to them to adopt r.p.m. as a condition of sale, even though they may in fact strongly favour r.p.m. as a trading policy.[1] It has also been found that if one manufacturer adopts r.p.m. as a condition of sale, all other competing manufacturers tend to follow suit, and conversely, if one manufacturer successfully drops r.p.m. others who are aiming similar products at the same market will normally also cease enforcing.

A number of other factors also tend to hamper any assessment of the extent of r.p.m. Not all outlets sell the same range of products and the importance of price maintained articles varies widely from shop to shop; thus a department store, such as Harrods, sells a much smaller percentage of manufacturer branded and price maintained lines than a small independent retailer who relies on such brands for his business. In recent years there has been a considerable increase in vertical integration in the manufacture and distribution of consumer goods with manufacturers opening their own shops and (more frequently) retailers adopting their own brand labels and either manufacturing themselves or arranging for suppliers to manufacture to their specifications. The Marks and Spencer organization is the classic example of the latter. This whole process has been appropriately termed by Mr Frank Friday 'direct price maintenance'.[2] The use of direct selling methods such as were employed by the Bloom organization also reduce the practical significance of resale price maintenance, as also does the growing tendency to hire rather than purchase certain consumer durables such as television sets. Chapter VIII considers various other forms of concealed price cutting such as high trade-in allowances which also tend to reduce in practice the importance of r.p.m.

A further complication arises in some trades where a 'quasi' form of r.p.m. is to be found. The manufacturer recommends a price and does not give the required notice that maintenance of this price is a condition of sale, but the price is still observed because it has always been the custom of the trade. This situation holds especially true in the fashion goods trade. In a number of others including further sections of the clothing trade and soft furnishings and furniture, replies to a questionnaire sent to

[1] The chemists goods trade provides a useful illustration of this point. Between 1956 and 1964 the Proprietary Articles Trade Association had between 220 and 260 manufacturer members but only a dozen or so found their products being regularly price cut.
[2] P. W. S. Andrews and Frank A. Friday – *'Fair Trade'* (London) 1960 p. 10.

manufacturers showed that many of these only recommended prices but that where cases of price cutting had been reported to them, they had taken appropriate action to prevent a recurrence either by a personal approach to the trader concerned or by cutting off supplies. In some trades, where wholesalers are not of much importance, the manufacturer can still effectively deal with price cutting by stopping supplies and so does not need to give the formal notice that r.p.m. is a condition of sale which legal action for an injunction under section 25 of the Restrictive Trade Practices Act requires. The register of applications for exemption from the prohibition of resale price maintenance under the Resale Prices Act 1964 gives further support to the view that many manufacturers insist on fixed resale prices being observed although they do not make r.p.m. a legally enforceable condition of sale.

As we have already seen (Chapter I), resale price maintenance really started in this country in the late 1890s and by 1900 only about 3% of consumer expenditure was on price maintained goods. As manufacturer branding increased, so the importance of r.p.m. grew. Besides some old-established trades adopting r.p.m., new industries such as photographic and electrical goods were adopting this as a policy from the beginning. A monograph written in 1933 by an American - E. T. Grether - showed that on groceries and confectionery there was then little r.p.m. but that r.p.m. was very effective in the book and photographic trades, whilst big outbreaks of price cutting were being successfully prevented in others.[1]

The *Manchester Guardian Commercial* published during 1938 and 1939 an important series of articles dealing with the extent of resale price maintenance. These contain much useful material and indicate that collective action to enforce resale price maintenance through the operation of a Stop List was then to be found in the grocery, ironmongery, cigarette, chemist, cycle and motor cycle, book, motor car, tyre and petrol trades.[2] The cycle and electrical equipment industries maintained lists of approved dealers where the effect was similar to a Stop List. A similar list

[1] E. T. Grether - 'Resale Price Maintenance in Great Britain' (Berkeley) 1935.
[2] Though it is doubtful whether an effective collective enforcement scheme existed on ironmongery and petrol.

of approved dealers had also existed in the sports goods trade but had ended in June 1936, after operating for a year and a half, because of the reluctance of manufacturers to refuse to supply a trader just because he was cutting prices on the products of another manufacturer.

Resale price maintenance was also enforced by individual manufacturers without the support of a collective scheme on radios, confectionery and to an increasing extent on drapery lines. The articles indicate that the steps taken by the manufacturers had been quite successful in controlling the price cutting which had existed a few years before. Undoubtedly the formation of several new collective enforcing bodies helped this, whilst there was also a growing tendency in many trades for manufacturers to collectively approve new retailer entrants before they could obtain supplies. This, too, helped keep out price cutters.

By 1938, the National Institute of Economic and Social Research estimated in evidence to the Lloyd Jacob Committee, some 30% of consumer expenditure was on goods which were price maintained.[1] Two other estimates tended to support this. Dr J. B. Jeffereys offered a 'rough calculation' that for the same year between 27% and 35% of all consumer goods, sold to domestic consumers in the U.K., carried a fixed or recommended price,[2] the present writer in an estimate based on a list of commodities in which r.p.m. amounted to over 50% of production in 1938, calculates that these products covered some 32% of all consumer expenditure on goods.

During the war and immediate post-war years resale price maintenance became increasingly important in theory as manufacturer branding and advertising increased, even though the scarcity of supplies meant that in practice, except in isolated cases, resale price conditions rarely had to be enforced. Dr Mark Abrams, in an article in *The Times* of 22 January, 1955, estimated that in 1954, 55% of all consumer goods were price maintained. In 1950, J. D. Kuipers made a careful study of the importance of r.p.m. in the grocery trade and estimated that roughly 20% of consumer grocery purchases were price

[1] *Op. cit.* **para. 5.**
[2] J. B. Jeffereys – '*The Distribution of Consumer Goods*' (Cambridge) 1950 p. 112.

maintained, the exact amount depending on the economic class of the family.[1] Even then, however, he found that some manufacturers were reluctant to act against price cutters, especially in areas such as East London where price cutting was the norm. The figure Kuipers gave seems to be rather on the low side, the reason being that in a number of cases where all the leading manufacturers enforced r.p.m. he did not include the products of the smaller manufacturers, though as we have already shown, there is no reason for them to enforce r.p.m. because there is no cutting on their brands.

Before the Restrictive Trade Practices Act was passed there were three methods of enforcing resale price maintenance. A supplier could withhold supplies, he could take legal action for an injunction and for damages for breach of contract from a trader who obtained supplies direct, or collective sanctions could be applied through a trade association. There was little recourse to the normal courts of law, for where a distributor was supplied direct, supplies could easily be withheld and in most of the trades where wholesalers exercised an important function, collective enforcement schemes existed.[2]

The Lloyd Jacob Report listed fifteen trades where resale price maintenance was collectively enforced, thirteen of these were concerned with goods normally bought by consumers; in four there was no Stop List and in a further five the Stop List was rarely used. This left four trades where collective enforcement by means of a Stop List was really important – chemists' goods, groceries, cigarettes and tobacco and motor vehicles and accessories. The Lloyd Jacob Report did in fact overlook two other collective enforcement schemes in operation at the time in the wines and spirits and sports goods trades. Neither was used to any great extent.

It is estimated that the proportion of all consumer expenditure going on products covered by the four main collective

[1] Kuipers *op. cit.* p. 215.
[2] In some trades such as ironmongery where wholesalers were important, no effective scheme for collective enforcement existed. Here in theory it was the responsibility of the wholesaler to give notice of the manufacturer's conditions of sale and to enforce them. In practice this was impossible because of the large number of lines handled and so the wholesaler would wait until he knew of a case of price cutting, would then warn the retailer and if he persisted, refuse to supply.

enforcement schemes was about 11% whilst the other trades where a Stop List was rarely used covered only another 2% consumer expenditure, so the direct influence of section 24 of the 1956 legislation in banning collective enforcement of r.p.m. would be felt on little more than 13% of all the goods and services purchased by consumers (17% consumer expenditure on goods alone).

An estimate as to the exact importance of resale price maintenance at the time of the passing of the Act is, for the reasons we have already discussed, very difficult. The 55% suggested by Dr Abrams seems to be rather high. Professor Yamey in his Hobart Paper published in 1960, arrived at a 'cautious estimate' that 25% of personal consumer expenditure was on price-maintained articles.[1] If we exclude from this figure services, house rents and rates, gas and electricity and other such charges then we might say that about one-third of consumer expenditure on goods alone was subject to r.p.m. In answer to Yamey's paper, which was a general attack on resale price maintenance, Andrews and Friday published 'Fair Trade' setting out the case for resale price maintenance. In the course of this, Friday made a careful estimate of the extent of r.p.m. and concluded that it covered 23% of expenditure on goods and services, with direct price maintenance covering a further 17%. If services are excluded, as we have done for Yamey's figures, a figure of 30% r.p.m. and 10% d.p.m. is arrived at. This figure Andrews and Friday regarded as a maximum. They said – 'We have had to define r.p.m. as sale under r.p.m. conditions whether or not the manufacturer has insisted on those conditions of sale. This definition has inevitably meant that sales have been included where there has not in effect been any enforcement of resale prices.'[2] The weakness in this calculation would appear to be that they have not taken into account those important instances where r.p.m. is not a legally binding condition of sale but where, nevertheless, the recommended price is treated as binding and any cases of price cutting are dealt with by the manufacturer cutting off supplies.

[1] B. S. Yamey 'Resale Price Maintenance and Shoppers Choice' (London) 1960 p. 8.
[2] Andrews and Friday op. cit. p. 7.

The time at which Yamey and Friday made their calculations was further particularly unfortunate, since by 1958 r.p.m. in the grocery trade had begun to break down, though they made no direct allowance for this in either of their calculations.[1] The table opposite indicates, so far as can be ascertained, an estimate of the approximate importance of r.p.m. in each trade at the time the Act was passed. Three gradings have been used for this purpose, thereby endeavouring to avoid the pitfalls of attempting too accurate a measure of a situation which no longer exists. An independent calculation of the extent of resale price maintenance suggests that in 1956 maybe some 34% of consumer expenditure was on goods and services where resale price maintenance was either legally enforced or was traditionally followed in the trade, 44% on goods alone. The major differences between this calculation and those of Friday and Yamey are an increase in the importance attributed to r.p.m. in the grocery and clothing trades.

Generally speaking, where a collective enforcement scheme was to be found, there wholesalers tended to be rather more important in the distributive system than in other trades, the only exceptions being in the cases of paint and wallpaper and hardware where no effective collective enforcement schemes existed, but where wholesalers were important and sports goods where, despite the existence of a form of collective enforcement, wholesalers were not important.

Thus we can summarize by saying that at the time of the passing of the Restrictive Trade Practices Act, schemes for the collective enforcement of r.p.m. covered about 13% of consumer expenditure on goods and services and on a further 15%-20% resale price maintenance was practised by individual manufacturers.

The 13% subject to collective enforcement would be directly affected by the prohibition of the use of Stop Lists, etc., but these self-same trades were those which stood to benefit most from the provision in section 25 which allowed resale price conditions to be imposed at law on third parties. So far as the remaining 87% of consumer expenditure on goods and services was con-

---

[1] Friday does offer a revised figure assuming that all r.p.m. on groceries had disappeared. *Ibid.* p. 7.

cerned, including the 15%-20% where there was individual enforcement of resale price maintenance, the direct effects of the change in the law on r.p.m. would be negligible though there might be indirect effects which could not be assessed in advance.

TABLE I

Resale Price Maintenance at the time of the Restrictive Trade Practices Act

	Collective Enforcement Scheme	Extent of R.P.M.
Food	Yes	b
Alcoholic drinks	Yes	b
Cigarettes and Tobacco	Yes	c
Paint and wallpaper	No	b
Furniture and floor coverings	No	a
Electrical appliances	Yes[1]	c
Soft furnishings	No	a
Hardware	No	b
Clothing	No	b
Motor vehicles including running costs	Yes	b
Cycles and motor cycles	No[2]	c
Books, newspapers etc.	Yes[3]	c
Stationery	Yes	b
Chemists goods	Yes	c
Other goods – photographic, sports, toys etc.	Yes[4]	b

Grading : a   0 – 25% sales subject to r.p.m.
        b   26% – 66% sales subject to r.p.m.
        c   67% – 100% sales subject to r.p.m.

Notes :
1. Both the British Electrical Appliance Manufacturers Association and the Electric Light Fittings Association operated a list of approved dealers which, in practice, achieved the same effect as a Stop List. There had been a Stop List on radio valves but this was dropped in the early 1950s during the Monopolies Commission investigations.
2. Although a collective enforcement scheme in the cycle and motor cycle trade was mentioned in the Lloyd Jacob Report, this was ended before the Restrictive Trade Practices Act was passed.
3. Books only.
4. Sports goods only.

D

CHAPTER IV

THE PROHIBITION OF COLLECTIVE ENFORCEMENT

Section 24 of the Restrictive Trade Practices Act prohibited the main forms of collective action at which so much public opposition had been directed in the six or seven years immediately prior to the passing of the Act. Two or more suppliers were no longer to agree to withhold supplies from price cutters, or to deal with them on less favourable terms and the use of private trade courts with fines and Stop Lists was also made illegal. As we have seen, collective enforcement procedures covered about 13% of all consumer expenditure in this country, many trades had provision for such a scheme though only in a few trades had it been frequently employed.

During the course of the Restrictive Trade Practices Bill through Parliament, many trade associations began to look carefully at those clauses dealing with resale price maintenance to discover exactly how they would be affected. The climax to their attentions came during the Committee stage of the Bill in the House of Lords, when the Lord Chancellor, Lord Kilmuir, stated –

> 'I hope it will be clear that trade associations will be able to assist individual manufacturers to enforce their resale price conditions without incurring any liability to registration under Part I of the Bill and – this is important – provided, first that there is no undertaking express or implied by the manufacturers to enforce their prices, and secondly, that such assistance is permissible under the ordinary law.'[1]

Thus, the appointment of a trade association to act as the agent of a manufacturer, in the enforcement of fixed resale price conditions, was given specific encouragement and it was highly unlikely that this view would be reversed in a court of law.

[1] *Hansard* vol. 198 (Lords) col. 1023.

Despite this, some trade associations did fold up because collective enforcement was prohibited. The Tobacco Trade Association was wound up immediately the Act was passed and each individual manufacturer promptly announced that he would continue to enforce resale price maintenance, and, apart from a small increase in the amount of price cutting in the last four months of 1956, no ill effects were felt and r.p.m. has remained strong. (One thing the ending of the T.T.A. did allow was the reintroduction of gift coupons. The members of the T.T.A. had all undertaken not to give them but directly the Association was wound up the manufacturers of Kensitas cigarettes reintroduced gift coupons.) In some industrial goods trades also, with which we are not really concerned in this book, it is known that the prohibition of collective enforcement has caused r.p.m. to be abandoned altogether and has caused trade associations to be wound up. An example of this is to be found in the edge tool trade.

In the grocery trade, the collective enforcing body - the Grocery Proprietary Articles Council - was ultimately wound up as a result of the Act. As early as 1951 the G.P.A.C. had indicated to the Board of Trade a willingness to drop its provisions for a monetary penalty and to restrict the use of the Stop List. Clearly they thought that without them there would be no material weakening of resale price maintenance in the trade. When the 1956 Act was passed the G.P.A.C. duly changed its Objects so as to remove all reference to collective enforcement of r.p.m. Their revised Objects were –

'1. The discussion of matters of common interest to those engaged in the manufacture, distribution and sale of grocery proprietary articles.

2. The furnishing to its members of advice, information and assistance (financial and otherwise) relating to matters of common interest.

3. The doing of all such other things as may be lawful and in the common interest of its members.'

The G.P.A.C. executive thought that they were well equipped to help manufacturers enforce their individual rights, though when the Objects of the G.P.A.C. are compared with the revised rules and objects of other collective enforcing bodies it may be felt that they erred on the side of being too neutral. While the G.P.A.C. managed to remain alive despite a steadily declining membership which fell from 80 in 1952 to 76 in 1956, 70 in 1958 and 55 in 1960, its influence had gone completely, many of the manufacturers who were still members in 1960 only remained for sentimental reasons, they had long since given up trying to stop price cutting. Those manufacturers of groceries who did take action under section 25 - Beechams and Cadburys - did not act through the auspices of the Council - Cadburys had never been members. The other manufacturer members were reluctant to act and new food manufacturers, especially the American-owned companies entering the British market for the first time, did not belong to the Council. So in September 1960, the G.P.A.C. was wound up, its power and influence completely removed by the prohibition of collective enforcement and by the reluctance of its members individually to enforce r.p.m.

However, in other trades the collective enforcing body remained powerful and active. Taking note of the encouragement given to them by Lord Kilmuir's speech, the trade associations concerned merely changed their rules to remove all mention of a Stop List and other evidences of collective enforcement and began to assist their individual manufacturer members to enforce. They collected evidence of price cutting, undertook negotiations on behalf of the individual manufacturer and, if the manufacturer decided to sue for an injunction, he would often use the association's solicitors.

One of the best examples of this is to be found in the motor trade. The British Motor Trade Association's Objects from 1910 to 1956 were -

'(a) To take such steps as may be deemed expedient to prevent price cutting or price inflation of trade goods.

(b) To secure throughout the Motor Trade observance of the terms contained in Manufacturers' and Concessionaires' Conditions of Sale relating to the regulation of prices and the supply and distribution of trade goods.'

After the Act they were changed to read -

'(a) To provide a service to all individual manufacturers and concessionaires and other suppliers of trade goods to secure throughout the motor trade observance of their respective terms and conditions as to the price at which their respective goods may be resold.

(b) To provide a service to all individual manufacturers and concessionaires and other suppliers of trade goods to secure observance of their respective terms and conditions (other than conditions as to price) relating to the supply and distribution of trade goods.

(c) To provide the means to attain these objects.'

These are more specific than the revised Objects of the G.P.A.C. and one is left in no doubt as to what services the B.M.T.A. intended to provide. Virtually all its former members remained in the B.M.T.A. and it quickly used its new powers; before the end of 1956 the Austin Motor Company had already obtained an injunction with the association's assistance.

Twice every year the association issued, on behalf of its members, the notice of conditions of sale which section 25 requires to be given before a price cutter can be sued. When the B.M.T.A. received a complaint about price cutting, it investigated and passed on its findings to the manufacturer for him to decide what action to take. The costs of investigation and of preparing a case were borne by the B.M.T.A., these are estimated to have amounted to about £5,000 a year. To meet the costs of legal actions, the Car Distribution Committee of the Association imposed a compulsory levy on dealers. Those dealers who refused to pay were denied supplies of cars and spare parts. When the matter was raised in the House of Commons, the President of the Board of Trade stated that the collective financing of legal actions was not unlawful under section 24 of the Act.[1] This also helped strengthen the position of trade associations assisting in the enforcement of r.p.m.

The B.M.T.A. assisted manufacturers in obtaining some thirty injunctions against price cutters, mostly over motor cars but in a few cases the injunctions related to accessories. Many other instances of price cutting were dealt with simply by means of a solicitor's letter. Thus the prohibition of collective enforcement certainly did not appear to weaken r.p.m. in the motor trade and

[1] *Hansard* vol 583 (Commons) col. 525.

the B.M.T.A. continued to play an important part in its enforcement.[1]

The Proprietary Articles Trade Association in the chemists' goods trade is another association which has continued to share in the enforcement of r.p.m. Even before the Restrictive Trade Practices Act became law, the P.A.T.A. had amended its constitution to meet the changed situation which it saw would exist. A new rule was introduced which stated,

Rule 31 – 'The Council or any sub-committee duly appointed by the Council may in any case where a member is or may be involved in legal proceedings relating to matters of common interest to Members authorize assistance (financial or otherwise) to be given by the officers, servants or agents of the Association in connection with such proceedings.'

This allowed the P.A.T.A. to assist in legal proceedings being taken by a manufacturer under section 25 and to defray his legal costs. In their Year Book the following notice was given at the head of the list of manufacturer members –

'Important Notice

(Restrictive Trade Practices Act 1956)

The Proprietary Articles Trade Association has been authorized by the manufacturer members whose names appear below to give notice on behalf of each of them that each of them individually supply for resale proprietary articles of a pharmaceutical, toilet or other nature, subject to conditions as to price, including a condition that they shall not be resold or offered for resale at wholesale or at retail at a price other than the appropriate price prescribed by each such manufacturer, plus the amount of purchase tax (if any) for which such products are liable.

Such conditions as to price are enforceable pursuant to the provisions of section 25 of the Restrictive Trade Practices Act 1956 . . .

Particulars of the conditions as to price prescribed by the respective manufacturer or distributor for the proprietary articles enumerated in this list may be obtained on application to the manufacturer concerned or his named distributor, or from the Association.'

[1] Though for a consideration of the situation regarding tyres see below ch. xi.

54

Although before suing for an injunction, a manufacturer, or the Association acting on his behalf, normally sent by registered post a further copy of the conditions of sale to a price cutter, the Goodyear Tyre case[1] showed that the general notice given by the B.M.T.A. and P.A.T.A. constituted sufficient notice of a condition of sale as required by section 25.

The majority of the manufacturer members of the P.A.T.A. gave the Association authority to act on their behalf in dealing with price cutting on their goods, those that did not were essentially those which had their own legal department and were therefore in a position to act alone. The P.A.T.A. provided a similar service to that given by the B.M.T.A. although the cost of investigation work carried out by the P.A.T.A. on behalf of its members was much lower – £1,413 in 1961 and £1,118 in 1963. By comparison the cost of such work by the P.A.T.A. before the war was in the region of £3,500 a year.[2] Rather less investigatory work has been carried out in recent years than immediately before the Act – for example, in 1963 the P.A.T.A. representatives made 1,443 visits to suspected price cutters and 349 test purchases as compared with 1,862 visits and 2,033 test purchases in 1955. Manufacturer membership has also declined – from 340 in 1955 to 300 in 1958, 270 in 1960 and only 211 in 1963.

There are a number of reasons for this decline in manufacturer membership since the passing of the Act. In the first place we have already noted that some manufacturers with their own legal departments preferred to act independently over the enforcement of r.p.m. There have also been some mergers which have tended to reduce the numerical membership – the parent company often being a member already, a few manufacturers have left because they have had to drop r.p.m. on their products[3] and, finally, a number of manufacturers left the association since the absence of price cutting on their products meant they did not require the main service the association provided. In fact the P.A.T.A. has never had to act on behalf of more than 20

[1] Goodyear Tyre and Rubber Co. (Great Britain) Ltd. v. Lancashire Batteries Ltd. (1958) L.R. 1 R.P. 22. This case is discussed in chapter v.
[2] 'The Story of a Crusade – P.A.T.A. 1896-1946.'
[3] See below ch. xi.

manufacturers and by 1964 they were only acting for about 12 whose goods were often subject to price cutting. The P.A.T.A. also, therefore, equipped itself well to play a part in the enforcement of resale price maintenance, in its trade. Despite declining membership, its influence has remained strong and its assistance effective.

A number of other trade associations also remained actively concerned with the enforcement of resale price maintenance though because of the small amount of price cutting to be found in their trades their scale of operation was much smaller than that of the B.M.T.A. and the P.A.T.A. The Publishers Association, British Cycle and Motor Cycle Industries Association and the Brands (Wines and Spirits) Protection Association all come into this category. The action taken has normally consisted of writing a letter on behalf of the manufacturer concerned to a price cutting trader drawing his attention to the conditions of sale and asking him to restore the fixed prices. In each trade such action has only occasionally been required. Legal action for an injunction has never proved necessary. The British Cycle and Motor Cycle Industries Association, however, faced a problem in that price cutting on bicycles tended to take the form of a fixed percentage reduction on all models and it was, therefore, sometimes difficult to avoid giving the impression of a threat of collective action by all manufacturers in dealing with the offending trader.

Whilst a number of other associations have passed back to manufacturers complaints about price cutting (associations of retailers have been especially active in this respect), so far as is known no other trade associations concerned with consumer goods have sought to take advantage of the opportunities offered to them to continue to play a leading part in the enforcement of r.p.m. since 1956.

A certain amount of objection was raised against trade associations acting on behalf of individual manufacturers to enforce fixed resale price conditions of sale. The suggestion was made that this implied an agreement between the manufacturer members to attach and enforce resale price conditions on their goods. The P.A.T.A. categorically denied that such an agreement existed.[1] But since the judgment in the Basic Slag case this controversy has been re-opened.[2]

British Basic Slag Ltd. (Basic) was a company set up and owned by a number of steel companies to sell their output of basic slag which was used as a phosphatic fertilizer. The court action arose because certain agreements between Basic and its supplying member companies had been held to be registrable by the Restrictive Practices Court. Whilst the major agreements do not concern us here, what is important is that in 1954 when their old agreements ended, each company entered into a new agreement with Basic that it would continue to sell its fertilizer output to Basic. These agreements were made, it was claimed, as a matter of independent judgment on the part of each company and not because of an agreement with the other companies. In the course of its judgment, the Court of Appeal held that by setting up Basic and entering into contracts with it in similar form and to the knowledge of each other, the steel companies were giving effect to an arrangement between themselves for a common selling organization and this was therefore registrable.

Following the lines of the Court's judgment, Mrs Korah has argued that the appointment of a trade association to enforce a member's individual rights under section 25 is suspect.[3] Her case is that in some trades pressure has been brought to bear on members to encourage them to preserve an orderly marketing system and impose and maintain resale prices. By appointing an association as enforcing agent a manufacturer is leading others to expect that he will continue to enforce r.p.m. and is inducing them to do likewise.

If, as Mrs Korah suggests, in some trades manufacturers have been pressed into enforcing r.p.m. then no doubt this would be registrable. However, where this is not so, and where a manufacturer has appointed an association as his enforcing agent, it would be hard to prove that this gave rise to a registrable agreement, though the dividing line in such cases would be difficult to draw. The fact that a manufacturer is perfectly free to leave

[1] *Quarterly Record* April 1963 p. 11.
[2] *British Basic Slag Ltd.* v. *Registrar of Restrictive Trading Agreements* (1963) L.R. 4 R.P. 116.
[3] V. L. Korah 'Registrable Agreements' – *Journal of Business Law* January 1964 p. 1.

an association and drop r.p.m. as some have done in the P.A.T.A. when faced with price cutting on competitors' products, suggests that no registrable agreement exists. Furthermore, whilst *Hansard* is, paradoxically, not a source of information to judges in determining what the intention of Parliament was in relation to a certain piece of legislation, there is no doubt that in view of the authoritative assurance from Lord Kilmuir that trade associations would be able to assist in the enforcement of r.p.m., so long as there was no direct evidence of an agreement providing for this or of pressure being brought to bear on manufacturers to appoint a trade association to enforce their rights, no court would readily interfere in such action taken by any trade association.

The main remedy for breaches of section 24 is the right of the Board of Trade to sue for an injunction. On a number of occasions the Board of Trade has either noticed reports in the press or received evidence from individuals which has suggested that a collective boycott was being organized. On some occasions the claim was not substantiated, on others the matter was satisfactorily settled. The Board has not actively looked for instances of breaches of this section – no active efforts have been made to ensure its conditions were observed but they would undoubtedly be informed by any trader or supplier who felt himself to have been the victim of a collective boycott.

The only occasion on which the Board of Trade have had to seek a legal remedy concerned the Northern District Council of Grocers' Associations. The Council were particularly aggrieved that certain manufacturers of branded groceries and allied products, namely Kellogg, Petfoods, Heinz, Crosse and Blackwell, Nestlé and Alfred Bird refused to enforce fixed price conditions on their products. The Council originally wanted to register an agreement under Part I of the Restrictive Trade Practices Act to the effect that they would not stock supplies of manufacturers who did not enforce r.p.m. On being advised by their lawyers that this had little chance of succeeding, they arranged a collective boycott against the six manufacturers.

The Board of Trade acted by obtaining an undertaking in the Chancery Court, under section 24(7), from the Council that they would not recommend their members to withhold orders or to discriminate in the handling of the goods of the manufacturers involved. Following this, the Secretary of the Council sent a letter to each manufacturer which was approved by the Board of Trade, assuring them that there was to be no discrimination against them. However, surprisingly the Secretary was allowed to add –

'I must add that unless you are prepared to take immediate steps to enable our members to be able to sell their goods at the same prices as their largest competitors, then the Council will consider recommending its members to refuse to stock your goods.'[1]

This must surely have still been close to a threat of collective boycott. Despite this strong worded action, the manufacturers involved seemed unconcerned and the breakdown of r.p.m. on groceries continued unhindered. If the Council really thought that the collapse of r.p.m. was causing harm, it would have been better had they registered an agreement as they had initially intended and really brought the issue of resale price maintenance into the open, quite apart from the fact that until the case had been heard they would have been able to carry out the terms of the agreement.[2]

It has often proved difficult for local grocers' associations and other groups of traders concerned about the breakdown of r.p.m. to avoid taking action which is either a breach of section 24 or else constitutes a registrable agreement under Part I of the Act. A similar situation arose with a local retailer buying group which had been unable to obtain Kraft products at wholesale terms, which they felt they were entitled to receive. A resolution was therefore passed that they would not stock Kraft products unless they were obtained on wholesale terms. The Private Grocers' Merchandise Association, hearing of the resolution, had to cause it to be withdrawn.

From this description of the consequences of the prohibition of methods of collective enforcement, it might be concluded that in fact it is the retailers who have been affected more than the manufacturers. They are now certainly powerless to act

[1] See *The Grocer* August 2, 1958 p. 23.
[2] Though such a boycott would surely have hurt the retailers more than the manufacturers.

together on any matter of a common trade interest without falling foul of either Part I of the Act or section 24.

As to the manufacturers, their private courts have, of course, disappeared. This was undoubtedly the main malpractice of which the Government disapproved. The disappearance of the Stop List, etc., caused some weakening in r.p.m. only on products such as groceries where conditions were such that it only needed something like this Act to cause a complete breakdown. In most other trades r.p.m. was not weakened by section 24 and the continued assistance given by a number of trade associations in dealing with price cutters seems to have been a more than adequate compensation for the prohibition of the former collective enforcement procedures.

The assistance of trade associations in collecting evidence of price cutting, writing the necessary threatening letters and, in some cases, even indemnifying the manufacturer should he take legal action is of value to all manufacturers. A fairly strong case can be made out on grounds of administrative economy that if r.p.m. is to remain on a product it is better that one trade association rather than a number of individual manufacturers should be responsible for its enforcement. It seems clear from Lord Kilmuir's speech quoted above[1] that this was what the Government intended and this is how it has worked out in practice. However, this has been achieved in some cases by allowing trade associations to retain a strong influence over the trading policy of their individual members. This has also been a defect in the operation of Part I of the Act and many commentators are unhappy about the situation. Trade associations undoubtedly play an important part in the British economy and will continue to do so, but a clarification of the functions which they are to be allowed to exercise seems called for.

[1] P. 50.

CHAPTER V

THE ENFORCEMENT OF R.P.M.–
I. THE DEVELOPMENT OF CASE LAW

When a statute is passed, it is often difficult to tell how effective it will be until a number of cases have been decided. The reason is that whilst Parliament makes a law, it is the Judiciary which enforces it. In most Acts there are certain words or phrases that can be given more than one meaning and decision as to the exact interpretation to be adopted rests with the Judge. In this chapter we shall consider the decisions of the courts in some of the defended actions brought for an injunction under section 25 of the Restrictive Trade Practices Act. The effectiveness of the supplier's powers to prevent price cutting on his products has largely depended on these decisions.

The first case of importance was brought by County Laboratories Ltd., part of the Beecham Group, against Mindel, a South London trader.[1] Once the Act came into force the manufacturers included on their price list a statement that – 'All goods marketed by us are sold subject to observance of the fixed retail prices published in our current price list.' The defendants conceded that they had received a copy of this and further conceded that in February 1957 they had sold a 2s 10d jar of Brylcreem for 2s 6d. The point at issue was whether or not the defendants should have known that the goods concerned were manufactured after the date on which this particular section came into force (November 2, 1956) for goods supplied before that date were not subject to resale price conditions enforceable under section 25. The plaintiffs said that by means of a secret code mark on each jar they were able to prove that the goods were manufactured after November 2, 1956. Mindel's argument was that to have 'notice' within the meaning of section 25(1) they had to have express knowledge; the plaintiffs claimed that so long as general

[1] *County Laboratories Ltd.* v. *J. Mindel Ltd.* (1957) L.R. 1 R.P. 1.

notice of the condition was given, express knowledge was not necessary.

The judge, Harman J., found in Mindel's favour. He agreed that 'taking with notice' meant 'taking with express knowledge' and that as Mindel did not know the supplier's code or how old were the wholesaler's stocks from which he obtained the supplies concerned, he concluded that Mindel did not know that the jar was manufactured subsequent to the appropriate date and was therefore subject to the resale price condition. In the course of his judgment the learned judge indicated that whilst the law had to be enforced, he certainly did not intend to unduly assist manufacturers in the enforcement of their resale price conditions –

'[this is] a section limiting the freedom of trade and therefore although I am bound to give it that effect which the language of it expresses I am not prepared to go beyond that and stretch it so as to produce an effect which the language does not warrant.'[1]

Dunlop also lost a similar action, against a trader who had been cutting the price of tyres.[2] The particular tyre over which the action was brought was manufactured in July 1956 and there was no evidence as to the date on which it was supplied to the trader. The judge held that it must be assumed that the tyre was acquired before November 2, 1956, and following the reasoning in *County Laboratories* v. *Mindel*, Lloyd Jacob J. held that retrospective operation should not be given to the section and therefore the case failed. In this case, however, Dunlop, having manufactured the tyre under letters patent, were able to obtain an injunction for an infringement of their patent rights.

These two cases were not of outstanding importance so far as the long term enforcement of r.p.m. was concerned, since they dealt only with goods which might have been supplied prior to November 2, 1956. After a while it would be reasonable to assume that stocks produced before this date would be non-existent and so in future all products would be covered by this provision. All it did was to make manufacturers delay taking

[1] *Ibid.* p. 5.
[2] *Dunlop Rubber Co. Ltd.* v. *Longlife Battery Depot* (1958) L.R. 1 R.P. 65.

action against price cutters until this legal technicality could be ruled out.

A further case also dealt with the meaning of the word 'notice'.[1] Goodyear were members of the British Motor Trade Association who, as we saw in the previous chapter, were responsible for sending out notice of conditions of sale on behalf of their members. In April 1957 the B.M.T.A. sent a circular to a large number of traders including the defendants, listing the products of manufacturers on which price maintenance was a condition of sale. Goodyear tyres, tubes and flaps were listed. The circular also said that details of the conditions as to price for any of the specified products could be obtained on application to the manufacturer or concessionaire concerned. In February 1958 the defendants advertised in an evening newspaper offering goods at a 2s in the £ discount. B.M.T.A. officials who made a test purchase obtained this discount and proceedings were commenced.

The defendants claimed that the B.M.T.A. circular was not, for the purposes of section 25, a notice of the condition as to price, since it did not expressly state the actual terms of the condition. The plaintiffs argued that the notice was in fact a substantial compliance with the terms of the section or alternatively, that as in patent law, it was sufficient to bring the attention of the trader concerned to the fact that there is a restriction and they supported this argument with a passage from a standard work on patent law,

> 'It is not essential that the purchaser should have notice of the precise restrictions concerned so long as he has knowledge of their nature and existence and means of knowledge of their exact intent.'[2]

The B.M.T.A. circular certainly complied with this requirement but Upjohn J. decided in favour of the defendants. He held that it was not intended that section 25 should place a trader in a worse position than if he had been a party to the original contract of sale, and it therefore required express notice of the actual terms and conditions sought to be enforced.

[1] Goodyear Tyre and Rubber Co. (Great Britain) Ltd. v. Lancashire Batteries Ltd. (1958) L.R. 1 R.P. 22.
[2] Terrell and Shelley on Patents, 9th ed. (London) p. 264.

'It does not seem to me that the notice issued gives such express notice of the actual terms, and therefore, it appears to me that for the purposes of the section the defendants have not received the requisite notice.'[1]

This decision placed in jeopardy the actions taken by both the B.M.T.A. and the P.A.T.A. in giving collective notice to traders that their members' products were sold subject to a condition as to resale price. Goodyear, however, appealed.

Although rejecting their argument based on patent law, since this refers to goods of which the patentee has a special proprietary right, Evershed M. R. adopted a more favourable view of the B.M.T.A. circular in the light of section 25. In his opinion,

'If Parliament had meant that the retailer must know the actual terms of the condition . . . Parliament would have said so.'[2]

The term 'notice' to a lawyer meant something less than full knowledge. In this case the defendants had been told that Goodyear tyres had a fixed resale price imposed upon them. They had also been told that details of the appropriate resale price for any particular tyre could be obtained on application to the manufacturer.

In Lord Evershed's view, this constituted sufficient notice of the condition. The lower court judge had decided that 'notice of the condition' must be interpreted as meaning 'express notice of the actual terms of the condition', but the Appeal Court held that 'notice of the condition' meant simply 'notice of the fact of the condition'. So on appeal, Goodyear won their case.

This decision therefore made the enforcement of r.p.m. for some manufacturers easier since the B.M.T.A. and P.A.T.A. schemes were now above doubt and even an individual manufacturer giving notice that r.p.m. is one of his conditions of sale could now give notice in more general terms than he would have had to have done had Mr Justice Upjohn's decision been upheld. Mr Grunfeld is of the opinion that it was this decision that facilitated the practical administration by business of the r.p.m.

---

[1] *Goodyear Tyre and Rubber Co. (Great Britain) Ltd. v. Lancashire Batteries Ltd.* (1958) L.R. 1 R.P. 22 at p. 29.
[2] *Ibid.* p. 36.

provisions of the 1956 Act.[1] Maybe this slightly overstates the importance of this particular judgment since many manufacturers have found it possible to effectively enforce r.p.m. without any such assistance from trade associations, but there is no doubt that where trade associations have assisted in enforcement activities they have made the task of the individual manufacturer much easier.

In both the Dunlop and Goodyear cases, the defendants had also challenged the use of trap purchases as means of obtaining evidence of price cutting, but in each instance the court had held that this was a justifiable procedure. The objection was to the fact that the B.M.T.A. representatives who made the test purchases would not disclose that they were acting on behalf of the Association. Obviously, if they had to disclose their actual identity, then it would be impossible for evidence of price cutting to be obtained. This, too, therefore, helped make the task of manufacturers in enforcing r.p.m. easier.

The Beecham group were also unsuccessfully involved in another early case - the 'Lucozade Case'.[2] The point at issue here was 'What constitutes a price cut?' At this time, the price of bottles of Lucozade included a 3d deposit which was repayable when the bottle was returned. The defendant reduced the price by 2d and when sued for an injunction under section 25 argued that there was no evidence that it was not his intention only to return 1d instead of 3d as deposit on the bottle. Since the bottles were hired rather than sold and as section 25 does not cover hirings, the plaintiffs lost their case and as a result ceased to price maintain their grocery products. With the benefit of hindsight we may argue that had the person responsible for the collection of the evidence returned the bottle empty and received a refund of 3d then Beecham would not have lost.

These early actions were important in that they provided a body of case law which showed manufacturers and their legal advisers exactly what steps had to be taken to ensure that they would be successful when they sued for an injunction. Success for the manufacturer in the Goodyear case was far more

[1] C. Grunfeld, 'Resale Price Maintenance – Notice to "Non Signers"', *Modern Law Review* vol. 21 (1958) p. 682.
[2] *Beecham Foods Ltd.* v. *North Supplies (Edmonton) Ltd.* (1959) L.R. 1 R.P. 262.

E

important in the long run than those setbacks suffered by other manufacturers over legal technicalities, though Beecham's defeat in the Lucozade case meant that one of the last bastions of r.p.m. in the grocery trade had fallen.

In 1960 and 1961, as the following chapter shows, there was something of a hiatus in manufacturer enforcement of r.p.m. In 1962 some further cases were heard which are more fundamental to the interpretation of the Act than those brought in 1957 to 1959 and show how stringent in practice the law is on price cutting.

Chronologically the first case was that between Kayser Bondor and Tesco.[1] It is also probably the most important, since there is considerable evidence that it was the success of Kayser Bondor in this case that encouraged other manufacturers to take a firmer line in dealing with price cutters. The trouble arose when Tesco opened their store at Leicester and started offering some Kayser Bondor products at cut prices. The local retailers complained and Kayser Bondor took the matter up with Tesco. After some contradictory statements from Tesco, first agreeing to stop cutting and then refusing, Kayser Bondor sought an interim injunction to restrain them from cutting prices.

Tesco obtained their supplies through a subsidiary – London and Midland Distributors Ltd. (L.M.D.), who had been regular customers of Kayser Bondor since 1957. When Kayser Bondor dispatched the goods that L.M.D. had ordered, at the same time, as was their traditional policy, they sent under separate cover an invoice which included the words, 'The acceptance of this invoice is an undertaking that the goods entered therein will be offered for sale at the prices specified upon the company's price list'. Tesco argued that the invoice did not arrive until after L.M.D. had sold the goods and that as the Kayser Bondor price list did not contain any notice of the resale price condition, they were not subject to any such condition.

Kayser Bondor argued on two grounds. First, they claimed that the goods were not sold until they were accepted by L.M.D. and that L.M.D. accepted the condition with them. The judge did not accept this as he felt the evidence was conflicting. Secondly, they argued that even if these particular goods were

[1] *Kayser Bondor Ltd.* v. *Tesco Stores Ltd. The Times* January 25, 1962.

resold before notice of the condition was received, since L.M.D. had dealt with Kayser Bondor for some years and knew that they adopted a policy of resale price maintenance, there should be implied in the contract made between L.M.D. and Kayser Bondor for the supply of the goods, a term that the goods were sold subject to a condition prohibiting their resale at less than the list price. Tesco argued that a long-established practice of sending notice of r.p.m. conditions did not constitute general notice so as to affect subsequent offers and acceptances.

The judge held that the defence plea neither accorded with common sense nor with a person's idea of fair dealing and furthermore he thought it was unsound in law. Accordingly an interlocutory injunction was granted. The judge (Cross J.) then made some comments about Tesco's position in this case. In substance, if not in law, they were the same person as L.M.D. and therefore could be regarded as standing in L.M.D.'s shoes, vis-à-vis the plaintiffs, and they knew that it was Kayser Bondor's intention to make the contract subject to a resale price condition. His Lordship was surprised that honourable men, such as the directors of Tesco involved in this case, should think it right to offer goods for sale at prices lower than those specified by the plaintiffs and to rely on the technical defence which had been put forward on their behalf. The point at issue was not whether r.p.m. was a bad thing, but whether business men should keep their word. Tesco did not have to buy from manufacturers who enforced r.p.m. but if they did, they should adhere to their conditions of sale.

Contrasted with Harman J.'s reluctance to stretch the meaning of this section at all (see page 62 above), Cross J.'s judgment was certainly helpful to the manufacturer. It meant that where a manufacturer traditionally imposed a fixed price condition of sale and this was known by the retailer, any oversight on a particular occasion in repeating notice of that condition would not justify the trader in price cutting. Furthermore, a policy of establishing a buying company to obtain resale price maintained goods which then resold to the trader without passing on notice of the conditions of sale did not constitute a valid defence to an action for breach of section 25. This decision can well be considered of major importance in contributing to the strength of r.p.m. in this country.

The next few months brought other cases of interest. British Xylonite obtained an injunction against a Northampton discount store operator I. D. M. Brierley and the wholesaler who supplied him – Jolley & Co. Ltd. – on the grounds that the price of their Bex Bissell Shampoo Master was being cut. The defendants then appealed on the grounds that the profit provided for in the fixed retail price was unreasonable.[1] In evidence, it was stated that the price at which the manufacturer sold to the wholesaler was 36s and the wholesaler's fixed reselling price was 45s. The fixed price at which the retailer had to sell to the public was 67s 6d. This provided a mark up of 50% to the retailer or, looked at another way, a gross margin of $33\frac{1}{3}\%$ off the list price. Brierley's argument that this margin was unreasonably high was rejected in the Court of Appeal by Pearce L. J., who held that there was a presumption in law that the provisions of a bargain made between business men were reasonable.

At the same time, Morphy Richards sought an injunction against the Bloom-owned Rolls Razor discount store.[2] Rolls argued that the hairdryers in question were bought in outer cartons of eight and notice of the resale price conditions was only on the individual carton holding each hairdryer. Therefore they claimed that when the goods were bought they did not have notice of the fixed price condition of sale. This, too, was rejected by the court and an injunction granted to Morphy Richards.

The following month, Cadbury Bros. Ltd. brought an action against an Essex supermarket company because they had been cutting prices on Cadbury's products.[3] Wallis argued that Cadbury's enforcement policy was inconsistent. They took action against some traders whilst allowing others to continue cutting. Since the grant of an injunction is at the court's discretion, it is open to the court to refuse an application for such a remedy if the supplier did not fulfil the requirements of equity, e.g. by failing to come 'with clean hands'. However, in this case despite Wallis's plea, an injunction was duly granted to Cadbury though

[1] *Hardware Trade Journal* March 2, 1962.
[2] *Morphy Richards Ltd. v. Rolls Razor Ltd. The Times* March 7, 1962.
[3] *Cadbury Bros. Ltd. v. F. J. Wallis Ltd. The Times* April 4, 1962.

it is not clear from the report of the case whether this was because the court refused to exercise their discretion not to grant an injunction or because they found Wallis's defence not proven.

At the end of the year an interim injunction was sought by Polycell against a discount supermarket because of price cutting.[1] The application was contested by the discounter who drew attention to the fact that the Polycell price list allowed a 10% discount to be given to bona fide decorators and submitted that there was no reason why do-it-yourself decorators should not be allowed this discount. The learned judge, Wilberforce J., upheld the discounter's argument and dismissed Polycell's application, commenting that there was an 'area of ambiguity' in the price list.

These decisions suggest that as compared with those heard in 1957-59, when the courts were prepared to uphold most technical legal arguments against the enforcing manufacturer, the cases determined in 1962 indicate a greater readiness on the part of the courts to enforce the spirit of the section – that where a manufacturer is opposed to price cutting he should have the right to prevent it. Undoubtedly they encouraged other manufacturers also to insist on the observance of their resale price conditions and contributed in large measure to the noticeable strengthening of r.p.m. again in 1962 and 1963. Polycell's defeat does not prove an exception to this reasoning. The weakness in their price list in allowing discounts for 'bona fide decorators' was a glaring error and no matter how anxious a court had been to enforce the spirit of the law, it could not have stretched the letter of the law so far as to be able to reject the defendant's argument. This case may in fact have encouraged other manufacturers to ensure that their price lists did not also provide such obvious loopholes.

Trading stamps were becoming of increasing importance in the retail trade and whilst these had already been treated by the courts as a form of price cutting, a Brighton store, S. Bellman and Sons Ltd., devised, with legal advice, an ingenious gift voucher scheme which it was thought constituted a lawful way round a manufacturer's resale price conditions. This was challenged by Bulpitt, the manufacturers of Swan Brand products,

[1] *The Ironmonger* December 22, 1962.

who had some months previously obtained an undertaking from Bellmans that they would not cut prices on their products. Bulpitt claimed that the new scheme was a breach of the undertaking previously given and sought a writ of sequestration.[1]

With each product bought, a number of coupons were given which could be exchanged either then or later for an article out of a range provided for this purpose by Bellman. On the back of each coupon certain conditions were set out, including the following –

'All gifts . . . are entirely voluntary and in the absolute discretion of [the defendants]. The certificate is not given or accepted as or by virtue of any condition or term of any purchase by the customer and is only given and accepted upon the basis that it does not give rise to any obligations in law.'

Evidence was given of the test purchase of a Swan Brand kettle for which the full price was paid, but in return for which 25 coupons were given, which were then exchanged for a casserole and stand said to have a retail value of 17s 4d.

The defence argued that the full price was paid for the article purchased and since the gift coupons gave no rise to an obligation in law they were genuine gifts. The plaintiff's conditions of sale did not prohibit the resale of their products together with something else at the full selling price. Bulpitt argued that the purchaser expected the coupons to be honoured and they were and therefore they had a value which must be deducted from the purchase price in order to arrive at the real cost of the kettles.

In his judgment, Ungoed-Thomas J. agreed that anyone had the right to try to avoid the provisions of section 25 and accepted as reflecting his own intentions, the opinion of Harman L. J. which we have already noted in which he refused to stretch the meaning of the section so as to produce an effect which the wording of the section did not warrant. However, despite an apparent sympathy with the defendants in this case, the judgment was given against them.

The crucial part of the section was,

'Where goods are sold by a supplier subject to a condition as to the price at which those goods may be resold' s25(1). 'Those goods' were the kettles only and the plaintiff's condition

[1] *Bulpitt and Sons Ltd. v. S. Bellman and Sons Ltd.* (1962) L.R. 3 R.P. 62.

was that the kettle alone should be sold at the stipulated price. The question, therefore, was whether the kettle and something else – the gift vouchers – were sold at that price. The judge held that the vouchers were associated with the sale and would not have been issued apart from the sale and therefore 'the coupons were part of the consideration for the price that was paid'.

Thus, at the fixed selling price the kettle plus the coupons were obtained. Rearranging the equation, the cost of the kettle to a purchaser was the fixed price less the value of the coupons. It was not necessary to establish the exact value of the coupons so as to fix the exact price which was paid for the kettle in order to succeed under section 25 and the court therefore found that the kettle had been sold below the fixed retail price and the defendants were in breach of their undertaking.

In an affidavit the defendants stated that they had not intended a breach of their previous undertaking, since they thought their scheme was not affected by section 25. In view of this no order was made on Bulpitt's writ except that the defendants were to pay the plaintiff's costs on a full indemnity basis.

In this chapter, we have seen, therefore, how, after certain teething troubles in the enforcement of their resale price conditions under section 25, the power of the manufacturers was greatly strengthened by the section. The courts became more willing to enforce the spirit as well as the letter of the law, the giving of notice on behalf of a number of manufacturers by a trade association had been upheld, and no trader had succeeded in devising a scheme for legitimately avoiding the provisions of the section. With this strong backing in the courts, manufacturers have proved willing to continue to enforce their fixed resale price conditions and thus in many trades the strength of r.p.m. was ensured.

It may be argued that the courts have gone too far in assisting manufacturers to enforce r.p.m.[1] The issues raised in the British Xylonite and Cadbury cases are of special significance in this respect. The preservation of unreasonably high profit margins is clearly undesirable. But what constitutes a reasonable profit? The common law courts have traditionally been unwilling to be drawn on the issue of fair prices. Now it seems likely that in

[1] See for example the editorial in *The Solicitor Quarterly* vol. 1 (1962) p. 191.

balancing detriments and advantages in the 'tailpiece' required by the Resale Prices Act, 1964, the Restrictive Practices Court will have to adjudicate on this issue.[1] With sections of retail distribution becoming increasingly dynamic there lies a potential conflict between the desire to approve a margin which allows the preservation of an adequate number of retail outlets where this serves the public interest and to encourage further growth of innovation in retailing as represented by those traders who claim to be able to work on lower margins.

Claims of victimization by manufacturers in their selection of traders against whom to take action have been voiced on several occasions. It has always been considered to be the prerogative of plaintiffs to choose their victims, and manufacturers frequently find that a successful action against one trader is a sufficient deterrent against other recalcitrant traders. However, there have also been manufacturers who have chosen to 'run with the hare and hunt with the hounds' over resale price maintenance. (It is not suggested that Cadburys fall into this category.) The question then arises whether manufacturers who are inconsistent in their enforcement of r.p.m. should receive the support of the courts in their actions. The line between exemplary action and victimization would be hard to draw but where resale price maintenance is allowed to continue this might be an issue that will have to be faced.

[1] As they have had to in cases arising under Part I of the Restrictive Trade Practices Act, 1956.

CHAPTER VI

THE ENFORCEMENT OF R.P.M.—
2. MANUFACTURER ACTION

Price cutting may take place on a product for a number of possible reasons. Suppliers or distributors may have taken an over-optimistic view of the prospects in a particular trade and created a situation where supply exceeds demand for the product and price cutting is seen as a means of reducing the size of stocks that have to be carried. Innovations in retailing with the development of new types of low cost distribution also increase the likelihood of attempts to cut prices.[1] This has, of course, happened with the development of self service stores and supermarkets and later of discount stores. In the case of alcoholic drink this tendency was further encouraged by the change in the Licensing Laws in November 1961, making it possible for supermarkets which had licences to sell liquor throughout the day.

On the other hand, there are instances where little or no price cutting occurs. Goods with a slow rate of stockturn, a marked seasonal pattern of demand or which are subject to changes in fashion are not normally subject to price cutting though the clearance sale is widely accepted as a justifiable means of disposing of such goods when they are left on the retailer's hands at the end of a season. Some products are retailed by very few distributors in any given shopping area and the existence of such a monopoly position means that little advantage may be obtained by reducing prices. Goods which come into this category are toys, sports goods, the more expensive types of photographic equipment, etc. In addition, in some trades the appointment of a retailer as sole agent in a town for a particular

---

[1] The insistence of manufacturers in imposing a margin in excess of that required by modern distributors and in some cases allowing them additional discounts too, merely exacerbates the problem.

manufacturer also helps to establish a monopoly position in which price cutting becomes unlikely. This is particularly important in certain sections of the clothing trade, especially on fashion goods and also applies to radio equipment. Although motor manufacturers also extensively use the franchise system, it is suggested that in this case the high cost of a car and the fact that a purchaser is already likely to have a car in which to travel from garage to garage means that the area of potential competition between dealers of the same make of car is greater and the monopoly position less secure.[1]

Price cutting may be either prevented or merely cured. Prevention can be achieved if manufacturers appoint sole distributors and make it clear that if price cutting did ensue it would result in the withdrawal of the franchise. Refusal to supply supermarkets and discount stores means that the major source of potential price cutting is controlled. Manufacturers who limit the size of margins and control the offer of quantity discount terms on their products have found themselves bothered less by unwanted price cutting than other manufacturers. One of the main reasons for the small amount of price cutting on confectionery in post-war years as compared with the early 1930s when price cutting was rife is that the size of distributors' margins has been reduced. When Beecham Foods dropped r.p.m. on their products in 1959 they also reduced the level of margin allowed for in the recommended price.

Until 1956 the cure normally applied for price cutting was the collective action of groups of manufacturers in refusing to supply the trader concerned. This was prohibited in the Restrictive Trade Practices Act and since 1956 manufacturers have had two remedies open to them. They could either refuse to supply a price cutting trader or they could sue him under section 25 for an injunction to restrain him from this breach of the manufacturer's condition of sale.[2]

---

[1] The large amount of local press advertising of used car prices also helps improve the perfection of the market.

[2] As a result of the passing of the Resale Prices Act 1964, both these forms of action have been prohibited since April 30, 1965 on goods which are not exempt from the ban on resale price maintenance. Suppliers of goods which are exempt still retain their rights either to refuse to supply or to sue for an injunction.

To be able to take action for an injunction under section 25 of the 1956 Act, adequate notice had to be given that r.p.m. was a condition of sale. We saw in the last chapter how certain legal decisions clarified exactly what this involves. Directly the Act was passed, a number of manufacturers amended their conditions of sale in order to allow them to take action where necessary under this section, but other manufacturers did not do so. This does not mean that they did not support r.p.m. It indicates simply that there was no threat to cut prices or that where there was price cutting, the manufacturer was sufficiently able to control supplies of his products that he did not need to resort to legal action to deal with a price cutter. In chapter XI we quote examples of a number of manufacturers who did not make r.p.m. a condition of sale until price cutting began on their products, whilst a number of other manufacturers did not make r.p.m. a legally enforceable condition of sale until the autumn of 1964 when they did so to obtain registration of an application for exemption under the Resale Prices Act.

The actual wording required to give notice of the condition of sale was quite simple. As we saw in the previous chapter, the courts held that it was sufficient to make the trader aware that a resale price condition was attached to the goods, it was not necessary to give express knowledge of the actual terms of the condition. Most manufacturers gave notice of their condition of sale regarding the maintenance of resale prices, as section 25 required, on their price lists or sales invoices. When the giving of trading stamps became a problem in 1963 some amended their conditions of sale to specifically prohibit this practice.

In the first two or three years after 1956 there was considerable doubt as to what use would be made of section 25. The motor manufacturers and Beechams had acted quickly in seeking injunctions against price cutters. But in other trades little enforcement action was noticed. Instances of cutting outside the food trade were, at this time, isolated and few grocery manufacturers were willing to take the necessary enforcement action. Where complaints from other retailers forced them to do something, they would often merely ask the trader concerned to desist. As the supermarkets became interested in chemists' lines in 1959-60, so the number of actions for injunctions rose appreciably.

In other trades cutting gradually became more frequent. This was especially true in the electrical goods trade, where a heavy investment boom in the middle 1950s had been followed by a falling off in consumer expenditure as the following table shows.

TABLE 2

Consumer Expenditure on Radio and Electrical Goods etc.

Year	Expenditure £million at 1958 prices
1957	346
1958	378
1959	449
1960	418
1961	402

Source : Preliminary Estimates of National Income and Expenditure 1956 to 1961 Cmnd. 1679 Table 9.

A similar falling off in expenditure on other consumer durable goods was also experienced and so manufacturers were left with little alternative than to allow price cutting in what was virtually a grand clearance sale.

By the end of 1960, a new type of retail outlet – the discount store – was coming into operation, specializing in cutting prices on branded consumer durables. In view of the weakness of r.p.m. at this time, their optimism was well justified. In May 1961, the Consumer Association publication *Which?* was able to report the existence of price reductions of up to 30% on electrical goods; and newspaper articles were being published marking the virtual collapse of resale price maintenance.[1] However, by the end of 1961 the slump in consumer spending was over and, spurred on by louder complaints from retailers about this new type of cut price activity, manufacturer opposition to price cutting began to harden. One or two successful cases for injunctions were sufficient to encourage other manufacturers to stand more firmly against price cutting. So in 1962 increasing use was made of section 25 and the discounting operations of the new discount stores were successfully curbed.

In 1964, when the President of the Board of Trade announced

---

[1] *E.g.* 'The Crumbling Facade of Resale Price Maintenance' *Financial Times* February 16, 1961.

his intention to introduce legislation to make resale price maintenance illegal, further outbreaks of price cutting were reported which has again caused a number of manufacturers to take firm action. An analysis of 138 cases recorded, giving details of the year of action, which were brought under section 25 shows clearly the year by year trend in the frequency of manufacturer action between 1956 and the passing of the Resale Prices Act in July 1964.

TABLE 3

Manufacturer action for injunctions under section 25

Year	1956	1957	1958	1959	1960	1961	1962	1963	1964
% of all injunctions sought	1	3	17	23	2	9	25	13	(to July) 7

Total – 100

Two distinct peaks will be observed – 1958-59 and 1962-63. The first reflects activity for injunctions in the food and chemists' goods trades, and the second is caused by a relatively large number of actions brought by electrical goods and hardware manufacturers to deal with a growing wish on the part of discount stores and supermarkets to cut prices on these products. Over two-thirds of the actions brought on chemists' goods arose in either 1958 or 1959 and more than one-half of the injunctions obtained by electrical goods manufacturers were sought in 1962. Since the beginning of 1964 cut price activities have been found on a more diverse range of commodities, and equally, therefore, enforcement action has been concerned with a greater number of products.

Information on instances of price cutting has usually been given to manufacturers by other retailers in the locality who feel that their trade is being harmed by price cutting. Some have been channelled through the retailer's trade association but others have gone direct either to the sales department of the manufacturer concerned or to the manufacturer's sales representative. Apart from the chemists' goods and motor trades, in no trade have retail outlets been actively 'policed' in an effort to trace cases of price cutting, though a member of the staff of the Imperial Tobacco Company Ltd. has been employed part-time to investigate complaints of price cutting made by other traders. In most trade associations, apart from the P.A.T.A. and B.M.T.A. which have always been r.p.m. enforcing bodies, the amount of time spent by officials on the enforcement of r.p.m. has amounted to a very small proportion of their actual working hours.

Where a complaint has been received by the manufacturer, the first step is for test purchases to be made and if price cutting is found, a letter is sent to the trader drawing his attention to the evidence obtained. A copy of the manufacturer's conditions of sale will be enclosed together with an undertaking which the retailer is asked to sign agreeing not to cut prices in future. If he signs, the matter is then dropped. In order to prove that the trader has received this communication, it is normally sent by registered post. So far all these steps will be taken by the manufacturer's own legal department or by a trade association, where this has been appointed agent for the manufacturer. If the trader refuses to give the required undertaking, the matter will either be placed in the hands of solicitors and proceedings for an injunction commenced or supplies will be stopped.

In practice, the great majority of instances of price cutting reported to a manufacturer have been dealt with internally and resulted in the cutter giving a private undertaking. On investigating allegations of cutting, the manufacturer has often found that it is not deliberate – or so he is told! The wrong price ticket may have been put on a particular article or the product may be one which is shop-soiled and therefore being sold off cheaply, although the public are not informed of this. In a number of cases, especially where small shopkeepers are involved, price cutting may have been unwitting. One manufacturer found that many retailers were not aware that by giving trading stamps they were committing a breach of his conditions of sale. In these cases the necessary adjustments have always been readily obtained.

A large number of manufacturers in a variety of trades report that a warning letter has usually sufficed, whilst in many instances this has been carried out on a purely friendly basis. There has not been the cut and thrust between manufacturer and retailer in the r.p.m. war that many journalists have led us to believe. When discount stores were first established in this country a number of their operators suggested that they were prepared to fight tooth and nail to defeat the manufacturers over this but after a number of failures they have been more willing to comply with the manufacturer's wishes.

A number of price cutters became unhappy when they felt that manufacturers were inconsistent in their enforcement action. The Independent Shopkeepers Committee protested that there were many occasions where a manufacturer took action against one price cutter and not against others. It has, however, often been deliberate policy on the part of the manufacturer to single out one trader for exemplary action, especially if he was important since this acted as a deterrent to other potential and actual price cutters.

The reputation of some manufacturers also tended to suffer if they merely made a token protest and failed to take the necessary action when cutting persisted. One important discounter sent to the Board of Trade Committee of Inquiry into Resale Price Maintenance a list of twelve manufacturers who, he said, had protested about his price cutting activities but had failed to take further action when he persisted. These covered a number of trades, including clothing, hardware and electrical goods. A few other manufacturers, all brand leaders in their own fields, have admitted to ignoring some instances of price cutting whilst taking enforcement action in others. As one person put it, 'the vicissitudes of business force you to procrastinate over the enforcement of resale price maintenance'. In some cases, the manufacturer agreed to a discounter continuing to cut prices, so long as he did not attract the attention of other traders by advertising the fact.

One manufacturer stated that on certain of his products, despite the fact that resale price maintenance was a condition of sale, a large multiple would be asked to stock the goods even if the trader intended to cut the prices. Needless to say, r.p.m. has now been completely dropped on this particular product.

The *Financial Times* claimed that some of the 'toughest' manufacturers on r.p.m. have turned a blind eye to price cutting so long as other retailers don't know. This, it argued, was driving discounting underground and was therefore bad.[1] In a number of articles this paper has quoted one particular instance, anonymously of course, where a certain 'tough' manufacturer has had a gentleman's agreement with a discount store that so long as price cutting was not advertised, it would be allowed. After supplying goods direct to this store since 1960, the manufacturer was, in 1964, threatening to sue for an injunction and also to stop supplies to other outlets owned by the same company. This seems a particularly deplorable situation and hardly furthers the case of those who support r.p.m.

Whilst manufacturers have failed in some cases to take the appropriate enforcement action – usually on products where there seems to be least justification for the continuance of r.p.m. – there are far more instances where the necessary enforcement action has been taken. In some trades, notably chemists' goods and hardware, successful injunctions or undertakings obtained have been reported in the trade journal either in the form of a news item or a letter to the Editor from the manufacturer taking the action. Manufacturers seem to have been very anxious to draw the attention of their retailer customers to the fact that they have successfully acted to prevent price cutting.

In trades where the manufacturer has traditionally supplied most of his goods direct to the retailer or where there are few wholesalers, manufacturers have preferred to stop supplies rather than take legal action. The more wholesalers there are, the more difficult this becomes and the greater the likelihood of the price cutter finding one who could be persuaded to supply him. The sanction of cutting off supplies has remained the most important means of action against price cutters on wines and spirits and electrical appliances. Some manufacturers have required their wholesalers to assist in enforcing resale price conditions by refusing to supply price cutters.

Some suppliers have taken particularly dramatic ways of stopping price cutting. When the Palace Discount House at Crewe began to cut prices on tools and, inevitably, the local traders protested, the manufacturers of Stanley tools bought back the whole stock of their products from the shop and then closed

[1] 'Discount Stores the Devil We Don't Know' *Financial Times* December 28, 1963.

their account. When the Tesco discount store in Leicester sold Gor-Ray skirts at 75s instead of 84s, Gor-Ray told all other retailers in Leicester to sell them at 69s and Gor-Ray promised to pay the difference.

When a manufacturer has taken legal action, he has normally sought three forms of relief from the court; injunction to restrain the cutter from continuing to cut prices on his goods, an inquiry as to damages and also payment of his costs in the case. The granting of costs is at the discretion of the court, though in these cases they have always been given. The great majority of applications for an injunction have been undefended and lasted only a few minutes in court. Unless the retailer had some legal technicality on which to argue, such as those discussed in the previous chapter, he has had little hope of succeeding. Though in view of this, it seems silly that the cutter should not have capitulated before court proceedings were instituted and so save himself having to pay the costs of the action. The reason why many traders have allowed themselves to be taken to court is that they consider the value of such publicity outweighs the extra cost involved.

Many cases have been heard on affidavit with witnesses not required. The court requires evidence on four points. The sales director of the company suing must assure the court that a condition has been imposed as to the price at which the goods may be resold. Evidence is then given of the results of test purchases (usually two are made), a representative of the company states that the goods on which the test purchases were made were in fact his products and, finally, he gives evidence of the date on which the price cutter was given notice of the conditions of sale attaching to the products concerned and he shows that the goods in question were supplied after the retailer received notice of the conditions of sale.

Each of these four pieces of evidence requires care in its preparation and a number of cases have had to be dropped because the evidence did not fulfil all these requirements. It has sometimes proved difficult to obtain evidence of price cutting, for once challenged, a cutter may switch to another product. Evidence of cutting on sales by wholesalers has also been difficult to obtain. Wholesalers occasionally receive complaints from their

F

sales representatives that sales to a retail customer were lost because another wholesaler offered the goods at a cheaper price. No retailer would provide the necessary evidence in such a case as this and sometimes such an accusation might simply be an excuse for a piece of poor salesmanship. Similarly, with sales to industrial users, it has proved difficult to obtain evidence of sales at a cut price so that an action can be brought. The need to prove that the goods which were the subject of a test purchase were supplied after notice of the condition of sale had been received has caused all products to be coded, and whilst most manufacturers do this as a matter of course, there are probably some for whom this created an extra problem. Because of the care with which evidence has to be collected to comply with the legal technicalities of the section, from the time that a case of price cutting has been notified, the time lag before an injunction is obtained has tended to be in the region of three to six months.

Whilst it is open to any plaintiff to ask for damages, it is difficult to prove that actual loss has been suffered as a result of price cutting, unless it can be shown that it has caused the manufacturer to lose the trade of other retailers. As a result, in very few reported cases has a manufacturer been awarded damages. If a manufacturer is serious about requiring damages from a trader, his best policy is to follow that adopted by Joseph Lucas (Sales and Services) Ltd., who, when they were enforcing fixed resale prices, required any person selling their products below the fixed price to pay liquidated damages of £20 in addition to any other remedy which was available against him.

The costs of an action depend very much on whether or not the action is defended. The sum total of the plaintiff's and defendant's costs will be at least £100 if the case is undefended, though one estimate puts it as high as £200. The greater part consists of the costs of the manufacturer and depends on how much legal assistance external to the firm or trade association has been provided. Where a case is defended, costs are much higher. It costs a trader at least £200 to fight a case and the manufacturer's costs may be even greater. The cost to one manufacturer of a case which was successfully defended was £1,600.

Although a successful manufacturer will have costs awarded in his favour, these will probably cover only about three-quarters of the actual costs of the action and will not take account of the time spent by company staff in preparing a case. In some instances, too, it may be difficult to recover the costs awarded from the defendant, especially if he is a market trader or some such trader who can readily move on to another area. Thus, absence of financial resources can cause a serious limitation on the amount of action taken by a manufacturer under section 25, especially is this true should a manufacturer not have his own legal department and/or be in a trade where no trade association is available to help meet part of the costs of the action.

Short of a census of all manufacturers, it would be impossible to present an exact statement of the frequency with which action has been taken. However, an attempt has been made to obtain a general picture from reports in the national and trade press and from information supplied confidentially from a number of other sources – manufacturers, retailers, trade associations and solicitors. No attempt has been made to 'gross up' these figures so they must be taken as a minimum, though it is believed that few cases where injunctions were granted will have been missed, so our 'minimum' calculation may not be very much below the true figure.

TABLE 4

Legal Action to Enforce R.P.M.

Product Group	Injunction or Undertaking in Court Approximate number
Food	10
Confectionery	3
Wines and spirits	1
Tobacco	5
Paint etc.	8
Furniture	–
Electrical appliances	30
Hardware	40
Clothing and draperies	3
Motor vehicles and accessories	30
Chemists goods	70
Other products*	10
Total	210

* Stationery, records, toys, clocks and watches etc.

In most trades several manufacturers have all taken legal

action – twenty manufacturers of chemists' goods, eleven manufacturers of electrical appliances and ten hardware manufacturers. They have all tended to be leading manufacturers in their own field. A few have obtained ten or more injunctions, the Beecham group with eighteen and Addis with fourteen lead the way.

The readiness with which manufacturers have resorted to the law courts for an injunction varies from manufacturer to manufacturer. Whilst some have sought an injunction in at least half the cases of cutting reported to them, there are others who, for every injunction granted, will have stopped price cutting by twenty or thirty more traders without going to court. An informed estimate is that at least 90% of all instances of price cutting reported and in which the manufacturer has started to take positive action, have been settled before reaching court with the trader voluntarily giving an undertaking not to cut prices in future. Such private undertakings have frequently been obtained in a number of trades. Chemists' goods, hardware and furniture manufacturers have often used this method, for example one furniture manufacturer has obtained over 100 undertakings, so, too, have at least two manufacturers of hardware. Manufacturers of stationery, confectionery, electrical goods and clothing have also frequently obtained private undertakings. Whilst in most trades some manufacturers have stopped supplies occasionally, it is only on electrical goods and wines and spirits and possibly confectionery that manufacturers really seem to have used this to any great extent relatively speaking, as compared with their use of actions for an injunction or obtaining a private undertaking.

We have seen that the first step has normally been a private approach to the price cutter by the manufacturer or by a trade association representing him. In some trades, negotiation (or 'intimidation and persuasion' as it is sometimes appropriately described) is all that is normally required. Even the frequency with which such negotiations have taken place varies widely. On such products as cycles and motor cycles, wines and spirits and drapery, there have been perhaps not more than fifty cases a year to be dealt with altogether. On others such as motors, furniture, hardware and cigarettes and tobacco, the number has run into hundreds, and on chemists' and electrical goods over a thousand complaints have been dealt with each year.

Thus we find that in those trades where most injunctions have been sought, the greatest use has also been made of negotiations and requests for private undertakings. While a number of manufacturers have refused to supply a price cutter, in only one or two trades is this a sanction which has been used frequently. To have successfully taken action for an injunction in one or two cases has normally been a sufficient deterrent to discourage a trader from persisting in price cutting and with the backing of the threat of an action for an injunction under section 25 as the ultimate sanction, manufacturers have often found little difficulty in obtaining a voluntary undertaking. If our informed estimate that in 90% of the cases a private undertaking has been given is right, then between 1956 and 1964 at least 1,800 of these undertakings were given and in many (probably thousands) more cases a trader will have been persuaded to stop price cutting without being asked to give even a private undertaking.

Thus, whilst maybe on average not more than twenty-five injunctions a year have been obtained under section 25, it is quite clear that it is the ultimate deterrent available to the manufacturer in this section that has enabled him, in most cases, to persuade a trader voluntarily to stop price cutting. Added to this is the fact that apart from cheap publicity, the trader has known that he has nothing to gain by allowing himself to be taken to court, since section 25 is so tightly drawn that only on a legal technicality will a manufacturer lose a case.

The great majority of cases have been brought by manufacturers against retailers. However, in one or two cases involving chemists' goods a wholesaler has also obtained an injunction, whilst on the other hand at least one manufacturer has obtained an injunction against both a retailer and a wholesaler.

A number of manufacturers have found that to insist on observance of their resale price conditions and to rigorously enforce them through the courts can create a lot of ill-will. Many price cutters have gained considerable publicity at the expense of enforcing manufacturers which at times has tended to become quite abusive. For example, *The Ironmonger* contained an account of the efforts of the manufacturer of Eclipse tools to force a Southsea trader to restore the fixed price. The trader placed all the correspondence, together with his own comments, in the shop window. Much abuse was levelled against the manufacturer which must have been damaging to his reputation in that area, quite unjustifiably. As Mr J. Hugh Neill, the managing director concerned, remarked, 'the enforcement of resale price maintenance is not an easy or pleasant task for the manufacturer'.[1]

Most discount stores, after failing in their initial attempts to break r.p.m., have been co-operative so far as price maintenance is concerned except where manufacturers were found to be acting in one case of price cutting and ignoring others and where the enforced margin was ridiculously high. It is, for example, difficult to see how a mark-up of $87\frac{1}{2}\%$ on cost can ever be justified on a simple household product. In instances such as these, it is not surprising that traders have felt aggrieved when action has been taken against them.

When asked to comment on the effects of their policy of enforcing r.p.m., most manufacturers consider that they have obtained more support from distributors, but far fewer are prepared to say that they believe that their policy has resulted in an increase in sales. In fact, some manufacturers in a variety of trades are of the opinion that their sales are lower as a result of the maintenance of resale prices.

Some manufacturers who actively enforce r.p.m. (or did do so) found that they have not received the support from retailers who want r.p.m. that they are entitled to expect. One manufacturer in the grocery trade was particularly angered to find that although for some time he stood firm in insisting on r.p.m. whilst his competitors did not, in the shops of small grocers it was the products of his competitors which were being featured. The moral of this is that if the independent trader supports r.p.m. and wants to retain this system, then he must ensure that he promotes the price maintained line rather than a competing brand which is being price cut elsewhere. This is especially important in respect of those goods of small unit value which require no service to sell. Here it is difficult to prove that to enforce r.p.m. confers any benefit on the manufacturer and those

[1] *The Ironmonger* August 17, 1963. p. 238.

who enforce r.p.m. on their products to support the small retailer expect him to reciprocate.

Why then have manufacturers continued to enforce r.p.m. over a large part of consumer expenditure? In some cases brought by manufacturers under section 25, evidence was given that price cutting was causing other traders to refuse to stock that manufacturer's products. As counsel for Morphy Richards in their case against Rolls Razor remarked,

'It is quite plain from letters that have come in that this kind of activity is doing grave damage to our business so far as relations with our customers are concerned.'[1]

Whether the manufacturer is wise to heed actions such as this depends on the importance of the retailers who are refusing to handle. In the case of a leading brand, the retailer is often doing more harm to himself by not stocking a product than to the manufacturer. Whilst the views of distributors of the products are important in determining whether r.p.m. is adopted as a sales policy, a sample of manufacturers revealed that this was only of secondary importance to the policy followed by manufacturers of competing brands. Analysis of the replies gave the following result –

TABLE 5

Determinants of Manufacturer Policy as Regards R.P.M.

Factors	%
Policy of other manufacturers	36%
Views of distributors	32%
Attitude of trade association	11%
Other reasons	20%
Total	99% (not 100 due to rounding off)

Most of those which listed 'other reasons' claimed that their decision was company policy uninfluenced by other factors. One manufacturer of furniture held that sales were greater under resale price maintenance. Some manufacturers who do not enforce say that enforcement action is now too difficult, whilst others say that there has never been any need for enforcement action to be taken.

[1] *Morphy Richards Ltd.* v. *Rolls Razor Ltd. The Times* March 7, 1962.

Analysing the replies to this question, by type of product, very little difference between products was found from the percentages quoted above. In the case of grocery manufacturers where r.p.m. has ended, the policy of other manufacturers was given a higher importance (44% of all replies) and the views of distributors a correspondingly lower significance (25% all replies). In the furniture and hardware trades, where r.p.m. covers only certain sections of the trade, the views of distributors are accorded greater importance. Manufacturers of chemists' products place a slightly greater emphasis on the attitude of a trade association but the figure of 16%, compared with the overall average of 11%, is lower than one might expect, bearing in mind the influence that the P.A.T.A. has had in this trade, though it does, perhaps, suggest that no agreement to adopt and enforce r.p.m. as a condition of sale exists between the manufacturer members of that association.

Thus, whilst both the policy of other manufacturers and the views of their distributors are shown to have a strong influence on manufacturer policy, the former is slightly the more important and experience in the grocery trade suggests that once r.p.m. begins to break down in a trade, the need to keep in step with manufacturers of competing goods becomes even more important.

The arguments in favour of resale price maintenance have been well set out in recent years[1] and it is not the intention of this writer to go back over the ground that these writings have covered. However, in closing this chapter it may perhaps be interesting to note some of the arguments put forward by manufacturers to this writer in favour of r.p.m. Whilst a few manufacturers consider the enforcement of r.p.m. to be unnecessary and claim that they have been forced to keep the system simply because of pressure from retailers and their trade associations, their number is not large and it is clear that many manufacturers genuinely believe resale price maintenance to be desirable.

A number of manufacturers fear that a breakdown in r.p.m. would have unfortunate consequences on their distributors. They

[1] Notably in Andrews and Friday *op. cit.* and P. W. S. Andrews *'On Competition in Economic Theory'* (London) 1964.

argue that the widest distribution possible is desirable and that cutting would cause some distributors to go out of business and others to cease handling price-cut products, especially those that were being used as loss leaders by non-specialist distributors. Cutting could also cause an increase in the number of bad credit risks. The preservation of a reasonable margin to ensure that distributors give adequate pre- and post-sales service is also important and this links up closely with issues of public safety. The danger that the public will be encouraged to carry out their own repairs to such things as television sets because of the availability of spare parts at cut prices in discount stores is considered a problem. Whilst there are increasing numbers of people who are competent to carry out many of their own repairs, there is still a much higher proportion of the population which needs to have servicing carried out for it by competent agents. The issue here is whether those members of the public who could not carry out their own repairs would be enticed, by offers of spare parts at cut prices, to ignore the services of competent dealers. The manufacturers fear they would.

There are also a number of manufacturers, especially in the clothing trade, who enforce r.p.m. on their goods because they produce a particularly wide range of sizes and fittings and by preventing cut price competition they hope to stop cut price traders creaming off the more popular lines and leaving awkward sizes, etc., on the hands of the other traders, to the dissatisfaction and inconvenience of customers. Quite apart from the issue of resale price maintenance, one manufacturer of children's wear - Pasolds - who use the 'Ladybird' brand name, have found it so difficult to persuade ordinary retailers to stock the full range of their products that they are now encouraging selected retailers to stock solely 'Ladybird' lines.

These arguments so far are all related to the distributive side of the trade and manufacturers fears that with the advent of price cutting the services provided by traditional retailers would suffer to the detriment of both manufacturer and consumer. Manufacturers fear, too, that price cutting will harm them directly. It is commonly held that price cutting on a branded line suggests an inferior quality good and it is argued that for the same product to be found in different shops at varying prices discredits that line. The security offered by r.p.m. enables orders to be placed well in advance by retailers for a product and this enables a manufacturer to achieve economies arising from long production runs. The fear of being left in the hands of a few large multiple distributors is also uppermost in the minds of some manufacturers who consider that the consequence of this will be to cause extra pressure on manufacturers' profits and hence a decline in the quality of the product as is argued has happened in the U.S.A. Thus manufacturer decisions to enforce r.p.m. have, in many cases, a strong philosophical background to them. It must be considered doubtful, however, whether, in the absence of a similar policy being pursued by their competitors and in the absence of pressure brought to bear on them by their distributors, they would continue to adopt such a policy.

CHAPTER VII

THE PRICE CUTTERS

Two types of trader have been responsible for the majority of price cutting which has caused manufacturers to take legal action. First, there are the market traders and other small retailers operating on a policy of price advantage whom we will call 'bargain stores'. These have existed for many years and even when supplies were scarce after the war would often be found cutting prices. They tend, inevitably, to concentrate their cutting on small products such as confectionery and chemists' goods. At the other extreme, we find the discount stores and supermarkets also engaged in price cutting. A number of the operators of these outlets started off twenty or thirty years ago as small cut-price grocery establishments or bargain stores. They have tended to have most of their conflicts with manufacturers in the fields of hardware and electrical goods. In both cases price cutting is a deliberate trading policy and is facilitated by the achievement of lower distribution costs than normal retailers experience through savings on overhead and/or operating costs.

Analysis of the type of business carried on by defendants to actions brought by manufacturers to restrain them from price cutting under section 25 of the Restrictive Trade Practices Act indicates that some 40% of the actions have been brought against market traders and 'bargain stores' and the other 60% have been brought against discount stores and supermarkets. More than half the actions listed have been against traders operating in the Greater London area, especially in East and South East London, where cut-price stores have traditionally flourished. In other areas small pockets of price cutting have existed, especially in the North West and North East. To some extent these reflect the development of discount stores in these areas.

For the remainder of this chapter attention will be concentrated mainly on the discount store since this is where the real future of cut price trading on non-foods probably exists. Discount stores in this country were first introduced in about 1960 and between 1960 and 1962 a number were opened up. Since then manufacturer enforcement of r.p.m. has retarded their development, since by definition a discount store devotes at least 50% of its selling space to branded non-foods and sells these at a saving of at least 10%. In fact, because discount stores are really intended to concentrate on branded goods, it is arguable that there are no such outlets at present operating in this country. However, for the purposes of this study we will assume that those stores whose trading policy is to cut prices on a wide range of non-food goods where at all possible are, in fact, discount stores. A number developed from grocery supermarkets whilst others were started by retailing companies which operated traditional department stores.

Self Service and Supermarket Annual Survey and Directory for 1964 listed only sixteen discount stores in the United Kingdom.[1] These are:

Grandways Stores	Leeds	Victor Value & Co. Ltd.	Bristol
Shoppers Fair	Leeds	Victor Value & Co. Ltd.	Romford
Tops Super Sales	Rotherham	Victor Value & Co. Ltd.	Acton
U-Save	Harrogate	Bath Co-operative Soc.	Bath
I.D.M. Brierley Ltd.	Northampton	Adsega Ltd.	Manchester
I.D.M. Brierley Ltd.	Peterborough	Payless Ltd.	Glasgow
Buyright Ltd.	Northampton	Payless Ltd.	Oldham
Supa Save	Southend-on-Sea	Grandfare	Glasgow

The size of store ranges from 7,200 square feet at U-Save to 40,000 square feet in Brierley's store at Peterborough. Few stores are over 20,000 square feet in size.

This list seems, however, a little too restricted. No outlets operating under the name Tesco are included, although their outlets at Leicester and Grantham are commonly accepted as being discount stores. Bellmans of Brighton also did at one time endeavour to operate as discounters and would be in a position to do so again once resale price maintenance was dropped. A

[1] The 1965 Directory lists a further eight, of which only the Cee-N-Cee store in Crewe is shown as being over 5,000 sq. ft. in size. Buyright Ltd. no longer appears in the list.

similar situation also applies in relation to some of the larger outlets of Anthony Jackson's Foodfare Ltd. Thus, whilst accepting that since r.p.m. is still in existence in this country no true discount store exists, if any stores are to be listed who are in a position to start discounting operations should r.p.m. end, then there are probably twenty-five or so outlets in all which should be included.

Study of the Self Service and Supermarket list of discount stores reveals that a high proportion are situated in the northern part of the country. This reflects a greater readiness on the part of people in the north to accept cut price goods than southerners. The operator of one discount store in the south reports that whilst consumers readily buy groceries in his discount store, they prefer to go to a nearby department store, which he also owns, to buy an identical non-food product to that which they could have obtained at a reduced price in the discount store. No doubt, given the breakdown of r.p.m., discounting will be able to gain ground but a more rapid expansion of discount stores in the north than in the south is still to be expected.

It is interesting to note that whilst the discount store movement is largely moving from north to south, the spread of supermarkets was from south to north. This difference is no doubt largely due to the fact that supermarkets are operated in chains and most of the early supermarkets belonged to companies with head offices in or near London, whilst any one company tends to own only one or two discount stores so dispersion from London becomes easier, but it also bears out the point just made that there is some reluctance on the part of those living in the south of England to provide a clientele for a discount store selling cut price non-food goods.

A discount store aims to work on a gross margin of about $17\frac{1}{2}\%$ to 20% instead of the 30% available to traditional non-food retailers. Wherever possible they buy in large quantities in order to obtain the best possible terms, which may mean in some cases buying at the price at which the manufacturer normally sells to a wholesaler. Despite this, to make price cutting pay, a large turnover has to be achieved and all services are cut to a minimum. The store operates on a self service basis and pre- or post-sales services such as demonstration, delivery or installation are not normally provided. Fittings in the store are kept to an absolute minimum and sites with low rents are sought. Some discount stores have opened in disused cinemas and others are out of the main shopping centres of towns. To obtain the fast turnover required to make the concern profitable, only fast selling lines are stocked – only popular brands and sizes of a product are made available. As a result they are able to achieve an overall rate of stockturn on non-foods of between eight and ten a year as compared with a normal stockturn on household goods, clothing, etc., of about five and a half.

A big problem facing many discount store operators is the difficulty of acquiring the ability to sell successfully products which they have never before handled.[1] Thus, to a company that formerly concentrated on foods, the difficulty is buying and selling non-foods especially clothing and consumer durables. Some operators overcome this by letting out parts of the store to concessionaires but Tesco have found this to be unsatisfactory and now acquire their 'know-how' by taking over retailing companies with experience in selling these particular goods.

There is some disagreement between operators as to what products best lend themselves to discounting. Food, toiletries, household products such as cleaners, detergents, polishes, are stocked by most supermarkets and by discount stores. Leading brands of hardware are also popular, so, too, are small electrical appliances such as toasters and irons. Some discounters would also sell large electrical goods such as television sets, cookers and washing machines but there are others who would not because of lack of space, servicing problems and the high proportion of such goods bought on hire purchase. For similar reasons, furniture does not assume any importance at present in the range of goods stocked or which discount stores would like to stock. Some doubts are also being expressed about branded clothing lines. At one time branded nylons, corsetry, shirts, underwear, etc., were obvious goods for a discounter to stock. As a result of manufacturer opposition some discounters now sell unbranded or own brand clothing and claim that these are proving even more satisfactory.

[1] Though this is not a problem to those discount stores which are owned by companies already operating department stores.

A few years ago when discount stores were opening, price cutting on brand leaders took place and from details given in various trade journals at that time, we can investigate the sort of price reductions that were being offered.

TABLE 6

Price Reductions offered by Discounters 1960-1962

Brand	Fixed Retail Selling Price			Discounter's Selling Price		
Morphy Richards Astral Refrigerator	£70	7	0	£62	14	0
Burco Tumblair Dryer	56	10	0	49	5	0
Dimplex Radiant Heater	10	18	0	9	15	0
Morphy Richards Automatic Toaster	5	11	8	4	15	6
Hotpoint Electric Blanket	5	14	3	5	2	11
G.E.C. Electric Kettle	5	1	7	4	10	0
Belling Fire	4	13	2	3	19	6
Bex Bissell Shampoo Master	3	7	6	2	9	0
Prestige Minit Mop	1	3	6		11	9

The majority of those reductions show savings of between 10% and 15%. These offers were, however, usually made at the time of the opening of the store and hence the reductions shown may perhaps be larger than could be normally expected if discounting became normal trading practice in this country.

By 1964, however, the situation was quite different. Manufacturer enforcement of r.p.m. had prevented price cutting taking place on most non-foods. The non-food lines sold were often unbranded or carried the retailer's own brand. Manufacturer branded goods, where they were still being sold, normally carried the maintained price though at least one discounter, as a matter of principle, has continued to cut prices in defiance of the manufacturer's wishes. Though as these price reductions were unadvertised and appeared, in most cases, to be for only a nominal sum, it is difficult to see just what this policy achieved.

TABLE 7

Price Reductions offered 1964

Brand	Fixed Retail Selling Price			Discounter's Selling Price		
Bex Bissell Shampoo Master	£3	7	6	£2	17	6
Wolf Electric Drills	5	19	6	4	7	6
Prestige Minit Mop	1	10	0	1	7	6
Aladdinique Convector Fire	9	16	1	9	8	0
Philishave Razor	8	12	6	8	2	6

Discounters claim at least a threefold increase in sales when a brand is price cut, while one stated that sales of certain hardware products rose eight times and sales of razor blades rose ten times as a result of price cutting. Another trader found that over three weeks his sales of cut price Scotch whisky amounted to £5,750 over nine branches, whereas previously only a few dozen bottles were sold. Cigarette sales also seem to react well to price cutting, this same trader, who had not previously sold cigarettes achieved sales of well over £12,000 in three weeks. Two other price cutters also experienced large increases in sales as a result of reducing the price of cigarettes. One in Bethnal Green found sales rose from 2,000 packets to 30,000 a week and one in Wolverhampton sold 140,000 packets in a week, compared with only 20,000 before he started cutting their prices.

To what extent these figures could be maintained or even reflect increases in total manufacturer sales is problematical. The experiences quoted above all related to a period of time immediately after price cutting had begun and as they all occurred on goods which at the time were still subject to r.p.m., a considerable advantage over other traders was obtained. Some of this increase in sales would no doubt ultimately be lost when the novelty had worn off because of the inconvenience of travelling further to shop. In the event of the abolition of r.p.m. on the products concerned (as has now happened on razor blades and spirits) other traders could fight back by also cutting prices without fear of incurring the opposition of manufacturers. The offer of a good at a reduced price may also have encouraged some people to buy sooner than they would otherwise have done and in the case of consumer durables this could not readily be maintained.

Cut price merchandising also requires considerable skill. The sevenfold increase in sales of cigarettes achieved by the Wolverhampton trader mentioned above still did not prevent his losing £160 a week and, in January 1962, going bankrupt. Ten per cent of the copies of a questionnaire sent out during the course of this study to a small sample of traders who were known to have had actions for price cutting brought against them by manufacturers, were returned by the Post Office on the grounds that the addressees had gone away, this compares with a figure of slightly less than 1% returned by the G.P.O. in a sample survey of grocers conducted at the same time. Small traders cutting prices indiscriminately run a considerable risk of going bankrupt but there is, as yet, no evidence that the larger discount operators are in any form of financial difficulty.[1] Evidence provided in the journal *Self Service* in April 1960 showed that despite a number of severe price cuts made by Anthony Jackson's Foodfare, in only one instance was their margin, shown as a percentage off their selling price, less than 20%. Examples given included:

TABLE 8

Margins to a Price Cutter

Brand	Cost Price	Fixed Retail Selling Price	Anthony Jackson's Selling Price	Margin to Anthony Jackson
Bex Bissell Carpet Cleaner	£1 15 0	£3 7 6	£2 15 0	36%
Addis Gift Set	1 7 11	2 9 6	1 15 0	20%
Prestige Minit Mop	16 4	1 10 0	1 0 0	18%
John Dickinson Writing Pad (dozen)	6 0	12 0	9 0	33%
Sylkett Gloves (dozen)	1 15 0	2 14 0	2 5 0	22%

From these figures it is clear that there is scope for traders operating with low selling cost to offer price reductions and still to be able to make a reasonable profit themselves.

Initially discount store operators realized that they would have to fight to break resale price maintenance. As a Tesco spokesman remarked at the opening of their store in Leicester – 'This is war, we are trying to break r.p.m. and we are going to be in and out of court over it.' It is doubtful whether this 'war' has really materialized, as most of the instances of price cutting have been dealt with by friendly negotiation. Some sections of the national and trade press have made more out of the matter than was really justified. As one trade journal commented, 'National publicity has turned Tesco into a sort of St George who is going to kill this awful dragon [r.p.m.].'[2]

What battle there was has so far undoubtedly been won by the manufacturers and the traditional types of retailer who favour r.p.m. Hostility and opposition has faced the discounters on all sides. In some cases they have been prevented from

[1] Though this does not apply to supermarkets, see below ch. ix.
[2] *The Grocer* December 16, 1961 p. 26.

G

advertising in local newspapers. One discounter found that the windows of his shops were being mysteriously broken once he started cutting prices. But the main difficulties have been with the manufacturers. Most manufacturers have refused to supply determined price cutters, so they have had to find alternative sources of supply. Wholesalers have sometimes helped, though where most of the supplies of a product go direct from the manufacturer to the retailer, the discounter has had to buy from alternative sources such as mail order houses or other retailers. However, since most manufacturers code their products, they have been able to trace the source of supplies stocked by the discounter and to take action against the wholesalers or other retailers who supplied them.

At one time the Grandways Store at Leeds had plain vans touring the country to buy goods for cash from any who would supply them. Even this, however, failed to ensure that they had adequate supplies and it further failed in its prime object which was to force manufacturers to supply discount stores direct. Such an uneconomic method of trying to obtain supplies could not go on indefinitely and eventually victory, in round one at least, was conceded to the manufacturer.[1] The number of injunctions obtained against any discount store varies; some have had five or six against them but in view of the virtual impossibility of winning a case under section 25, most have chosen to give private undertakings to manufacturers to save themselves the additional cost and bother of fighting a case. Some have given thirty or more private undertakings and until the Resale Prices Act stirred some into action again, most had given up challenging manufacturers over r.p.m.

The reaction of discounters to the enforcement of r.p.m. on a good varies. Some refuse to stock the product at all, preferring merely to sell cheap imports or their own brand instead. In other cases, the retailer may still continue to stock the line and to sell

[1] An Association of Independent Discount Stores was formed at one stage in an effort to overcome this problem of the refusal of manufacturers to supply. A condition of membership was that the trader must sell at least 95% of his merchandise at 'a realistic discount'. It intended that all members should seek to help each other by providing supplies where another trader had his stopped by the manufacturer. This failed when in 1962 a number of discounters decided that they would no longer cut prices on price maintained goods.

it at its fixed price, especially if it is thought necessary to continue to stock the line in order to retain consumer support. Sometimes cheap unbranded lines are placed next to the price maintained goods and marked as being of special value.

On certain products, such as transistor radios and shirts, cheap imports form very satisfactory alternative lines to stock. In other cases the retailer prefers to introduce his own house brand. Amongst discounters, Tesco were the pioneers of this method of avoiding r.p.m. (though Marks and Spencers, Boots and similar stores have for a long time adopted a similar policy), and they backed their own brand name – Delamere – with heavy press and television advertising. Manufacturers who enforce r.p.m. are often found to be very anxious to pack 'own brands' for such retailers.[1] The usual advantages of 'own brands' – improved store image and hence greater customer loyalty and a good quality product at a lower selling price but with a good return to the retailer – occur and it is hardly surprising that some discounters are doubtful whether on certain lines they will ever revert to manufacturer brands.

Some of the more aggressive price cutters have looked for other ways of avoiding manufacturer enforcement of r.p.m. Two ingenious schemes were tried by Grandways of Leeds and U-Save of Harrogate. Grandways cut the price of the product and then imposed a hire charge of 1d per quarter to last for twenty-one years on top of this. The hire charge was of course never implemented. However, they were advised that they were still contravening a manufacturer's fixed price conditions of sale and so dropped the scheme. U-Save attempted to accept goods such as old toothbrushes in part-exchange for new goods and counted the good taken in part-exchange as being of the value of the price cut offered on the product purchased. They, too, were advised that this was still actionable under section 25 of the Restrictive Trade Practices Act and so the idea was dropped.

One or two discounters still insist on price cutting and they have agreements with some manufacturers that so long as the price cuts are not advertised, the manufacturer concerned will

[1] A sample survey of manufacturers carried out in connection with this study revealed that nearly one-half of those replying supplied goods for retailers to brand.

not take action. One smaller price cutter displays price maintained lines but with no price marked on them, when a customer enquires the price a reduced price is quoted.

Discount store operators have a number of complaints, some of which are well founded. The willingness of some manufacturers to act against them but to allow other traders to continue to cut prices is in their opinion inequitable. The margins enforced by manufacturers (in some cases as a mark up they range from 66% to 100% on the cost price) provide good publicity for the discounter as a champion of the consumer. In some cases, it is clear that these margins are excessive and provide a high profit to a retailer who does very little in return, especially in the case of hardware and stationery products where little or no service is required. Some manufacturers, whilst enforcing fixed price conditions, favour the use of premium offers, when their product is purchased another good is given free or made available at a reduced price. This, too, is seen as being inconsistent with resale price maintenance and so angered the director of Supa Save that when two such manufacturers, Morphy Richards and Thermos, sued for injunctions against him because he persisted in cutting the price of their products, he stated that he would no longer stock them.

The impact of the discount store on the British retailing scene, which seemed to be so promising in 1960 and 1961, has faded considerably over the last three years. Whereas then it was possible to achieve substantial savings by purchasing consumer durables from discount stores and carrying them away oneself, this opportunity no longer exists.[1] The main reason for the failure of discounting is, as we have seen in this chapter, manufacturer insistence on r.p.m. supported by the tightly-drawn section 25 of the Restrictive Trade Practices Act. There are other reasons, however, which hinder any future development of discounting. One is the supposedly traditional British suspicion that a cut price good is an inferior good. Where the products involved may cost a man's wages for a month or more, this is a suspicion that can be less readily overcome than a similar suspicion on cut price

---

[1] Since the Resale Prices Act the situation has eased a little but discount stores have still not made a major impact on the British retailing scene as most goods are still subject to r.p.m.

groceries. Maybe discounters should be prepared to give a form of guarantee when they sell the goods.

Discounting largely depends on the existence of cheap sites since rents constitute a high proportion of the selling cost. In the United States of America this problem has been solved by siting discount houses in 'out of town' areas. This is not likely to be as successful in this country. In the first place, whereas there is one car to every two and a half persons in the U.S.A., the ratio is only one to seven here. Furthermore, in Britain, especially in the large conurbations such as Greater London, the Midlands, the North East and the North West, as town merges into town there just is no 'out of town' area to be utilized in this way. Thus discount stores would have to be built within urban areas. Even here, the lower car ownership ratio presents problems in moving large consumer durables out of the shop, whilst pressure on land in town centres prevents the provision of parking space for those who do have cars and inflates site rents.

The main hindrance so far, however, to the development of discount stores has been the continued strength of resale price maintenance. In so far as the Restrictive Trade Practices Act has helped keep r.p.m. strong, it has therefore denied the public the benefits of new and cheaper methods of distribution which discount stores seemingly offer.

CHAPTER VIII

CONCEALED PRICE CUTTING

In addition to allowing a supplier to enforce a condition as to the price at which his goods were to be resold, the Restrictive Trade Practices Act also allowed him to treat any condition as to discount, the price paid for other goods taken in part exchange and the letting of goods on hire purchase as a condition as to the price at which the goods were to be resold and therefore enforceable under section 25. This was clearly desirable if r.p.m. was to remain a viable system in any trade. Whilst at the time of the passing of the Act the Co-operative Societies feared that these provisions would be used by many manufacturers against the Co-operative dividend (the dividend was already banned on many price maintained goods), this has not happened and the only form of 'concealed' price cutting which manufacturers have, on the whole, attempted to prevent has been the giving of trading stamps.

Trading stamps are by no means a new phenomenon in this country. As early as 1933 a Committee set up by the Board of Trade had investigated the giving of gift coupons and trading stamps.[1] It found that neither practice was detrimental to the public interest though it was suggested that trading stamp schemes run by local traders might be preferable to schemes run by independent trading stamp companies. An eminent economist on the Committee – Professor D. H. Macgregor – however, dissented from the general approval given to schemes run by independent trading stamp companies. This report did not consider the position of trading stamps in relation to resale price maintenance though it is of present interest that the Committee suggested that retailers might find it beneficial to agree amongst themselves not to give trading stamps!

Whilst trading stamp schemes have had a continuous existence

[1] *Committee on Gift Coupons and Trading Stamps Report* 1933 Cmd. 4385.

since then, the present boom only dates from 1958 with the introduction of Green Shield stamps. This was reinforced in October 1963 by the appearance in this country of an American trading stamp company – Sperry and Hutchinson. Whereas in 1957 it was estimated that the total turnover of some thirty stamp companies was between £1m. and £2m. a year, by 1965 turnover was £11m. a year, of which Green Shield were estimated to be responsible for 65% and Sperry and Hutchinson for a further 25% and 30,000 retail outlets including garages were giving trading stamps. The basis of a trading stamp scheme is that for every sixpence spent the consumer receives one stamp.[1] The stamps are collected by consumers in books provided by the stamp company and when the book is completed it may be redeemed for one of a range of gifts offered by the stamp company. Many of the gifts offered are the products of leading manufacturers and the most popular are hardware, holloware and other household utensils which account for more than one-quarter of the gifts redeemed by Green Shield, followed by soft furnishings and draperies and small electrical appliances.

The number of books of stamps required to obtain a gift depends, of course, on the normal retail price of the good, though the Consumer Association, in a study of the value of gifts offered by trading stamp companies, found that for every £100 spent by the consumer for which stamps were received, gifts varying in value from £1 1s to £2 8s could be obtained according to the stamp company concerned.[2] It is estimated that when a completed book of stamps of one of the two leading companies is redeemed a gift with an average value of 15s is obtained. Since 1,280 stamps are required to fill one of their books this indicates that by receiving trading stamps on the purchase of a good an advantage of nearly 2½% is available to the consumer. In reality the advantage is less than this due to the reduced number of stamps given on petrol purchases[3] and since bills frequently do not come to an exact multiple of 6d more than the minimum expenditure of £32 to fill a book with 1,280 stamps would be

[1] Except in the case of petrol where because of the high purchase tax content in the price of petrol, five stamps per gallon are normally given.
[2] *Which ?* May 1960.
[3] Garages are at present responsible for 20% - 25% turnover of the leading stamp companies.

required, though this would to some extent be offset by the current tendency to give double and even treble stamps on purchases.

The Trading Stamps Act 1964, the major provisions of which came into force on July 31, 1965, requires all stamps to carry a cash value and makes it obligatory on the stamp companies to redeem their stamps for cash if required to do so by any person holding stamps with a cash value of more than 5s.[1] Green Shield and Sperry and Hutchinson have both decided on a cash value of 0·075d per stamp, giving a cash redemption value of 8s per book, which is much lower than the value when a book is exchanged for a gift. In the light of American experience where similar provisions exist they are expecting only a small proportion of their redemptions to be for cash. A smaller company, however – Thrift Stamps – has fixed a cash value of 0·125d per stamp and is anticipating a much higher rate of cash redemption.

By giving trading stamps a retailer is incurring additional costs, estimated to amount to about 2% of his turnover. Thus for stamps to be worthwhile an increase in turnover sufficient to compensate for this extra cost has to be achieved. Why then do retailers give trading stamps? Commentators have tended to see this as an aggressive action, attempting to gain some competitive advantage for the retailer concerned. In some cases this view has also been related to the existence of r.p.m. in a trade preventing the distributor offering a direct price reduction. Thus in an early article, Dr (later Professor) W. A. Lewis argued that trading stamps were the product of r.p.m.[2] In her recent study on trading stamps, Mrs Christina Fulop has taken a similar point of view, claiming the case of petrol as an example,[3] though she also recognizes that in some cases manufacturer enforcement of r.p.m. has prevented trading stamps being given.[4] Walter Taplin has put forward the interesting suggestion that the boom in trading stamps reflects the growth in importance of the consumer which is forcing retailers to compete for custom and to

[1] Trading Stamps Act 1964 c. 71.
[2] W. A. Lewis – 'Competition in Retail Trade' *Economica* vol. 12 (N.S.) 1945 p. 228.
[3] Christina Fulop – 'The Role of Trading Stamps in Retail Competition' (London) 1964 p. 23.
[4] *Ibid*. p. 20.

do this they must offer some concessions.[1] Whilst the time is not yet ripe for unrestricted concessions such as across-the-board price cuts, argues Taplin, trading stamps represent a step away from restricted concessions towards unrestricted concessions.

Clearly, trading stamps are used by many distributors as aggressive weapons, though to suggest that they are the retailer's answer to r.p.m. is incorrect since it is the enforcement of r.p.m. which has stopped stamps being given on many goods. The case of petrol is difficult though it is not correct to claim that stamps are used here to avoid r.p.m. since this has not been a practical issue for many years.[2] It is probably in relation to petrol that Taplin's suggestion is most significant since here the offer of trading stamps seems to be the first step towards cut price competition between garages.

On the other hand, this writer would suggest that trading stamps may also be used defensively. The trading stamp companies operate a franchise arrangement which means that in any shopping area only one retailer of a given class of goods will be allowed to give the stamps of a particular company.[3] This means that the outlet of a retailer giving those stamps will be differentiated from the others. Thus, it is argued, by giving trading stamps the retailer is creating an imperfection in the retailing market and thereby reducing the impact of competition, especially price competition, in his trade. It would seem that it is for this reason that many small grocers (especially those outside the voluntary group movement) have chosen to give trading stamps.

However, although a trader may decide to adopt trading stamps for reasons either of offence or defence, ultimately the consumer is sovereign and stamps will only be successful if consumers choose to collect them. Much promotional activity has been concentrated on creating consumer interest in stamps. The existence of 'families' of retailers giving stamps has helped,

[1] Walter Taplin – 'Why Trading Stamps Now?' *District Bank Review* September 1963 p. 3.
[2] As the Monopolies Commission *'Report on the Supply of Petrol to Retailers in the United Kingdom'* 1965 para. 67 makes plain.
[3] Though the aim is to build up in that area a 'family' of varied retail outlets each giving the same stamps.

making it possible to fill books of stamps more quickly; so, too, has the establishment by the leading stamp companies of a number of Gift Houses in large towns where completed books can be exchanged for gifts which can be inspected before a final selection is made. The consequence is that a large measure of consumer support has been obtained for stamps. Already it is estimated that more than half the housewives in this country are collectors despite the existence of a number of obstacles placed in the way of the expansion of the trading stamp movement. Three obstacles should be noted. These are, (1) the difficulty experienced by Sperry and Hutchinson in establishing themselves in this country, (2) the opposition encountered from manufacturers who treated the giving of trading stamps as a breach of resale price maintenance, and (3) the existence of restrictive agreements between traders that they would not give trading stamps.

In their attempt to enter the British market, Sperry and Hutchinson recognized the desirability of rapidly achieving a national distribution of their stamps by arranging for Fine Fare, the Garfield Weston supermarket chain, and Blue Star Garages to give their stamps. This was not successful as both groups dropped the stamps and a certain amount of consumer support for trading stamps in general was lost. However, this ground has now been reclaimed and Sperry and Hutchinson have retrenched themselves by taking over the retail accounts (including Victor Value) of King Korn stamps, another American company, who have now left the British market.

At present it is estimated that 80% at least of the turnover of the trading stamp companies is obtained from outlets in the food and petrol trades. This is at least partly due to the attitude of those manufacturers who enforce fixed resale price conditions on their goods, most of whom treat the giving of trading stamps as a form of price cutting and have therefore prevented trading stamps being given on most non-food purchases. Only a few actions for an injunction under section 25 have been brought to the courts by manufacturers seeking to prevent trading stamps being given on sales of their products. However, as with actions against direct price cutting, the value of the few cases that have been brought to court, together with the decision in the *Bulpitt*

v. *Bellman* case,[1] has been to have a deterrent effect and discourage other traders from attempting to give trading stamps with price-maintained goods.

Two instances in which manufacturers successfully prevented the giving of trading stamps with their products without needing to sue for an injunction received wide publicity. Harrison Gibson, who own a few furniture shops in the South East of England, began to give King Korn trading stamps. Within a few days, the Branded Furniture Society, acting on behalf of twelve r.p.m.-enforcing furniture manufacturers, informed Harrison Gibson that supplies from all twelve manufacturers would be stopped if trading stamps continued to be given. Since three-quarters of Harrison Gibson's sales consisted of these products they had no alternative but to cease giving stamps altogether. The second instance arose in November 1963 in relation to Cadbury's products. Cadbury had not, originally, taken any action to prevent trading stamps being given with their goods, but when Tesco began giving Green Shield stamps other multiple traders, notably Waitrose – part of the John Lewis Partnership, and Melias, a multiple based in the North West, began to cut prices on Cadbury products to compensate. This caused Cadbury to rewrite their conditions of sale to prohibit the giving of trading stamps and when attempts to bring these multiples into line failed, supplies were stopped until they agreed not to cut prices or give trading stamps on Cadbury products.

In practice the greatest difficulty in preventing the giving of trading stamps has been that facing the manufacturers of goods such as confectionery and cigarettes which are still subject to r.p.m. but which are increasingly sold through grocery outlets. Since r.p.m. is now a dead letter on branded groceries many retailers have chosen to give trading stamps. This has meant that the manufacturers of confectionery and cigarettes have had to try to ensure that stamps are not given on their products whilst they are given on all other goods. Cadbury have acted over this, so, too, have Gallaher who have obtained several injunctions against retailers giving trading stamps on sales of their cigarettes. Where a number of goods are purchased at the same time and paid for at a self service checkout this becomes particularly

[1] See above chapter v.

difficult. There is always the possibility of the cashier making a mistake and inadvertently including these lines with all other purchases in calculating the number of trading stamps to be given.[1] Or if the manufacturer is not prepared to accept that the giving of stamps on his products was a mistake, the retailer could always plead that they represented a bonus issue on some other product purchased at the same time. It is likely that some grocery retailers will have succeeded in giving trading stamps on sales of price maintained goods because of the difficulty of proving where a number of products are purchased together that the issue of stamps was related to the purchase of a particular price maintained article. However, it is true to say that, in general, manufacturers of price maintained goods have treated trading stamps as a breach of their conditions as to the price at which the goods might be resold and have thereby prevented the expansion of trading stamps into trades where r.p.m. remains an important trading practice.

A further hindrance to the growth of the trading stamp movement has been the existence of agreements between traders that they would not give trading stamps. Such agreements are registrable under Part I of the Restrictive Trade Practices Act. When the controversy over trading stamps was at its height in November and December 1963, it seemed that many such agreements or arrangements were being made and would have to be registered as restrictive trading agreements. However, a recent inspection of the Register revealed just over a dozen agreements relating to trading stamps.

In most cases a group of traders had passed a resolution not to give stamps. In some, manufacturers or wholesalers agreed to refuse to supply retailers who gave stamps and two contained an agreement between retailers not to obtain supplies from the Weston group whilst Fine Fare gave trading stamps. A few have already been rescinded and, no doubt, when referred to the Court, the others will not be defended.

This shows up very clearly a weakness in the first part of the

---

[1] Though such an error does not constitute a defence in law – see *Gallaher Ltd.* v. *Supersafe Supermarkets Ltd.* (1964) L.R. 5 R.P. 89 where the fact that the defendants had instructed their cashier not to give trading stamps on cigarettes did not prevent an injunction being granted.

Act. Where a controversy such as that on trading stamps arises, it should not be possible for traders or manufacturers to be in a position where they can make an agreement and have the benefit of it for three months before they even have to register it. These three months' grace are vital to agreements which seek to prevent the introduction of a new method of trading. Once the agreement has been made, it is likely that even if it is later rescinded, the parties to it will continue to act in a spirit that is in keeping with the agreement. This is clearly what happened in the case of trading stamps. By agreeing in the first place not to adopt or allow trading stamps, it was possible for traders and manufacturers to stand firm in weathering the initial storm. In any future amendment to the Act it would be desirable to make all new agreements registrable immediately they are made. This would probably discourage some from being made at all and would enable the Registrar to make an immediate reference to the Restrictive Practices Court when an important new agreement arises.

The Co-operative dividend has long been a bone of contention, with a large number of manufacturers refusing to allow the dividend to be given or even going further and refusing to supply Co-operative Societies. The situation at the time of the passing of the Restrictive Trade Practices Act was that they were not allowed to give a dividend on drugs, cosmetics, toilet preparations, books, stationery, petrol, vacuum cleaners and other electrical apparatus, photographic apparatus and films and certain proprietary brands of wearing apparel. They were unable to obtain supplies for resale to the public of newspapers, motor vehicles, records, certain brands of bicycle, radio sets, gramophones, hand tools and toys and games. In many, if not all, cases this policy was adopted by manufacturers as a result of protests by other retailers and their trade associations that the Co-operative dividend was tantamount to a price reduction and was therefore a form of unfair trading. The only resale price maintained products on which the dividend was unchallenged were cigarettes and tobacco, groceries, confectionery and electric lamps.

In many cases, in order to be able to sell the prohibited goods, the Co-operative Societies manufactured and sold their own brands. It is not, therefore, surprising that the Co-operative Union fought hard against the implication that a manufacturer could take legal action against a Co-operative Society if it allowed a dividend on his products. Since 1956 it would seem that there has in fact been an improvement in the position regarding the Co-operative dividend. Only on motor cars, photographic goods and records has manufacturer opposition to the dividend remained strong, though some manufacturers in the clothing trade have still refused to allow a dividend to be given; on at least one occasion a number of manufacturers of fashion goods have refused to supply the West End store of the London Co-operative Society.[1] In Societies where there is still a high dividend often of between 1s and 2s in the £1 (these are mainly to be found in the North of England and in Scotland), the advantages from shopping in a Co-operative Society store and receiving such a dividend on a price maintained article are strong, and it is not surprising therefore that other traders have sometimes complained to manufacturers and urged them to ask the Society concerned to cease allowing a dividend on their products. No manufacturer has sought an injunction against a Co-operative Society on the grounds that the dividend is a breach of a fixed resale price condition, though many would strongly oppose the offer of a double dividend on their price maintained goods or the advertising of the fact that a dividend was allowed on such a line.

Why should manufacturers who enforce fixed resale price conditions allow Co-operative Societies to give a dividend? Different manufacturers offer different answers to this question. There are those who will admit that they have never felt inclined to prohibit the dividend because Co-operative Societies are important distributors of their products, in many cases having been in existence longer than the manufacturer. Others see the purchaser in a Co-operative Society store as a shareholder and therefore just as entitled to his share of the profits as a shareholder in any other public company. Linked to this is a third argument, that the reduction is not at the time of sale but is a deferred payment and as such deserves to fall into a different category to other price reductions. The Co-operative Union argues that the

[1] *Financial Times* November 26, 1959.

Co-operative voucher is merely a receipt for goods purchased and is not in itself a right to a dividend, neither do the vouchers have to be produced to obtain payment of the dividend (except in the few instances where the Eccles system is used – here the receipt has to be stuck in a book and the book presented at the end of the year to receive payment of the dividend). The growth of competition between manufacturers and their desire to achieve as wide a distribution of their goods as possible and the successful competition in some fields such as radio from the Co-operatives' own brands, are clearly also other reasons why manufacturers are now more willing to accept the system of trading of the Co-operative Societies.

Where distributors, anxious to offer some competitive advantage to consumers, are prevented by manufacturer insistence on r.p.m. from reducing prices, they are forced either to compete on service or to look for some way of offering a 'concealed' price cut. Besides trading stamps and the Co-operative dividend, free gifts, high trade-in allowances, discounts to professional associations and failure to charge a full rate of interest when goods are bought on hire purchase all fall into this category and in each case manufacturers have had the power to prevent these actions which are, in practice, tantamount to a breach of r.p.m. In a number of trades the annual or twice yearly clearance sale also offers an opportunity for goods that are normally subject to r.p.m. to be sold at a reduced price, though they are intended as a means of selling off goods where the quality has deteriorated or the article was imperfect in the first place or where production is ending on a particular line in order to dispose of out of date stocks. Sales are particularly important on fashion goods and in the clothing trade in general but are also to be found on furniture, photographic goods and electrical appliances, whilst even the book trade has a National Book Sale to sell off slow-selling titles cheaply. All manufacturers are agreed that clearance sales are important both to the retailer and to the manufacturer and make no attempt to prevent them, though they tend to look with disfavour on retailers who buy up large stocks of perfect goods just before a sale or extend a sale for a long period of time.

To keep demand for consumer durables at a high level, consumers are nowadays urged to change one piece of equipment for another before it has worn out. To encourage this, retailers offer to take in the old model in part exchange for a new one. In no trade has there been any attempt by manufacturers to control the size of part exchange allowances, though such a scheme did exist in the motor trade between 1935 and 1939.[1] The absence of any limitation by manufacturers as to size of trade-ins to be allowed by dealers has tended to create a serious practical breach in resale price maintenance. For example, it is estimated that more than 90% of all new car sales include the part exchange of an old car and it is well known that in order to achieve the profitable new car business a distributor may even offer an allowance on the old model larger than the price at which he can reasonably expect to resell it. This means, therefore, that on less than 10% of new car sales was resale price maintenance effective whilst it was being enforced in this trade. In other consumer durable trades a similar situation has existed. For example, traders may offer a £15 to £20 part exchange allowance on the purchase of a new television set or large electrical appliance. Even on smaller items such as an electric razor or hair dryer, the keen shopper has often been able to obtain a substantial part exchange allowance. Admittedly, part exchanges are not as important on these goods as on motor cars, but as the market approaches saturation so such breaches in resale price maintenance are likely to become wider. Again, so far as is known no manufacturers attempt to control the growing policy of some retailers of allowing consumers to acquire goods on hire purchase at low rates of interest. Similarly, mail order houses who have to sell at the manufacturer stipulated prices do not charge for the credit they give. In each case the purchaser is therefore obtaining some advantage by dealing with that particular trader.

In some trades a further way of giving the consumer some advantage on a price maintained line is for the retailer to make a free gift of some other complementary item. Thus a tobacconist may give a box of matches with a packet of cigarettes, a photographic dealer may include a film when a camera is bought and a television retailer may provide a free aerial when a television set is installed. The conditions of sale of some manufacturers

[1] K. C. Johnson-Davies – 'The Practice of Price Maintenance' (London) 1955 p. 6.

include a specific prohibition against any gifts being given in conjunction with the sale of a price maintained article. Despite this, the practice certainly continues, in some cases with the retailer unaware that he is contravening the conditions of sale and with the manufacturer unconcerned and often unaware of what is going on so long as the retailer does not advertise the fact that he is offering these free gifts. Once such an offer is advertised, then the opposition of other traders is raised and the manufacturer is forced to act.

An increasing number of people, especially members of professional staff associations, are also tending to obtain direct discounts on purchases. The active member of these bodies will usually find that his executive has arranged for a number of local traders to supply him with his furniture or washing machine at discounts ranging up to 25% or more off the list price. Requests for such discounts sometimes engender hard feeling on the part of local traders who see them as a suggestion that the traders should accept a reduction in their earnings. To the trader who agrees, this is presumably good business, the offer of a discount, advertised free to a large number of potential customers, being more than compensated for by the possibility of increased turnover. In some cases the trader offering a discount may be a wholesaler and even larger reductions may be obtained.

Some shops will grant discounts off a bill for paying cash, whilst others will grant a discount to anyone who has the courage to ask for it! Other members of the public who belong to certain types of club, such as sports, gardening or motor clubs, will usually manage to obtain their equipment at a discount. Some workers are able to obtain the products of their own firm at a low price, whilst some firms also negotiate for their employees to obtain the products of other firms at specially reduced rates.

Thus there are many trading techniques which in practice amount to price cutting. Many of these have been going on for a large number of years and the traders concerned would be most offended if it were suggested that they were price cutters. It would be very difficult, if not impossible, to assess the quantitative importance of these advantages obtained when price maintained goods are purchased. It is quite clear that they are of considerable importance, a widely accepted estimate being that

H

at least 10% of consumer goods are bought at a discount, whilst *The Economist*[1] concluded that about one quarter of the country's shoppers benefit from such discounts. Since that article was written, the proportion has undoubtedly risen further.

To summarize, we find that manufacturers have normally had it within their power to treat the major forms of 'concealed' price cutting as a breach of their resale price conditions and actionable under section 25 of the Restrictive Trade Practices Act. Whilst they have effectively acted against trading stamps and prevented their penetration into most non-food trades, the other practices have been allowed to continue virtually unchallenged. Though this absence of manufacturer action is due rather to lack of knowledge of these instances than to any unwillingness to act. The evidence is, however, that more traders are becoming able and willing to offer some advantage to consumers and more members of the public are taking advantage of this situation.

[1] *The Economist* March 19, 1960.

CHAPTER IX

THE BREAKDOWN OF R.P.M. IN THE GROCERY TRADE: CAUSE AND EFFECT

The grocery trade was the first to show signs of a weakening in resale price maintenance after 1956. Opinions as to just how important the practice was in this trade differ widely. Undoubtedly there have always been traders who cut prices, some of them without attracting manufacturer attention, others having done so less successfully found manufacturers cutting off supplies. At least two of the important supermarket chains of today, Tesco and Anthony Jackson Foodfare, started off as small cut price traders.

Collective enforcement was through the Grocery Proprietary Articles Council (G.P.A.C.) which had a membership of around eighty manufacturers. Some of these were leaders in their own particular field, e.g. Cerebos, Horlicks, Huntley and Palmer, Kraft, Schweppes, Shippam, Weetabix, etc. Some were manufacturers of 'fringe' goods such as polish, paper products and toiletries. A further forty or more leading manufacturers were also enforcers of resale price maintenance, though not belonging to the G.P.A.C. - such manufacturers as Cadbury, Rowntree, Oxo, James Robertson, some of the Unilever companies and the leading tea manufacturers. Nestlé, too, were active enforcers of r.p.m. in the early 1950s.

The Lloyd Jacob Report contained an estimate that in 1947 25% by turnover of all branded grocery products were on the G.P.A.C. protected list and they, too, noted the fact that many manufacturers who were not in the G.P.A.C. individually enforced r.p.m.[1] In the post-war years the normal method of enforcement was to ask a price cutter to stop cutting and if

[1] *Op. cit.* p. 50.

necessary to refuse to continue an account with him. Until rationing ended in 1953-54, there was little incentive to a trader to cut prices and resale price maintenance appears to have remained quite strong. It would, however, be true to say that by about 1955 a state of 'cold war' had been reached between some multiple retailers who wanted to cut prices and manufacturers and other retailers who did not want them to do so. The reason for this was clearly the growth of self service outlets. In 1947 there were only ten of these in existence and in 1950 - 600, 90% of which were establishments of Co-operative Societies. By mid-1955 the figure had grown to approximately 2,500 of which only just over 60% were owned by Co-operative Societies.

The self service method of distribution offered a saving on labour costs to the retailer, and housewives, encouraged by the popular press, were beginning to look for this saving to be passed on in the form of lower prices. Some traders did try to cut prices. W. G. McClelland, in reviewing B. S. Yamey's *Economics of Resale Price Maintenance,* tells how in July 1953 his group of shops in the North East - Laws Stores - began to cut 6d off the price of all fruit squashes.[1] The leading manufacturers received complaints from other traders but accepted further orders. In December 1953 the local grocers' association took the matter up formally with the manufacturers, who stopped supplies until Laws undertook to restore the normal price. McClelland used this to argue that manufacturers only actively enforce r.p.m. when an organized group of retailers bully them into doing so. This may or may not be so but what it does make clear is that grocery suppliers were still prepared to take action against price cutters at this time. In the summer of 1954 another retailing company, which was well to the forefront in the development of self service, began to cut prices on soap powders and toothpaste. They, too, were forced to withdraw under threat of collective action, this time by the P.A.T.A. If further evidence is needed that price cutting was not the norm in the early 1950s, there was a letter printed in the trade journal *Self Service* from Mr Patrick Galvani which asked manufacturers to assist the development of self service by marking the price of the good on the pack - to make it easier for the cashier

[1] In *Stores and Shops* May 1954.

to calculate the bill.[1] Nowadays, of course, a manufacturer is preferred not to mark a price on the pack so that the retailer can stamp on it his own price.

Awareness of the need to reduce prices was shown early in 1956 in a talk by L. J. Phillips of Waitrose[2] who stated –

'Eventually the public must have something more than convenience and novelty [in self service stores], that "something" must be price advantage. We are not undercutting but we must offer a price advantage in due course.'

The first serious price reductions were made on 'safe' articles such as provisions and imported goods in the summer of 1956 whilst at the same time several multiples were reported to be giving 2 lb. sugar away free when goods to the value of (for example) more than 15s were bought. Thus it is quite clear that there had been no breach in resale price maintenance in the grocery trade before the passing of the Restrictive Trade Practices Act. What it is true to say is that the ending of food rationing in 1954 was encouraging High Street shops to compete for custom and the development of self service stores, assisted by the lifting of building controls at the end of 1954, was encouraging retailers to realize that the time would soon be upon them when savings in distribution costs would have to be passed on to consumers in the form of lower prices.

Selective price cutting on some branded groceries began early in 1957 with the more aggressive retail chains leading the way. The small grocers in local grocers' associations were pinning their hopes on manufacturers using the legal powers available to them under section 25 to prevent this gaining ground. When Beechams took positive action to deal with price cutters, they received the approbation of the small trader, though not any greater support.

One of the first products to be price cut was Nescafé. Nestlé had originally been anxious to prevent price cutting and for a time attempted to discourage it but they found so many retailers already cutting prices that effective action was impossible. Further reasons why Nestlé allowed price cutting were given in a letter sent to the Bristol Grocers' Association which argued

[1] *Self Service* February 1952.
[2] Quoted *Self Service* April 1956 p. 64.

that to take legal action could have serious repercussions on their business, both by its effect on the public and also on their competitors.[1] One of the difficulties, they claimed, was the intro-duction into this country of Maxwell House coffee on which there was no resale price maintenance and the willingness of the suppliers to allow price cutting on this brand forced Nestlé to stop trying to enforce r.p.m. themselves. Fruit squashes were also price cut, the reason here being that competition between manufacturers, especially after the development of comminuted squashes in about 1955, encouraged them to allow a margin of profit - 25% off the list price - which was much higher than that usually obtaining in the grocery trade.

In the opinion of many observers in the grocery trade, it was in the twelve months between June 1957 and June 1958 that resale price maintenance really ended on most branded groceries, though the main benefits were then only felt in and around London where the self service movement had developed most. A number of the more diehard manufacturers still refused to allow retailers to cut prices; some allowed them to stock their lines but not to cut, others refused even to supply potential price cutters. In March 1958, Garfield Weston agreed that for three months his Fine Fare shops would not cut prices on the products of a number of manufacturers so long as other shops agreed to do the same. But despite clearly increasing price cutting not one of the seventy or so manufacturers in the G.P.A.C. took any legal action (Beechams were no longer members) and by mid-1958 only the products of Cadbury, Beechams and Van der Bergh (Stork margarine, etc.) and a few less important manufacturers, were not being price cut. Even on Beechams products it was noted that there was no attempt to maintain the prices of their fruit squash - Quosh - which was subject to severe competition from competing brands.

Other developments also showed that r.p.m. in the grocery trade had ended. In April 1958 the Ministry of Labour began to include cut price retail outlets in the sampling frame used in the compilation of the Retail Price Index. July 1958 saw Sainsburys cutting prices on leading manufacturer brands and in September 1958 the London Co-operative Society began to cut prices. The

[1] Published in *The Grocer* June 29, 1957.

Consumer Association carried out a study of manufacturer policies over the enforcement of resale price maintenance and found that 32% of those replying enforced their retail prices, 45% recommended a retail price but did not enforce and 23% did not even bother to suggest prices.[1] Those manufacturers who still enforced were those which did not have to fear a shift in demand to the products of a competing manufacturer. Manufacturers of some grocery products, such as cocoa and health foods, managed to retain r.p.m. on their products for a long period of time after the general breakdown for the simple reason that there was no cut price alternative readily available.

A study carried out by Research Services Ltd. in December 1958[2] which was, however, weighted in favour of large towns, revealed that 50% of the shops included in the survey were cutting prices. 85% of multiples were price cutting, so, too, were 43% independents and 42% Co-operatives. They found that 75% of the price cutters were reducing the price of instant coffee but that not more than one-third of them were cutting the price of any other of the wide range of products included in the investigation. Normal pricing policy seemed to be to select just a few items on which to cut prices, the average number of cut price lines was 4·40 though multiples were found to be price cutting on average nearly 6 items per shop and their cuts were the deepest. Thus, although price cutting tended to take the form of a limited number of special offers rather than the 'across-the-board' cutting we have come to expect today, it is quite clear that by late 1958 on a wide range of groceries fixed resale prices were no longer enforced and a fairly substantial number of retailers were taking advantage of the opportunity to cut prices. The breakdown came rather quickly, as a writer in *Self Service* remarked in 1958,

'Only last year the words "cut price" were felt to be an opprobrious epithet, almost a term of abuse. In less than twelve months the climate of opinion has changed enormously, albeit grudgingly, and "cut price" (by that or any other name) is now practically synonymous with "go ahead".'[3]

---

[1] 'Cut Price Groceries' *Which ?* Summer 1958.
[2] *'Enquiry into the extent of price cutting among retail grocers.'*
[3] *Self Service* October 1958 p. 64.

Some manufacturers found that by insisting on retailers observing their fixed prices they suffered. We have already seen that Nestlé had to drop r.p.m. once Maxwell House coffee came on to the market. The problem facing manufacturers who wanted to retain r.p.m. was whether or not the traditional retailers would compensate for sales lost through cut price outlets. Schweppes attempted to meet this difficulty by adopting a dual policy – price maintenance was to remain on their Roses and Schweppes brands which were clearly aimed at the traditional grocer and chemist and cutting was to be allowed on Suncrush and Kia-Ora lines. Their statement in the trade press at the time showed a clear grasp of the problem –

'. . . it must also be admitted that unless a manufacturer is really dominant in a particular field he is reluctant to withhold supplies from a retailer whether a multiple or independent who cuts the price. If he does so, the retailer concerned merely switches to a competitor's product in respect of which the manufacturer may take a slightly more elastic view on price maintenance. And some of the multiple retailers who cut prices are not customers a manufacturer will lightly turn over to a competitor.'[1]

Several manufacturers are known to have lost sales to competitors because they supported r.p.m. and in May 1959 the Trade Customs and Commodities Committee of the National Grocers' Federation found that independent traders failed to compensate manufacturers who continued to enforce r.p.m. and they therefore decided that the Federation 'cannot with honesty ask manufacturers to support us by a price maintenance policy when we fail to offer any tangible return'.[2]

This decision marked the end of any real attempt to retain price maintenance in the grocery trade and now the small retailer who was the strength of the National Grocers' Federation could also cut prices without the fear of being cast out from his local association as a renegade. In September 1959 even Beechams Foods, who had actively enforced r.p.m., dropped this condition of sale, the reasons given being that the court decision in the 'Lucozade case' placed difficulties in the way of enforcing r.p.m.

[1] *Soft Drinks Trade Journal* January 1959 p. 40.
[2] *The Grocer* May 30, 1959 p. 29.

and also the growing prevalence of price cutting showed that margins were sufficiently generous to allow this. Only a few manufacturers persisted in enforcing r.p.m. after this.

Having begun in the latter part of 1957, by mid-1959 the breakdown of resale price maintenance in the grocery trade was virtually complete. Why did it occur at this particular time? The collapse followed quickly upon the return to normal conditions after the war with the ending of rationing and the removal of building restrictions. In addition there was, as we have seen, the development of self service and popular pressure for reduced prices. After the Co-operative Societies had pioneered self service, it was taken up by a number of the new growth multiples, e.g. Tesco, Fine Fare, Anthony Jackson, which had sprung up in this trade. Their owners had seen, in the United States, the possibilities for supermarket development based on cut prices. The increase in packaging meant that more goods could be sold by self service and the growth of manufacturer branding meant that the offer of a well-known brand at a cut price would attract the attention of a wide range of consumers.

Competition between manufacturers caused them to allow and even encourage price cutting. At about this time the American food firms, of whom there are now a large number in important market positions in this country, e.g. Kellogg, Nabisco Foods, Heinz, Maxwell House, began to introduce the concept known as 'brand management'. Their problem became one of moving goods out of the shop. Whereas previously they had aimed to persuade the retailer to stock their product, now they also had to make the consumer ask for their particular brand. So the special offer was introduced and once this became accepted, the way was clear to permit general price cutting. There were also English companies who were not brand leaders who, in order to increase sales, found it profitable to allow their products to be featured as special cut-price offers.

These were undoubtedly important influences contributing to the breakdown of r.p.m., but what part did the Restrictive Trade Practices Act play? There appears to be a disagreement on this issue between two of the leading specialists in the economics of distribution - Professor Yamey and W. G. McClelland. Yamey says -

'The collapse of r.p.m. in the grocery trade cannot be ascribed to the legislation: in its early stages it preceded the legislation and its main cause was strong competition on the manufacturing side coupled with the strength and scale of operation of those retailers who wanted to be free to compete on price.'[1]

McClelland, on the other hand, finds that –

'The Restrictive Trade Practices Act of 1956, which outlawed the collective enforcement of resale price maintenance was a help [to the growth of supermarkets] for without price flexibility the supermarket cannot build up sales volume quickly.'[2]

Again –

'The collective enforcement of resale prices ... was rendered illegal in 1956, and partly as a result of this, the practice has crumbled in the grocery trade.'[3]

In the view of this writer, the opinions of McClelland are more in keeping with the facts than the view of Professor Yamey – though it is not disputed that, as Yamey says, competition between manufacturers and the strength of retailers who wanted to cut prices have also helped in the breakdown of r.p.m. We have already noted that despite attempts by retailers to cut prices before 1956, there is no evidence that any success was reached, witness the opinion of Mr Jack Cohen of Tesco in the B.B.C. television series 'Challenge to Prosperity' in 1961, who remarked that until 1957 price cutting had been very difficult.

In a large number of discussions with people concerned with the grocery trade in all its stages, very few were prepared to argue that the Act had no effect in the breakdown of r.p.m. In the first place the Act was made a focal point by those traders who wanted to cut prices. Manufacturers who took action against such price cutters found themselves the recipients of adverse publicity, being accused of keeping prices unnecessarily high. Some claimed that action under section 25 was difficult, the need to give adequate notice, to police outlets and to obtain proof

[1] B. S. Yamey *'Resale Price Maintenance and Shoppers' Choice'* (London) 1960 p. 41.
[2] W. G. McClelland 'Economics of the Supermarket' *Economic Journal* vol. 72 (1962) p. 161.
[3] W. G. McClelland *'Studies in Retailing'* (Oxford) 1963 p. 13.

were thought to prove insurmountable problems which caused some manufacturers who had previously strongly supported r.p.m. to change their policy.

The prohibition of collective boycotts was also important. Whilst collective enforcement was the norm it was quite simple for a manufacturer to be cajoled into enforcing r.p.m. with others. Conversely, of course, it was possible for a local grocers' association to threaten to arrange a collective boycott of the products of a manufacturer if he allowed another trader to cut the prices of his goods. Once collective enforcement was forbidden, manufacturers had to stand alone and risk possible bad publicity claiming they were keeping food prices unnecessarily high.

At least, we would argue, the Act had a catalytic effect, speeding up by one or two years the breakdown of r.p.m. which, because of manufacturer competition and the strength of price cutting retailers, was inevitable. Those manufacturers who had never really favoured r.p.m. could now drop it openly, others who would have liked to keep it were put off by what they thought were the serious difficulties of proving a case under section 25 and of facing adverse publicity. The G.P.A.C. amended its rules and constitution to allow itself to provide an efficient machinery and financial or other forms of assistance to manufacturers who wanted to take legal action under section 25 but it was not strong enough and its members not sufficiently willing to take legal action. As a result it lost all influence in the trade and was ultimately wound up by common consent in September 1960.

Thus we conclude that the Act was at least a major factor in causing the breakdown of resale price maintenance in the grocery trade. Whilst other factors are also clearly to be taken into account, to the prohibition of collective enforcement and the supposed difficulty of acting under section 25 must be attributed at least a catalytic effect.

Having endeavoured to discover the causes of the collapse of r.p.m., we must now investigate its consequences. There is no evidence that when price maintenance is dropped the manufacturer loses support, a few small retailers may refuse to handle the line but this is normally more than compensated by greater sales through price cutting outlets. It was, in fact, the failure of the independent retailer to give preferential display space and selling effort to price maintaining manufacturers that caused many of them to drop r.p.m. in the first place and it was hardly a sensible policy for these same retailers to refuse to stock the brands once they were decontrolled; those that did do this quickly realized their mistake. One manufacturer who wrote to all his direct account customers announcing that he was dropping r.p.m. received thirteen replies only, five were abusive, e.g. 'R.I.P. decent trading', whilst the other eight were from large retail chains asking for the company to arrange for a representative to call to arrange for a special offer promotion. Thus it would seem on balance the manufacturer immediately gained by his action.

The actual effect on sales as a result of price cutting is really impossible to quantify, so many other factors also affect the level of sales of a product. We may, however, note that there are two different elasticities of demand to be taken into account. The first is the normal price elasticity of demand for a good. This will be high where the product tends to be just too expensive to be a regular purchase. So a large increase in sales will often be obtained from a small fall in price, i.e. where the price reduction brings a good down from the 'luxury' class to the 'necessity' class for a large group of consumers. Secondly, there is the elasticity of demand for a particular brand or product in a particular shop. This will be high for products which are bought frequently, although the overall demand for many of these items, such as basic foodstuffs, tends to be inelastic. In this situation cut price competition will be beneficial to consumers though, by definition, the overall level of sales of the product will remain substantially unaltered. It is also true that the effects of price cutting are to encourage a higher level of purchases of all foods. The reason is that a given sum of housekeeping money will buy a greater number of goods when prices are reduced. The manufacturers of semi-luxuries, such as condiments and preserves, are probably the main beneficiaries here.

Fruit squashes and instant coffee appear to have shown the largest overall increase in sales as a result of price cutting. Previously the price of the brand leaders in each case was over 3s[1]

[1] Taking a 2 oz. tin of coffee.

and this was rather beyond the purse of many consumers, nowadays the usual price of each is well below this figure. In the case of squashes it was necessary for the manufacturers to stop imposing a 3d deposit on the bottle to encourage supermarkets to stock, for they were not interested in handling something where money had to be returned later and empty bottles collected and stored. Having dealt with this the manufacturers found price cutting on squashes to be – 'a marked stimulus to demand' to quote the chairman of Thomas and Evans Ltd.[1] The instant coffee market has grown from £7 million a year in 1954 to £32 million in 1964. Whilst instant coffee was a relatively new product in 1954, it is hard to see it having achieved such a large increase in the market over so short a period of time unaided by price cutting.

Other products have shown less startling results though most manufacturers in the food trade agree that their level of sales has been higher as a result of price cutting. Many manufacturers are very pleased with the extra interest shown in their products by price cutting retailers and where special promotional offers are arranged a very considerable increase in sales is expected. One supermarket chain expects that for the duration of a special offer, sales of that line will be about ten times the normal level. In 1960, when Tesco held a national advertising campaign on Independent Television featuring three lines – Daz, Lifeguard and Libby Red Salmon, they found that one year's sales on each of these was covered in two weeks.[2]

In present day economic conditions where there is a buyers' market in many products including food and where there is probably excess manufacturing capacity in the food trade, manufacturers are anxious that their goods should be regularly featured as special cut price offers in the large supermarket chains. To encourage this they will offer extra large discounts to the retailer and will bear up to one-half of the cost of any special advertising of the offer on his brand. This is treated as a way of using part of the manufacturer's advertising appropriation, though recently on some goods the emphasis has changed again, away from direct cut price offers to special premium offers

[1] F. D. Armstrong in *Soft Drinks Trade Journal* August 1960 p. 837.
[2] See *Self Service* October 1960.

of low priced records, silver spoons, artificial flowers, etc., in the continual battle to retain consumer loyalty. Small retailers often complain that the discounts given to large retailers are too great but these protests are largely unavailing, an exception being in the case of biscuits where manufacturers tightly limit the size of quantity discounts and so deep price cutting is rarely found.

Two other consequences of the ending of r.p.m. from the manufacturer's point of view need to be observed. In the first place, price cutting tends inevitably to be concentrated on the brand leader because this line is a good 'traffic builder' in that a reduced price here has the greatest appeal to consumers and therefore attracts more into the shop and encourages them to buy other goods, too. This makes it difficult for a small manufacturer to gain a real foothold in the market for a product. Secondly, the ending of r.p.m. has meant that a new type of sales representative is required. His visits to retailers are no longer merely social calls to take an order, his function now is to sell his product to the retailer and advise on the best merchandising policy to follow in order to obtain the best return. It has taken some time to obtain the right sort of person for this job, but the problem has now apparently been overcome.

The structure of retailing has also been affected by the breakdown of r.p.m. making possible the expansion of self service stores and supermarkets based on price appeal. As we have already shown, there is little doubt that the Restrictive Trade Practices Act contributed to the breakdown of r.p.m. in the grocery trade and this encouraged a rapid expansion of self service (see Table 9, opposite).

A supermarket is defined as a store with at least 2,000 sq. ft. sales area, with three or more checkouts and operated mainly on self service, whose range of merchandise comprises all food groups, including fresh meat and fresh fruit and vegetables, plus basic household requirements (i.e. soaps and cleaning materials).

We have already seen how the Co-operatives led the way in the development of self service and were then followed by a large growth of self service multiples. In the last five years independents and small multiple retailers (those with less than ten branches) have also recognized the advantages of the self service method of operation and are now responsible for a sizeable proportion of the total (see Table 10 below).

The growth of self service stores and supermarkets can best be shown in the following table:

TABLE 9   *Growth of self service retailing and supermarkets*

Year	Approx. no. of self service stores (incl. supermarkets)	Rate of growth p.a.	Approx. no. of supermarkets	Rate of growth p.a.
mid 1947	10			
		196		
1950	600			
		366		
1953	1,700			
		433		
1956	3,000			
		950		
1959	5,850		286	
		1,660		189
1962	10,830		854	
		1,940		338
end 1964	15,680		1,700	

Source – from *Self Service and Supermarket Annual Survey and Directory* 1965.

TABLE 10   *Distribution of self service grocery outlets by type of operator*

Year	Co-operatives %	Large multiples %	Independents and small multiples %	Other* %
1953	66·0	18·0	16·0	
1956	59·6	25·3	15·1	
1959	52·2	31·9	12·4	3·5
1962	36·8	33·2	27·7	2·3
1964	32·9	36·5	28·6	2·0

Source – *Self Service and Supermarket Annual Survey and Directory*.

  * 'Other' are self service outlets in department stores and Naafis. Super-markets are included in this table but mobile shops and non-food shops are excluded.

Having started in the Greater London area, self service stores and supermarkets have now spread to all parts of the country, though not to an equal extent. There are still far more per head of population in the south and south east than in other areas. The reason for this is that most branches of multiple retailers are kept to within a day's return lorry drive of the Head Office and as most companies have their Head Office in or near London so the growth of supermarkets in other areas is slow. In 1964, however, the rate of growth of all self service outlets was greater in the north than in the south so it seems the imbalance may eventually be corrected.

TABLE II

Distribution of Self Service Grocery Shops and Supermarkets by Nielsen Region 1964

Nielsen Region	All self service grocery shops	Ratio of population per outlet	Supermarkets	Ratio of population per outlet
1 (Northern)	No.: 929	1 : 3,553	No.: 84	1 : 39,288
2 (E. & W. Ridings)	1,010	4,198	89	47,640
3 (N. Midlands)	1,123	3,411	129	29,689
4 (Eastern)	1,231	3,224	130	30,531
5 (South Eastern)	820	3,763	100	30,860
6 (Southern)	987	3,318	131	25,000
7 (South Western)	890	3,724	97	34,165
8 (Wales)	601	4,453	72	37,167
9 (Midlands)	1,188	4,146	122	40,377
10 (North Western)	1,840	3,584	214	30,818
11 (Scotland)	1,284	4,055	125	41,656
12 (Greater London)	2,388	3,428	285	28,726
Total and National Average	14,291	3,681	1,578	33,338

Source – Self Service and Supermarket Annual Survey and Directory 1965.

The figures differ slightly from those given in Table 9 because self service outlets in the Channel Islands, Irish Republic, Northern Ireland and the Isle of Man are, in this table, excluded. Also the totals in Table 9 represent an allowance for outlets which were not included in the Directory, whilst Table 11 is based on recorded outlets only.

In 1961, according to the Census of Distribution, those grocery shops which were fully self service accounted for about 20% of sales in all grocery establishments.[1] In 1957 the figure had been only 9% or 10%. Now it is estimated that all self service stores are responsible for 40% of grocery sales of which supermarkets alone take nearly 14%.[2] Thus, self service stores have really taken a firm grip in the grocery retail trade of this country today. Their expansion has been facilitated by town centre redevelopment and rising site rents which have enabled them to take over from the independent retailer. The development of packaged

[1] Board of Trade Journal vol. 185 (1963) p. 1372.
[2] Self Service and Supermarket Annual Survey and Directory 1965

products has also been an essential prerequisite to their growth, so, too, has the breakdown of r.p.m., as we have seen.

Self service stores have benefited considerably in that turnover per person employed is much higher than in non-self service outlets. The Census of Distribution, 1961, showed turnover per person engaged in 1961 to be £6,200 p.a. or £119 per week in a fully self service shop and £4,674 p.a. or £90 per week in non-self service outlets, a difference of nearly one-third. Persons employed on a part-time basis were counted as half a full-time worker in each case. A similar study by A. C. Nielsen Co. Ltd. in 1962 also reached a similar conclusion.[1] The consumer favours self service outlets because they are considered to offer (in order of preference) a wider selection of goods, greater hygiene and lower prices.[2] The opportunity of doing all the shopping in one place, more quickly and in some cases in the evening is also considered advantageous. It has been found that in the first twelve months after conversion to self service, a shop will show on average a 25% increase in turnover, compared with the present 5% p.a. increase in turnover in the grocery trade as a whole.[3]

TABLE 12

Concentration of Buying Points in the Grocery Trade

Type of outlet	Buying points 1960 Number	%	No. of shops 1961 %	Grocery Turnover 1961 %
Multiples	500	0·6	11·8	27·9
Co-ops.	889	1·1	7·6	20·5
Independents in buying groups	230	0·3	28·6	27·8
	1,619	2·0	48·0	76·2
Independents not organised	78,000	98·0	52·0	23·8
	79,619	100	100	100

Source – The Statist July 13, 1962.

Besides providing benefits to consumers, the development of supermarkets, allied to the growth of voluntary groups, has

[1] *Nielsen Researcher* July/August 1962.
[2] Though the J. Walter Thompson study – *'Shopping in Suburbia'* carried out in October 1963 found lower prices to be a long way down the list of advantages claimed for supermarkets.
[3] *Nielsen Researcher* March/April 1963.

I

benefited the manufacturer. He is now able to cover a wide proportion of the grocery trade by selling to few buying points. A study made by Southern Television in their area early in 1963 showed that 1% of the grocery outlets were responsible for 15% of grocery purchases. An earlier study on a national basis published in *The Statist* also showed the concentration of a large part of the trade in a few buying points (see above, Table 12).

It is not surprising in view of this that many manufacturers choose to direct any special offer promotions they may arrange at the multiples and voluntary groups, since, through their small number of buying points, outlets responsible for more than half the total grocery turnover can be covered.

The pricing policy of supermarkets is based on cut prices and they have caused almost all other retailers to follow suit. It is noticeable that when a supermarket is opened all other traders within its catchment area also make special cut price offers. The aim in a pricing policy is to attract customers into that shop so the products on which prices are cut most are those which are bought most frequently and where the customer is most price conscious. This has been rationalized in the U.S.A. into a general principle known as the Dorothy Layne Principle. According to this, about 85% of customers know the prices of about ten lines which are bought most frequently, these have to bear the deepest cut, even down to cost in some cases; 15% of customers know the price of an additional thirty or forty lines, so these should also be cut, though not to the same extent as the first ten. Short period promotions on other lines can also be made.

Although some stores do exist which operate a reverse system, selling staple lines at a full mark-up and others at cut prices, the majority of retailers seem to follow fairly closely the Dorothy Layne Principle. Thus, sugar may often be bought near to cost price and coffee also yields a low return to the retailer. Some supermarket chains go well beyond the Dorothy Layne Principle and price cut most of the goods in their stores. The idea of short period promotions of products which are not always purchased (called 'suggestion' items by McClelland[1]) has met with the approval of manufacturers and fits in well with their policy of arranging special offers of their goods at cut prices.

[1] W. G. McClelland *op. cit.* ch. vi 'Pricing for Profit in Retailing'.

In an effort to combat price cutting some Co-operative Societies have stopped giving the normal deferred dividend on grocery
sales, preferring just to cut prices. The fact that price cutting
tends to be more severe in some areas than in others caused
some multiple retailers to introduce a flexible pricing policy with
the manager of each branch allowed to fix his own price according to the state of competition around him. This seems not to
have proved successful in many instances and prices in most
supermarket chains are centrally determined at the company's
head office.

The effect of price cutting has been to lower the gross margin
taken on branded groceries from about 20% to 14% or 15%.
This can, of course, be more than offset by a much faster turnover. The Census of Distribution results published in the *Board
of Trade Journal*,[1] reveal some interesting data on rates of turnover and gross margin. For fourteen multiple grocery organizations with self service in all their branches, the rate of turnover
was 18·3 and the gross margin 13·9%. For other multiples with
no branches operating on self service, rate of turnover was 12·2
and the gross margin 19·3%. This suggests, therefore, that a
policy of cutting prices is rewarded with a faster rate of turnover which compensates for the lower margin per unit taken.
However, supermarket expenses are rising and consequently
their financial performances are at present somewhat disappoint-
ing. They are therefore tending to look more and more to
non-foods which offer higher margins than groceries to help
combat this difficulty and it is not unusual for them now to aim
to achieve at least 10% of their total turnover from non-food
sales.

A number of reasons may be offered in explanation of the
troubles of some supermarkets. In the initial wave of enthusiasm
to expand in the period 1958-1961, many took on premises which
were really too large, whilst others chose bad sites on which to
build. Premier Supermarkets, a subsidiary of Express Dairy, have
closed down three large supermarkets which they opened – in
Croydon, Slough and Wimbledon, because they were not profitable, and in March 1964 Premier Supermarkets were sold to
Mac Fisheries, though Express Dairy denied that this was

[1] December 20, 1963.

because they were not making sufficient profit. Rising site rents in town centres have also made for difficulties, so, too, has the insistence of some town planning authorities that a car park be provided. There has also been the problem of obtaining the right sort of shop manager. The Weston organization's decision to bring in Canadians to manage many of their Fine Fare supermarkets indicates the difficulty here.

Although in May 1963 an offer of 650,000 2s shares at 12s 6d in Pricerite Ltd., a small multiple supermarket company in the south, was oversubscribed 137·2 times, generally speaking the City has shown a reluctance to provide capital for supermarket companies. Despite, in most cases, continuing increases in trading profits, a number of the leading companies have been unable to maintain their overall performance at the high level achieved in the early years after the breakdown of r.p.m. on groceries.

TABLE 13

Earnings of certain supermarket companies
Earnings on Ordinary Capital (Less Tax)

End of company year	Melias Ltd.	Tesco Stores (Holdings Ltd.)	Victor Value (Holdings Ltd.)	Pricerite Ltd.
	%	%	%	%
1956	55·7	66·7	72·2	
1957	70·0	*	84·9	
1958	84·6	74·1	73·2	
1959	102·5	98·3	70·0	
1960	126·5	91·7	60·6	
1961	54·6	65·5	60·8	
1962	33·8	65·8	48·7	59·7
1963	32·1	64·7	47·3	80·1
1964	5·1	58·8	49·1	109·9

Source – Exchange Telegraph Co. Ltd. Daily Statistics Service.

Notes : * no figure because change in company year.
　　　　Pricerite only became a public company in 1962.

A recent statement by the chairman of Melias provides interesting evidence of the problems which are having to be faced. Speaking of their supermarkets, he says,

'The expected turn round has not taken place; indeed, overall results of these units have shown a further deterioration. In some locations sales have been affected by the appearance of new competitors in the near vicinity and, in the struggle to retain trade, gross profit margins have inevitably suffered.'

Melias have decided to sell some of their supermarkets.

The problems facing the supermarkets are very much of their own creation. When resale price maintenance began to end, the fear was for the survival of the independent retailer and also the wholesaler who supplied him. The multiples did in fact take trade away from the Co-operatives and Independents – whilst between 1957 and 1963 the multiples increased their share of the grocery trade from 24% to 33%, the shares of the Independents and Co-operatives fell from 54% to 49% and 22% to 18% respectively.

The breakdown of r.p.m. has not, however, had the catastrophic effect on the small retailer that was expected, though no exact statistics are available on this point. While the report of a London company of stockbrokers says that the opening of each new supermarket causes between six and nine small traders to close down, the available data does not bear this out. The Census of Distribution indicates that there was a small decrease in the number of establishments of grocers and provision dealers between 1957 and 1961 from 150,552 to 149,548 and over the same period bankruptcies rose from 118 to 202 per annum. However, other traders such as hardware and electrical dealers showed a faster increase in bankruptcies, whilst there was a larger decline in the numbers of some non-grocery establishments as in the case of confectioners, tobacconists and newsagents, where a decline from 77,437 to 70,802 was recorded by the Census of Distribution. A comparison of data provided in the 1950 and 1961 Censuses of Distribution shows that taking twenty-seven large boroughs in all parts of the country, in 72% of them the decline in the number of grocery establishments has been less (or the rise greater) than that in the number of establishments classified as 'other food retailers', whilst each group over all nearly doubled its turnover. There are exceptions. Slough, a town with very keen cut price competition and several supermarkets, is one – here with a turnover that nearly trebled there was a decline of about 4% in the number of grocers and provision dealers, whilst a doubling in the turnover of 'other food retailers' was accompanied by a small increase in the number of establishments falling into this category.

Thus, on balance some small retailers have gone out of business, in some cases they sold their premises to the supermarket companies. The fact that the Census figures show a fall in the number of establishments indicates that with the multiples opening up new branches there must have been some overall decline in the number of independent retailers in business. Some of this is due to cut price competition from the multiples but many commentators are of the opinion that the decline of the small shopkeeper has been due as much to town planning as to price cutting. Everyone is agreed that far fewer have succumbed than was expected.

Why have so many managed to survive? Those shops which are situated in residential rather than High Street areas have the advantage of convenience which tends rather to take them away from the general cut price fray in the High Streets of large towns.

The services provided by small grocers such as taking orders over the telephone, delivery and giving credit also help them to compete. A steadily rising grocery trade – turnover is increasing on average by 5% a year – also helps the independent to survive; although his share of the trade is declining, it is at least a declining share of an expanding total turnover. The main reason, however, why independent retailers have survived in such large numbers has been the advantages offered to them by their membership of trading groups.

The wholesalers in the grocery trade saw that their future depended on the survival of the independent trader. To arrest the falling off in each of their sales, the voluntary group movement was developed. Voluntary groups look for their membership to independent retailers who have a weekly turnover of at least £100 and a desire to expand. In other words, voluntary groups were not to save the 'stick in the muds' but would benefit the go-ahead trader. They provide assistance to the retailer in modernizing his outlet, advice on selling techniques and sometimes credit is provided for conversion to self service which is necessary if the independent is to compete with the multiple on such important matters as display and cleanliness. By 1964 it is estimated that about one-fifth of all self service outlets were operated by voluntary group members.[1]

The benefits of voluntary group membership are important to the retailer. Time that would otherwise be spent seeing numerous manufacturer sales representatives is saved, so, too, is the trouble of checking several deliveries each week. Only one cheque now needs to be written. The retailer obtains his supplies on better terms - one estimate suggests that this adds another 1%-2½% to his profit margin. Special cut price promotions are arranged by the group for its members and advertising material is provided in support. One group normally aims to have at least six special offers running at any one time.

Although the first voluntary group in this country was formed in 1954, it was not until 1957-58 when price maintenance broke down that the movement really went ahead. It started in the south of England and has now spread over the whole country. Two possible explanations may be offered for its slow development in the early stages. Either its members were so bound up with the struggle to keep r.p.m. that they failed to take stock of the true position, or it may have been because of the initial opposition of the National Grocers' Federation to any form of buying group on the grounds that bulk buying facilitates price cutting and would therefore weaken price maintenance. Probably both are valid explanations in this case.

TABLE 14

The Growth of Voluntary Groups

Year	Wholesalers in voluntary groups	Retailer membership
1954	3	120
1959	109	12,000
1962	134	nearly 24,000
1965	143	26,000

Source – The Group Grocer.

The 26,000 independent retailer members of wholesaler sponsored voluntary groups in 1965 represented just over 21% of all independent grocers in existence and were estimated to be responsible for 42% of the share of the grocery trade held by independents which is equivalent to about 21% of the national

[1] Much of the statistical data on the voluntary group movement has been obtained from the Group Grocer and their most valuable 'Group Grocer Census'.

grocery trade. There are twenty-one such groups, the largest - Mace - has over 5,000 retailer members, Spar has over 3,000 and V.G., A.I.G. and Danish Bacon Co. Ltd. all have over 2,000 retail members. Most groups have a large number of wholesalers collaborating, there are thirty-one in the Spar Group.

The position of the wholesaler is now much stronger, thanks to the success of voluntary groups and also because more manufacturers are realizing that it is uneconomic to supply many outlets direct. Whilst the wholesaler's margin has dropped in the last seven or eight years from $8\frac{1}{2}\%$ to about 7%, the rationalization afforded by voluntary groups has helped him to reduce his operating costs to about 6%. To deal with the problem of the uneconomic small drop, cash and carry warehouses have been set up of which there are now over 200. The really small retailer is able to obtain the stocks he needs from these warehouses at cost price, plus a small percentage to cover the cost of administration and overheads.

We should not overlook the benefits offered to the independent retailer by retailer buying groups. These are retailer owned and run, often without a warehouse, and operating on drop shipments. There are at present about ninety retailer buying groups with a total membership of some 8,000 retailers. The largest company - Londis Grovisions Ltd. - has over 700 members. The Private Grocers' Merchandise Association was formed in 1958 to co-ordinate the various groups, many of whom also belong to the national B.O.B. scheme which is also run from the P.G.M.A. though it originated in Scarborough.

Whilst retailer sponsored buying groups are generally not as effective or important as wholesaler sponsored groups, they, too, have enabled the independent retailer to rationalize his purchasing arrangements and hence to obtain better terms and so to meet price cutting with price cutting. By the middle of 1963, it was estimated that independent retailers who were members of retailer and/or wholesaler sponsored buying groups (a few belong to both) were responsible for 28.6% of total grocery sales, this represents just over 57% of the sales of all independent retailers.[1]

Having seen how the growth of cut price supermarkets and self service stores has affected the retail grocery trade in this

[1] *Nielsen Researcher* July/August 1963.

country and the attempts made to combat this, we must finally note a development which is tending to reduce the significance of the breakdown of r.p.m. 'Own brands' were introduced originally by retailers who wanted to offer a lower price product and were prevented by resale price maintenance from merely cutting the price of a manufacturer brand. Since the ending of r.p.m. the use of own brands appears to have increased rather than decreased, though their function seems to have changed. Many of the large retailer multiples sell own brand lines and find that they sell well. Sainsburys and David Greig are two who lead in this respect. Most voluntary groups also feature their own brands – Spar have eighty-four own brand products, including electric lamps, nylons and tissues, besides groceries, with an annual turnover of £3½ million.

It is estimated that own brands account for some 12% of the total market for instant coffee and maybe as much as 6% or 7% of all sales in supermarkets. Besides allowing the retailer to offer a lower price for a product of a quality comparable to that of the manufacturer brand, by placing a large manufacturing order and eliminating all advertising expenditure on it, the retailer is able to obtain a higher margin despite the lower selling price. Thus an own brand coffee selling at 1s 9d yields a margin to the retailer of 18½%, while Nescafé, sold at 2s 5d only returns a 10% profit margin.

Own brands are also an important way of creating and retaining customer loyalty to a particular shop. For example, you can buy Heinz soups in any shop but if a retailer or voluntary group own brand of soup is found to be cheaper and equally satisfactory, the customer tends to return to the same shop in order to be able to have the same brand again. Thus, besides offering a lower price good and obtaining a larger profit margin, by using own brands the retailer is creating a form of market imperfection. He is taking some of the emphasis away from price cutting on manufacturer brands and is therefore helping to reduce the severity of cut price competition arising from the breakdown of r.p.m. in the grocery trade. With voluntary groups increasingly using own brand lines they are therefore providing further protection to the independent retailer and enhancing his chances of survival.

CHAPTER X

THE LEVEL OF GROCERY PRICES

Since resale price maintenance ended on branded groceries, much interest has been shown in the saving which price cutting offers to consumers. Several different organizations have investigated this. In 1958 the Consumer Association carried out a survey in Croydon in which they found that twenty-one specified items whose cost at manufacturer recommended prices was £1 13s 5½d could be bought for £1 11s 2½d - a saving of 1s 4d in the £.[1]

A larger survey was carried out by Garland-Compton Ltd. in February and March 1961 covering 100 stores in the Greater London area.[2] On twenty-three branded products whose manufacturer recommended prices amounted to £1 18s 6d, they found that the average price paid was £1 16s 5¼d - a saving of 4.7% or 11¼d in the £. In arriving at this estimate, the value of the Co-operative dividend was deducted from the prices prevailing in outlets owned by Co-operative Societies. Garland-Compton further analysed their results by ownership of store and method of operation. As was to be expected, the multiples and super-markets offered the greatest saving as the following table shows.

TABLE 15

Reduction on Manufacturer Prices

By ownership group	Saving %	By service group	Saving %
Multiples	6·0	Supermarkets	7·1
Co-operatives	5·8	Self service	5·7
Independents	2·9	Counter service	3·7

Source – Garland-Compton Inquiry 1961.

Interesting though the above studies are, their importance is limited by the fact that they applied to only a limited geographical area and one where price cutting was probably at its greatest. At about the same time the A. C. Nielsen Company investigated

[1] *'Which ?'* Summer 1958.
[2] *'The cost of the "Shopping Basket"'* June 1961.

the geographical spread of price cutting, taking three products only - coffee, soft drinks and toilet soaps. They found that price cutting on one or more of these was to be found in 50% of all grocery outlets in the country, though the proportion was much higher in and around London than in other areas.[1]

TABLE 16

Regional Distribution in Number of shops offering one or more of three products at a reduced price

Area	%
Greater London	68
Eastern, South Eastern, Southern	63
Yorkshire and Northern	54
Midlands	49
Lancashire and Cheshire	41
Scotland	39
Wales and South Western	32

Source – Nielsen Researcher.

Manufacturer price reductions were ignored in all the inquiries discussed above.

That there was more price cutting in the south than in the rest of the country was also shown in an inquiry by Alfred Bird & Co.[2] Their findings suggested that what price cutting there was tended to be concentrated on only a few products. Whilst more than 60% of buyers obtained coffee below the recommended price and 50% or more bought soap powder cut price, only one-third could obtain breakfast cereals and tinned soups at a reduced price and only 22% bought tea below the recommended retail price.

A later survey carried out by Nielsen suggested that by December 1, 1963, on a range of twelve branded food products, retailer price reductions amounted to 5·3% off the manufacturer recommended price with multiples offering a saving of 9·1% and Co-operatives and Independents a saving of 3·5%.[3]

In order to try to obtain further evidence on the extent of price cutting the present writer prepared a mail questionnaire sent to a sample of 1,000 retail grocery establishments. This

[1] *Nielsen Researcher* July/August 1961.
[2] *'Mrs. Housewife and Her Grocer'* May 1961
[3] *Nielsen Researcher* March/April 1964.

specified popular sizes of leading brands of twenty-nine products commonly sold in grocery outlets and asked the recipient to indicate the price being charged for these goods on May 26, 1964. Further questions investigated the number of other branches owned, whether the outlet operated on a self service basis for grocery sales, whether trading stamps were given, the value of the dividend given by the Co-operative Societies replying and whether the respondent was a member of any form of wholesaler or retail buying group. In order to weight the replies, a final question was included on the size of turnover achieved by the outlet.

In the final analysis three products included on the questionnaire – tinned peaches, aerosol and paper tissues – had to be ignored because of inadequate information. This left twenty-six products suitable for analysis. They were:

Commodity	Brand	Commodity	Brand
Sugar	—	Strawberry Jam	Robertsons
Tea	P.G. Tips	Processed Cheese	Kraft Dairylea
Instant Coffee	Nescafé	Jelly	Rowntrees
Horlicks	—	Sauce	H.P.
Orange Squash	Sunfresh	Salt	Saxa
Margarine	Stork	Self Raising Flour	McDougalls
Bread (white sliced)	—	Corn Flakes	Kelloggs
Rich Tea Biscuits	McVitie Price	Custard Powder	Birds
Assorted Biscuits	Peek Frean	Toothpaste	Macleans
Baked Beans	Crosse & Blackwell	Toilet Soap	Imperial Leather
Tomato Soup	Heinz	Soap Powder	Daz
Evaporated Milk	Libby	Carpet Cleaner	1001
Paste	Shippam	Dog Food	Pal

In the absence of an adequate sampling frame, the sample had to be constructed from a number of different sources – members of the National Grocers' Federation, *Self Service and Supermarket Annual Survey and Directory* 1964, *Stores and Shops Directory of Multiples* and from directories to a number of towns included in the sample of constituencies used by the National Food Survey in 1960. Two hundred and eighty-one questionnaires were returned which were suitable for analysis. Although the rate of response was low, it was expected to be so in view of the nature of the information sought and does in fact compare very closely with a similar study carried out some years ago in the United States.[1]

Analysis of the replies suggests that, due to the difficulty of tracing the large number of very small grocery establishments, the response is biased somewhat in favour of the larger store.

TABLE 17

The Distribution of Respondents to a Price Survey 1964, compared with the Actual Distribution of U.K. Grocers 1961

Turnover Group £ per week	Sample Survey 1964		Actual Distribution 1961*	
	% establishments replying	% turnover	% establishments	% turnover
0 – 100	6·5	0·6	22·8	4·0
101 – 300	33·5	6·7	40·5	22·0
301 – 500	27·3	14·4	16·2	15·5
501 – 1,000	16·4	16·3	14·5	25·3
1,001 – 2,000	9·4	18·7	4·4	16·5
2,001 – 5,000	4·0	18·3	1·3	11·2
Over 5,000	2·9	25·0	0·3	5·5
	100	100	100	100

* Based on Report on the *Census of Distribution* 1961 Part I Table 7.

However, with turnover in the grocery trade growing by some 5% a year, allied to the natural growth of the larger retailing establishments, if figures of the actual distribution of grocery retailers in 1964 were available they would undoubtedly show that large retailers had increased in importance since 1961. The bias in the sample returns does not come from an under-representation of independent retailers as a whole since their share of the total turnover covered by the sample coincides almost exactly with their overall importance in the U.K. grocery trade in 1964. Whilst initially the results will be presented without allowing for the possibility of bias, the more important figures will then be re-presented having been recalculated to try to correct any bias.

Weighting the replies received from each establishment by their weekly turnover, a national average cost for the twenty-six

[1] H. J. Ostlund and C. R. Vickland – *'Fair Trade and the Retail Drug Store'* (Chicago) 1940 referred to in M. Frankel's 'The Effects of Fair Trade: Fact and Fiction in the Statistical Findings' *Journal of Business* 1955.

products included in the analysis of £2 os 6d was arrived at.[1]
This compares with a total cost at manufacturer recommended
prices of £2 4s 0½d[2] and represents a saving of 8% or 1s 7d in
the £. As was to be expected, self service stores proved to be
cheaper than establishments without self service and establishments that were part of a multiple retailer organization offered
lower prices than Co-operative Societies and independent
retailers. Turnover-wise the large shops were cheaper than the
smaller ones.

TABLE 18

Saving on Manufacturer Recommended Prices

	Cost	Saving %
Analysed by service		
Self service outlets	£1 19 8½	9·8
Non self service outlets	£2 1 8½	5·3
Analysed by ownership		
Multiples	£1 18 9	12·0
Co-operatives	£2 0 7½	7·8
Independents	£2 1 3½	6·2
Analysed by turnover £ per week		
Over £5,000	£1 18 6	12·6
2,001 – 5,000	£2 0 7½	7·8
1,001 – 2,000	£2 0 8	7·7
501 – 1,000	£2 0 8½	7·6
301 – 500	£2 2 0½	4·5
101 – 300	£2 1 10	5·0
0 – 100	£2 2 2½	4·2

These results indicate clearly that although the larger shop
offers greater savings, all types and sizes of grocery outlet now
offer to the consumer reductions on manufacturer recommended
prices. One interesting feature is the way in which, when
analysed by turnover, the establishments fall into three categories so far as price savings are concerned. Those with turnovers
of over £5,000 a week are easily the cheapest and these are
essentially the real supermarkets. The next category is of

[1] Following the practice adopted in previous studies of this kind, the value of
the Co-operative dividend was taken into account in calculating the actual cost.
[2] On sugar and flour retail selling prices were not recommended and, on the
basis of evidence and advice from numerous sources, estimated recommended
prices of 1s 8d and 2s 1d respectively were taken. For bread where no brand
was specified a recommended price of 1s 2½d was assumed. This was the price
recommended at the time by the leading plant bakers though there is some
evidence that smaller bakers were recommending a higher price.

establishments with turnovers ranging from £501 to £5,000 a week. These are mainly other self service outlets – in fact 80% of replies in these categories were from establishments which operated on a self service basis. The remaining group of outlets with turnovers from £0 to £500 a week were predominantly counter-service shops (only 15% of those replying in this group had self service).

In recent years, as we saw in the previous chapter, the breakdown of resale price maintenance has encouraged the independent retailer to join some form of buying group in order to compete on better terms with the multiples. Replies to the questionnaire were further analysed to investigate the effect which membership of these groups had on the prices charged by independent retailers. The results suggest that traders who belong to wholesaler sponsored voluntary groups offer lower prices than other independents and from the available data this appears to apply at all levels of turnover where independent retailers are important. The aim of the symbol groups is to encourage their member retailers to convert to self service and to become more competitive and they are obviously succeeding in their objective.

TABLE 19

Prices in Establishments owned by Independent Retailers Analysed by Membership of Buying Group

Type of Group	(No. of replies)	Cost	Saving %
Wholesaler voluntary group or chain	(77)	£2 0 10	7·3
Retailer buying group	(85)	£2 1 11	4·8
Member of both wholesaler and retailer groups	(15)	£2 1 6	5·8
Unaffiliated independents	(50)	£2 1 2	6·5*

* That this figure is so high is due to the existence of a small number of unaffiliated independents with large turnovers who are keenly competitive on price. If these were to be excluded, the saving offered by unaffiliated independent retailers would be less than 2%.

Sixteen or nearly 6% of the establishments replying gave trading stamps. Numerically, the majority were small independents and in view of the wide spread of these few respondents both geographically and by turnover, it would not be meaningful to compare a weighted average price for these shops alone with the national average. It is better to compare prices in these outlets with prices in other outlets which have a comparable turnover and are in the same geographical region. On this basis it was found that in ten of the sixteen cases, prices in shops giving trading stamps were lower than the average price for all shops of the same turnover group in the same Nielsen region. Thus we would tentatively state that there is no evidence to support the claim that shops which give trading stamps are necessarily dearer than other comparable outlets which do not, though, it must be emphasized, this is on the basis of a limited amount of evidence.

Comparing the cost of the specified products in each Nielsen region separately, we find that there is a difference in costs of 3s 4d between the highest and lowest priced regions.

TABLE 20

Total Costs of Products Analysed by Nielsen Region

Region	Cost
1. Northern	£2 0 0½
2. East and West Ridings	£1 19 2
3. North Midland	£2 0 0½
4. Eastern	£1 19 11½
5. South Eastern	£2 0 5
6. Southern	£2 2 4
7. South Western	£2 0 11
8. Wales	£2 2 2½
9. Midland	£2 2 6
10. North Western	£2 0 6½
11. Scotland	£2 0 1½*
12. Greater London	£1 19 2
National Average	£2 0 6

* The high level of Co-operative dividend still obtaining in Scotland has contributed to the low total cost for this region.

Compared with a saving of 8% on the national average cost, consumers in the lowest priced regions are able to obtain a saving of 11·1% = 2s 2½d in the £, whilst those in the highest priced regions only save about 3·5% = 8½d in the £, on the manufacturer recommended prices. Thus it would seem that consumers in all regions are able now to benefit to a greater or lesser degree from cut price competition in the grocery trade. What then determines where the greatest price reductions are to be obtained? The most important factor would seem to be the development of either self service stores and/or supermarkets in a particular region. Therefore we would look for some positive correlation between the level of prices and the number of self service outlets or supermarkets per head of population.

Using the figures given in the previous chapter indicating the ratio of population to self service stores and supermarkets,[1] we are able to rank these in order of size, a low ranking indicating a high proportion of outlets per head of population. Ranking can also be given to each region, according to the total cost of the articles included in the questionnaire, in this case a low ranking indicates a low total cost. Then, correlating the ranking by price with the other rankings in turn, it is possible to see whether our expectations are upheld.

TABLE 21

Ranking of Nielsen Regions by Cost and Development of Self Service Stores and Supermarkets

Nielsen Region	Ranking by total cost	Ranking by ratio of population per self service store (including supermarkets)	Ranking by ratio of population per supermarket
	Column 1	Column 2	Column 3
1	4	5	9
2	1	11	12
3	4	3	3
4	3	1	4
5	7	8	6
6	10	2	1
7	9	7	7
8	11	12	8
9	12	10	10
10	8	6	5
11	6	9	11
12			2

: of Rank Correlation

; the nearer to +1 it
direction, the nearer
erse manner. Results

ERRATUM

The formula at the foot of page 145 should read:

$$\rho = 1 - \frac{6 \Sigma \, d^2}{n(n^2 - 1)}$$

near o indicate little correlation between the two sets of ranking.

Applying the formula for columns 1 and 2 we obtain a coefficient of o·34 and for columns 1 and 3 a coefficient of o·04. Thus, supermarkets alone do not appear to influence the overall level of prices in a region. Even the extent of self service outlets as a whole does not, on the face of it, appear to exert a very strong influence on the level of prices and the coefficient obtained is not statistically significant. However, closer inspection reveals that there are only two regions – regions 2 and 6 – which spoil the closeness of fit between the rankings of columns 1 and 2. In all the other regions there is a close relationship between the rankings in columns 1 and 2, thereby suggesting that in most areas the extent of price reductions available to the consumer is closely related to the extent of the penetration of self service outlets.

The replies to the questionnaire contained a certain amount of bias. Self service outlets were over-represented in the replies compared with their importance in the total grocery trade at present. Multiples were somewhat under-represented and Co-operative Societies correspondingly over-represented. In terms of turnover the replies contained a marked bias in favour of the large store.

It is possible to correct for any errors caused by such bias by recalculating our average price for the goods concerned, using as weightings the national distribution of grocery turnover by the various categories of retail outlet instead of the sample replies. Thus, independent retailers now have 49% of the grocery trade, multiples 33% and co-operatives 18%.[1] Of their total grocery sales it is estimated that between 50% and 60% of the trade of both multiples and co-operatives and 10%-15% of the sales of independent retailers were achieved by self service outlets. Thus we now have six categories of retail outlet (multiples with and without self service, co-operatives with and without self service and independents with and without self service) for each of which the sample inquiry provides data on the level of prices. If these prices are then weighted according to the share of each of the six categories in the total national grocery trade, a revised national average cost for the twenty-six products under

[1] *Nielsen Researcher* March/April 1965.

investigation of £2 0s 8d is obtained.[1] It will be observed that this does not greatly differ from the original estimate of £2 0s 6d.

An alternative calculation can be made on a turnover basis using the distribution of turnover indicated in the 1961 *Census of Distribution* (see Table 17 above). A higher figure of £2 1s 1d is thereby obtained, though in view of the general expansion of grocery sales between 1961 and 1964 and the growth in importance of large scale retail outlets, the use of 1961 figures for weighting purposes means that small retail outlets are accorded more importance than their actual position in 1964 would warrant and therefore the revised figure obtained by this method is clearly somewhat too high.

Thus we conclude that on the basis of an inquiry conducted by means of a mail questionnaire sent to grocery retailers the cost of the twenty-six products included in the analysis is between £2 0s 6d and £2 1s 1d with £2 0s 8d the best estimate we have. This indicates a saving on manufacturer recommended prices of about 7.7% or 1s 6½d in the £. Comparing the results of this inquiry with earlier analyses it seems, therefore, that cut price competition has become more general and more severe.

Replies to the questionnaire also indicate that price cutting is tending to take place on a wider range of products. Whilst previous surveys have shown that only on a very few goods such as coffee are more than, say, a third of all retailers cutting prices, the present inquiry reveals that a large majority of the lines included were being price cut by more than 30% of all retailers replying who sold that particular brand (see below, Table 22).

Whilst the saving throughout the country as a whole is estimated at about 7.7%, there are certain towns where larger savings are supposedly obtainable. One such place is the town of Slough, which has within a space of about half a mile along its High Street nine self service grocery outlets. Five of these belong to leading supermarket chains - Fine Fare, Tesco (which has two), Waitrose and Sainsbury. Premier Supermarkets also owned an outlet but sold it to Tesco in 1963. Three are branches of older multiple grocers - David Greig, Lipton and International Tea

---

[1] The revised figures for each ownership group after correcting for the extent of self service become – Multiples £1 19s 0d. Co-operatives £2 0s 3d, and Independents £2 1s 11d.

Stores[1] and there are two other local retailers - one a small multiple and the other an independent. As a consequence of this abundance of grocers, there is keen price competition.

TABLE 22

Proportion of Retailers Cutting the Price of Particular Products

Products being price cut by:

More than 50% retailers	*41% – 50% retailers*	*31% – 40% retailers*	*0 – 30% retailers*
Coffee	Paste	Soup	Sauce
Squash	Carpet Cleaner	Tea	Rich Tea Biscuits
Baked Beans	Processed Cheese	Corn Flakes	Margarine
Jelly	Evaporated Milk	Horlicks	Soap
	Jam		Salt
	Dog Food		
	Soap Powder		
	Custard Powder		

Notes : At the time of this study a '3d off' manufacturer special offer was running on Macleans toothpaste which it has not proved possible to separate from retailer price reductions. The proportion of retailers reporting a price for assorted biscuits was small. Both these have therefore been excluded from this analysis, so too have the three products for which no manufacturer recommended prices existed.

On the same day to which the questionnaire related, a close study was made of prices in these Slough shops using the same products that had been included on the questionnaire. The average price in Slough for these goods was £1 18s 6½d - a saving of 12·5%.[2] The outlet offering the lowest overall prices was the Sainsbury supermarket, where the goods would have cost £1 18s 0½d, a saving on manufacturer recommended prices of 13·6%. Sainsbury's also offered the considerable advantage that they were the only outlet where all the products listed could be obtained at the time. By shopping around and obtaining each product in the outlet where it was at the lowest price a further 2s could have been saved, making a total possible saving of 8s od or 18·1%. However, to achieve this extra saving, it would be necessary to shop around all the outlets first to compare prices and then to go back to each outlet to obtain the cheap product. It is estimated that this would take at least two hours and there-

[1] In the spring of 1965 International Tea Stores also closed their outlet.
[2] In this case as turnover figures were not available prices were weighted by size of selling area in each outlet.

fore is certainly not worthwhile, since to be prepared to seek the extra possible saving of 2s, the housewife must value her time at less than 1s per hour.

At the time of this survey, both Fine Fare and Tesco were giving trading stamps. Taking the value of the stamps when exchanged for a gift as 2½% and deducting this from the total cost of the goods in the shops concerned, Tesco became cheaper than Sainsbury's but Fine Fare remained somewhat dearer. Even if a cash value of 1¼% for trading stamps were taken, Tesco remained slightly cheaper than Sainsbury's over the range of goods which they both stocked.

There are some who argue that price cutting does not bring to the consumer the unmitigated benefits that have been suggested so far. We will now consider some of their arguments. First, they suggest that whilst prices of branded groceries may have been cut, these will be offset by higher prices on unbranded goods. This may or may not be correct. Whilst there is no evidence that on unbranded goods such as, for example, meat the self service store is charging higher prices than the traditional butcher, because of the virtual impossibility of defining a standard article no adequate price comparison on these goods could be made.

The complaint is also made that false price reductions are offered. It is reported that one multiple raised the price of all shampoos by 20% before 'cutting' them back to the normal recommended price. The National Pharmaceutical Union also collected evidence of similar practices:

TABLE 23

False Price Reductions

Article	Normal price	'Cut from'	Sold at
Liquid Shampoo	10½d	1s 0d	10½d
Liquid Shampoo	3s 4d	3s 8d	3s 2d
Hand Cream	2s 3d	2s 6d	2s 2d
Headache Powders	2s 0d	—	2s 1d
Hair Cream	1s 10d	—	2s 0d
Baby Shampoo	9d	—	10d
Baby Powder	2s 0d	2s 6d	2s 3d

Source – National Pharmaceutical Union *'Supplement'* August 1963.

It is not disputed that such examples do genuinely arise. This is a hazard that those who wish to see the breakdown of resale price maintenance have to face. This form of deceitful double pricing is, however, most objectionable and some form of action to deal with such offenders would be desirable. Equally objectionable is the practice of advertising goods at a cut price but not making any available to the consumer. Two such instances were found in Slough. In one shop, jars of coffee were advertised at 4s but all were marked at 4s 9d, whilst another outlet offered small jars of paste at 7d but charged 9d.

Simple overcharging is another matter. When a manufacturer recommends a price but does not enforce it, it is not to be wondered at if some retailers decide to charge above the recommended price. In fact it may be economically justifiable for some small retailers to charge a higher price in order to achieve a reasonable margin of profit. To put this in economic terms – if the maintained price is fixed on the basis of the average costs of all retailers, when left free to determine his own selling price, the high-cost retailer will now fix a higher price. This is not a new phenomenon. One manufacturer of branded groceries, who has never enforced fixed resale prices, found as long ago as 1950 that for the same size of the same product the price charged ranged from 11d to 1s 9d. The present inquiry revealed a number of examples of 'overcharging'. In all, out of more than 6,000 prices recorded, in eighty-eight instances prices above the manufacturer recommended level were recorded. Each time they amounted to a mere halfpenny or penny above the recommended price. Eight of these came from Multiples, five from Co-operatives and the remaining seventy-five from Independents. Most shops were only 'overcharging' on one of the specified brands, though in two or three cases three products were being sold above the manufacturer recommended price.

No instances of overcharging were found on tea, soup, evaporated milk, toothpaste or dog food. All other products were charged for at more than the recommended price in at least one outlet. The highest number of times on which overcharging was found was on Corn Flakes (13 times), Rich Tea Biscuits (11) and Soap Powder (10). (Sugar, bread and flour could not be included in this analysis since they do not carry a standard recommended price.)

There may be some who will claim that price cutting has only been made possible by manufacturers increasing the margins they allow. This, too, is not substantiated. For thirteen of the products included in the questionnaire, it has been possible, with the aid of The Grocer 'Buff List', to compare trade and retail prices prevailing at May 19, 1956. and May 2, 1964. In five cases the margin has risen, in five it has fallen and on three it has remained exactly the same.[1] The average margin for these thirteen lines was 17.85% in 1956 and 17.73% in 1964. While this does not deny the possibility that quantity discount terms available to large purchasers have increased or that more retailers are buying on better terms than the trade price listed, it does show that price cutting has not been achieved by an overall widening of the retailer's basic margin.

Small retailers sometimes complain that large self service stores are retailing products at prices lower than they can obtain the same lines. With the aid of the retail prices collected from our mail questionnaire and the trade prices listed in The Grocer 'Buff List', this was investigated. It was found that some 6% of all the prices recorded were below what we might call 'the worst trade terms'. Almost all products were sold below this level to some extent but only on three or four could this be described as a serious problem. It was found that 52% outlets selling Nescafé, 32% selling Sunfresh orange squash, 20% selling Bird's Custard Powder and 9% selling Heinz tomato soup sold at prices below the worst trade terms available to the smallest retailer. The practice of selling below such prices was by no means confined to the multiples since a number of independents also pursued the same policy helped, and in some cases encouraged, by their membership of wholesaler- or retailer-sponsored buying groups.

Thus we conclude that on balance the consumer has benefited from the breakdown of resale price maintenance in the grocery trade. The exact extent of the saving available varies from region to region and depends largely on the penetration of self service into each area. Taking the country as a whole, on the basis of information from a mail questionnaire survey, the saving to the

[1]The margin being calculated as a percentage of $\dfrac{\text{Retail price} - \text{Trade price}}{\text{Retail price}}$ for each time period.

consumer as a result of price cutting on *brand leaders*[1] in the grocery and allied fields is in the region of 1s 6d in the £.[2] The importance of this saving depends on the proportion of total consumer expenditure which goes on groceries. The poorer the family, the higher the share of the family income which is spent on food and so it is these families which have benefited most from the breakdown of r.p.m. in the grocery trade.

In return for this saving, the consumer is exposed to certain possible abuses such as overcharging and misleading double pricing. At the present time this does not appear a serious problem and may be considered a risk worth accepting in return for the savings obtainable. One thing is certain, more skill is now required from the housewife in her shopping expeditions if the benefits are to be obtained.

There is no evidence that price cutting has only been made possible by manufacturers widening normal trade margins, nor that large traders normally retail goods at prices below those at which the small independent retailer can buy. It is certain, however, that the pressure of cut price competition has encouraged wholesalers and independent retailers to rationalize their purchasing procedures in order to take advantage of the quantity discount terms available from manufacturers which enable price cutting to take place and this rationalization has been to the benefit of manufacturers, distributors and consumers.

[1] If less popular brands were taken the saving would be smaller and the likelihood of overcharging increased.

[2] It is not, strictly speaking, correct to say that all this saving is due to the collapse of r.p.m. since some of the products included in this inquiry were never price maintained. However, as the previous chapter indicated, it was the general collapse of r.p.m. in the grocery trade that facilitated the development of self service stores who have been mainly responsible for the growth of cut-price competition.

CHAPTER XI

OTHER CHANGES IN THE EXTENT OF R.P.M. 1956-1964

In addition to the breakdown of resale price maintenance on branded groceries, the period 1956-1964 also saw a number of other changes in the extent of r.p.m. in various trades. As we saw in chapter VI, there was a time in 1961 when it appeared that the system would collapse altogether, this did not materialize and resale price maintenance has remained a trading policy of importance over a large sector of consumer expenditure.

Whilst in some trades resale price maintenance has increased in importance, in others it has decreased. On some goods r.p.m. has only been enforced since 1956. The growth of manufacturer branding has ensured that a larger proportion of consumer spending on some goods has been on price maintained products. This trend has been most significant in the clothing trade and especially on footwear where new manufacturers have adopted a policy of fixed resale prices on their products. New household lines, such as aerosols, were initially price maintained though this did not last once distribution through supermarkets became important.

In the hardware trade also, several manufacturers only began to prescribe fixed resale prices after 1956. One leading manufacturer reported that it was only the new powers provided by the Restrictive Trade Practices Act that made it possible for such manufacturers to enforce r.p.m. Trade journals also contain letters from manufacturers stating that they would, from a certain date, impose a condition as to the price at which their products were to be resold. In most instances the reason given for the new policy was that for the first time there was price cutting on these goods. This supports still further our argument in chapter III that many manufacturers only make resale price maintenance a legally enforceable condition of sale when forced to do so by an outbreak of price cutting. Whilst the most important increases in the extent of resale price maintenance have occurred on hardware goods, some manufacturers of electrical appliances, furniture and stationery also began to formally price maintain their products after the passing of the 1956 Act.

The breakdown of resale price maintenance in the grocery trade made possible the development of a new type of grocery retailer, who used cut prices as a form of sales promotion to build a large turnover. As this method of trading rapidly gained public acceptance, so the operators moved from small self service stores to large supermarkets and so, too, they widened the range of goods which were stocked in such outlets so that now all 'consumable'[1] household items can be bought under one roof. This has been a major revolution in the retail trade of this country. The following table indicates the extent to which grocery outlets had encroached into the territory of other types of retailer at the time of the Census of Distribution in 1961.

TABLE 24

Grocers selling non-groceries

Item	% all grocers and provision dealers selling	Grocers and provision dealers selling as % all outlets selling
Chocolate and sugar confectionery	91	59
Cigarettes and tobacco	94	57
Electric light fittings and bulbs	19	41
Drugs and medicines	32	60
Face powder, face cream etc.	20	49

Source – *Board of Trade Journal* September 20, 1963.
These proportions will undoubtedly have increased still further since 1961.

The first supermarket challenges to non-food manufacturers over r.p.m. came on detergents and certain toilet preparations such as toothpaste. The breakdown started with the introduction of special cut price offers for a limited period of time but quickly led to general price cutting. In both these fields there is very keen competition between suppliers and the market is approaching saturation point. It is therefore an unwise policy on the part of a manufacturer to refuse to allow supermarkets to stock and

[1] 'Consumable' in the sense that they are quickly used up and further purchases are frequently required.

price cut his product when they are allowed to do so on competing goods. A recent study on non-foods normally sold in grocery outlets such as toilet soaps, polishes, detergents, etc., showed that 60% of consumers, when unable to find the brand they require, will buy a substitute brand rather than go to another shop.[1] Thus, to have his brand missing from a supermarket with a large turnover imposes a considerable penalty on the manufacturer. One manufacturer found that by 1964, 64% of his sales of toothpaste were through grocery outlets – an increase of one-third since 1959, whilst grocery outlets were, by then, also responsible for 50% haircream and 44% shampoo sales. Thus, with the trend of chemists' goods into the grocery supermarkets, the manufacturers have been forced to accept the inevitability of price cutting on their products. A further difficulty which suppliers faced was that, having allowed supermarkets to sell their products whilst they were still subject to r.p.m., much time was spent in trying to ensure that price cutting did not take place. One manufacturer was receiving up to 400 telephone calls a week complaining about price cutting and found as a result that his sales staff were spending their time trying to control price cutters instead of promoting sales. Except for a very few manufacturers who have continued to persistently enforce r.p.m. against the supermarkets, this means that once supermarkets became a normal channel of distribution for a product, r.p.m. quickly became a dead letter.[2]

Price maintenance on other household goods such as paper products, cleaners, disinfectants and soaps has also ended since 1956. A further major breach in the ranks of those manufacturers who enforced r.p.m. came in April 1963 when Chesebrough-Ponds Ltd. removed many of their products from the P.A.T.A. protected list. Chesebrough-Ponds had been strong enforcers of r.p.m. having obtained injunctions in at least eight instances, but they were forced to change their policy when they found that price cutting was being allowed by manufacturers of competing brands and this was placing the Chesebrough-Ponds brands at a disadvantage. Some cosmetics manufacturers still insist on r.p.m. and even in some cases continue to refuse to

[1] *Nielsen Researcher* May/June 1963.
[2] Though r.p.m. has been retained on confectionery and cigarettes and tobacco.

supply likely price cutters. So, too, do the manufacturers of patent medicines, though it is claimed that where certain brands are offered in supermarkets at cut prices, the manufacturers merely turn a blind eye.

Thus it is clearly the pressure placed on manufacturers by the supermarkets handling their products which has caused the breakdown of resale price maintenance on toiletries and other household products. Because of the frequency with which they are purchased and the small unit cost of the articles, they were an obvious choice of product for the supermarkets to choose to stock and now sizeable savings are available to consumers purchasing them in grocery outlets. The non-food lines included in the price study discussed in chapter X above show an average saving on manufacturer recommended prices of 7% overall, compared with the average saving of c. 8% for all products included in the survey.

Manufacturers have benefited from the additional interest shown by supermarket operators in their products once they allowed price cutting. Some chemists have refused to stock products which are being price cut in supermarkets but the trend in sales of these products is so much away from the chemist's shop and into the supermarket that this does not hurt the manufacturer, though the chemist is probably harming himself. To reject a line just because it is being aggressively promoted in a grocery outlet is not a sensible policy on the part of chemists, they only lose sales which they would otherwise have been able to make. So far as the feared disastrous consequences of the breakdown of r.p.m. on chemists' goods are concerned, it is interesting to observe the comments of a group of Australian pharmacists on a visit to this country who were quoted as having found that cut price competition from non-pharmacists had not, by the summer of 1963, had the drastic effect on the turnover of pharmacists that had been feared.[1] The only undesirable consequence arising from the breakdown of r.p.m. reported by a manufacturer was that as a result of the use by supermarkets of special offers on competing brands as well as on his own, the level of sales tended to fluctuate unevenly, being higher when his goods were featured and lower when those of his competitors

[1] *Chemist and Druggist* August 31, 1963.

were promoted. This makes production planning difficult and can lead to stock holding problems. If this difficulty is not overcome, it may well prove to be a detriment arising from the breakdown of r.p.m. Though since no food manufacturer claimed that this was a problem and as r.p.m. has been ended longer on groceries than on toiletries and household goods, this may prove to be of passing importance only.

In practice resale price maintenance also ended on pneumatic tyres. In theory the manufacturers still retained r.p.m. as a condition of sale[1] but for several years failed to take any effective enforcement action. There are two reasons for the breakdown of r.p.m. on these goods. In the first place a new form of trader - the 'tyre specialist' - has grown up. He does not have the large overheads of the normal motor dealer and by offering cut prices he is able to attract a large custom and thereby to qualify for sizeable quantity discounts from the manufacturers which make price cutting easier. The second reason is that there are more manufacturers than are really needed to meet present demand. Under such circumstances, to take action against a price cutter is to invite another manufacturer, who is less anxious to see resale prices maintained, to capture an extra part of the market. This shows, once again, just how imperative it is for a manufacturer to be in step with his competitors if, and when, resale price maintenance is abandoned in a particular trade.

Thus there are three types of product on which resale price maintenance broke down between 1956 and 1964: branded groceries, toiletries and household goods and tyres. In each instance the same basic reasons can be given - the growth of a new type of distributor for the product able to operate on a lower margin, and the realization of manufacturers that to ignore this development would cause them to lose sales to other manufacturers who would supply.

The prohibition of collective enforcement of r.p.m. certainly aided the breakdown of r.p.m. on these goods. It did so by removing the security that manufacturers had previously felt by knowing they would all, where necessary, withhold supplies from price cutters. Once such collective actions were prohibited there was a greater likelihood that one supplier would find them

[1] Until the Resale Prices Act came into force.

acceptable outlets and this would cause the rest to follow suit. By contributing to the growth of supermarkets through the breakdown of r.p.m. in the grocery trade, the Restrictive Trade Practices Act also created the situation where the encroachment of supermarkets into the distribution of non-food household items and the breakdown of resale price maintenance on these products, too, became inevitable.

In other trades there are a few suppliers who report having dropped resale price maintenance during this period. In most cases they are manufacturers of lesser known brands who were not troubled by price cutting. They were until 1956 members of collective enforcement schemes and on the passing of the Restrictive Trade Practices Act did not find it necessary to take an individual stand on resale price maintenance. The only other instance we need to note where a manufacturer stopped enforcing fixed price conditions of sale concerns Esso petroleum. They formally dropped r.p.m. in December 1963. This is not of great significance, however, since resale price maintenance on petrol has not been of consequence for many years and this move merely brought them into line with the other petrol companies.

Even where resale price maintenance outwardly remained strong, ways of offering a price advantage to the consumer were developed. In chapter VIII we considered the use of trading stamps, the co-operative dividend and clearance sales, as ways round r.p.m. More important, perhaps, we noted the growth of discounts to members of professional associations which may be given in up to 10% of all sales of consumer durables and the offer of high trade-in allowances by dealers anxious to make a sale of a new car or large electrical appliance.

Some manufacturers also now allow package deals, where two products together are offered at a lower price than the combined price of the goods involved. Dixons, the camera retail chain, have successfully featured such offers of a camera and films, whilst Woolworths have sold packages of different items of confectionery at a reduced price. Premium offers also are being increasingly employed by manufacturers. These involve an arrangement between two manufacturers that a purchaser of a product of the one will be able to obtain the product of the other at a reduced price. Thus, a little while ago a purchaser of

Cadbury's drinking chocolate was able to obtain a Pye Golden Guinea record for 17s. In another instance a purchaser of a packet of Kraft Dairylea cheese was entitled to buy direct from the manufacturer a Brimtoy train set for 22s 6d instead of at the normal retail price of 29s 11d.[1] Inevitably, this sort of offer upsets the retailers who traditionally handle the products which are being offered at a reduced price, since they feel it deflects sales away from them.

This is further evidence that beneath the surface resale price maintenance has weakened in all trades. Progressive retailers have become anxious to provide a price advantage to attract the customer and a number of r.p.m.-enforcing manufacturers are now party to trading policies which are tantamount to a cut price offer.

Any attempt to quantify the importance of resale price maintenance in the economy in 1964 ought therefore to make an allowance for these factors, as well as to take note of the problems discussed in chapter III of allowing for the importance of some manufacturers who, whilst supporting resale price maintenance in theory, did not find it necessary to make it a specific condition of sale. Nevertheless, estimates still continue to be made. It will be remembered that Professor B. S. Yamey calculated that for 1960 about 25% consumer expenditure on goods and services was subject to resale price maintenance, and Mr Frank Friday estimated a maximum of 23% with a further 17% subject to direct price maintenance. The Resale Price Maintenance Co-ordinating Committee claimed that by 1964 only 20% of consumer expenditure was on price maintained goods and services and suggested that even this probably overstated its importance.[2]

During the debate on the Second Reading of the Resale Prices Bill, the President of the Board of Trade suggested that resale price maintenance covered as much as 38% of consumer expenditure on goods - a total of up to £5,000 million a year.[3] *The Economist* entered the discussion by publishing a table headed 'Where R.P.M. Matters'.[4] Analysis of the items included in this

[1] *The Times* November 18, 1963.
[2] In *'Resale Price Maintenance and the Public Interest'* (1964).
[3] *Hansard* (Commons) volume 691 col. 258.
[4] *The Economist* February 29, 1964.

table showed that according to *The Economist,* some 24% of consumer expenditure on goods and services was on goods where prices were 'mainly fixed' and a further 8% or 9% was on products where prices were 'partly fixed'. This would suggest that about 40% of consumer expenditure on goods alone was on products which were price maintained, which closely agrees with Mr Heath's statement on the matter. Working from our own independent estimate given in chapter III that 34% consumer expenditure on goods and services in 1956 was on products subject to resale price maintenance, we calculate the net effect of changes in the extent of r.p.m. between 1956 and 1964 to be a decline of about 6% indicating that, at the time of passing of the Resale Prices Act, about 28% consumer expenditure on goods and services or 36% consumer expenditure on goods alone, was subject to resale price maintenance.

This figure takes account of the decline in the extent of resale price maintenance on groceries and a smaller decline (as a proportion of all consumer expenditure) on household products and tyres, offset to some extent by small increases in the importance of resale price maintenance in the furniture, clothing and hardware trades. The importance of food purchases as a share of total consumer expenditure has declined slightly, whilst there have been greater purchases of price maintained durable household appliances. An attempt has been made to take these into account also. The various forms of concealed price cutting discussed above such as high trade-in allowances and cash discounts probably account for at least 2% of all consumer expenditure on goods and services and to allow for this would reduce the estimated figures of the extent of resale price maintenance to 26% and 33% respectively.

CHAPTER XII

R.P.M. AND THE RESTRICTIVE PRACTICES COURT

In the course of its investigations into restrictive trading agreements, the Restrictive Practices Court has, in three cases which were fought out, had to adjudicate on restrictions containing provision for resale price maintenance. In two of these, cement[1] and standard metal windows[2] the agreements providing for r.p.m. were treated by the court as restrictions ancillary to the main restrictions under section 21(1)(g)[3] and as standing or falling according to the success of the main price restriction. The case on the Net Book Agreement[4] was a direct consideration of an agreement to enforce resale price maintenance and is therefore the most important of the three.

In so far as r.p.m. was concerned, both the cement and standard metal window cases were very similar and are best considered together. The cement industry agreement consisted of a common price scheme incorporating a basing point system to determine delivery costs throughout the country. Of the further restrictions contained in the Federation's 'White Book', one provided for resale price maintenance –

'In respect of cement supplied for resale each member will individually enforce such specified prices by means of any lawful remedy available to it either under Sec. 25 of the Restrictive Trade Practices Act, 1956, or otherwise.'

The Association argued under s21(1)(b) that the common price agreement conferred a number of benefits including lower prices and the avoidance of the wasteful use of transport. The further

[1] *Re Cement Makers' Federation Agreement* (1961) L.R. 2 R.P. 241.
[2] *Re Standard Metal Window Group's Agreement* (1962) L.R. 3 R.P. 196.
[3] 'That the restriction is not unreasonably required for purposes connected with the maintenance of any other restriction accepted by the parties . . . . which is found by the Court not to be contrary to the public interest.'
[4] *Re Net Book Agreement 1957.* (1962) L.R. 3 R.P. 246.

parts of the agreement - deferred rebates and standard conditions of sale including r.p.m. - were defended by the Federation
under 'gateway' (g) as being reasonably necessary for the maintenance of the main price restrictions.

The Court found in favour of the price fixing scheme on the
grounds that the industry was efficient, that without it higher
profits would have to be made and that to encourage the necessary capital investment prices would have to rise by between
25s and 40s per ton. Although the agreement did not contain
any formula as to how prices were to be fixed, the Court assumed
that they would continue to be fixed in a reasonable way and the
Federation promised to co-operate with the Registrar by providing him with the costs and profits data used in fixing prices
should he wish to apply to the Court again under section 22 on
the grounds that there had been a material change in circumstances. The Court held that the condition providing for the
enforcement of resale price maintenance was,

'. . . Reasonably necessary for the purposes of a scheme
which provides for fixed prices on sale to the ultimate consumer. This condition is likely to have the effect of keeping
down the price to the ultimate purchaser in what will continue
to be a sellers' market and is, we think, reasonably necessary
for the purpose of the main restriction.'[1]

The Standard Metal Window Group's agreement provided
for the fixing of minimum prices and agreed discounts and
included an agreement between the manufacturers that they
would ensure that merchants (who, acting as wholesalers,
handled one-third of the total sales of the Group) should observe
fixed resale prices. The Group were responsible for 42% production of standard metal windows and were in keen competition
with Crittalls, who had 43% of the market, other manufacturers
outside the group who had the remaining 15% of the market,
and also with manufacturers of wood windows.

The Group claimed that, as a result of the agreement there
had been an open exchange between members of operational
information and technical know-how which had kept costs, and
therefore prices, lower than they would otherwise have been.
This was accepted by the Court who held that the agreement had

[1] (1961) L.R. 2 R.P. 292.

made the manufacturer members more competitive in the market for windows and thus prices had been lower as a result of the agreement. This situation was expected to continue into the foreseeable future. So the Court came to the slightly paradoxical conclusion that competition would be stronger if the price fixing agreement were allowed to continue than if it were brought to an end.

In dealing with the provisions for the enforcement of r.p.m., Megaw J. pointed out in his judgment that this particular restriction had not been referred to in the submissions on behalf of the Registrar. He went on –

'No doubt the reason was that it was treated in this case as being an integral part of the price-fixing scheme and as standing or falling according to the court's conclusion as to that scheme as a whole. In the circumstances it is not necessary for us to deal separately with it. In so far as it is properly to be treated as a separate restriction, it is entitled to be upheld under paragraph (g) of section 21(1).[1]

These two cases are of interest from a number of points of view. In the first place they represent two of still only a small number of cases in which the Court has found in favour of the association – in only nine cases out of the first thirty argued before the Court have the main restrictions to an agreement been accepted.[2] However, in a study on resale price maintenance it would be an unwarranted digression to attempt to assess the merits or demerits of the Court's judgments.[3] What does concern us here is the position of resale price maintenance in these findings.

First of all we should note that r.p.m. was treated by the parties concerned as an ancillary restriction necessary to the main price restriction and so was defended under s21(1)(g). This tended immediately to withdraw r.p.m. from the main arena of the case and so far as can be seen the Registrar made no attempt to alter this situation. Certainly this was so in the Standard Metal

---

[1] (1962) L.R. 3 R.P. 243.
[2] To June 1964. In one other instance the restrictions in an agreement were declared by the Court to be not contrary to the public interest though here the Registrar did not argue a case against the agreement. See below p. 175.
[3] This has now been competently done in R. B. Stevens and B. S. Yamey – 'The Restrictive Practices Court'. (London) 1965.

Window case and in the Law Report on the Cement case no reference to r.p.m. can be found in the summary of the Registrar's pleadings.

Was the Registrar justified in not attacking r.p.m.? Probably he was. R.p.m. was clearly of lesser significance than the common price fixing schemes which constituted the major restriction in each industry - in the case of metal windows any decision by the Court against r.p.m. would have affected only 14% sales of metal windows. Further, it should be remembered that the Monopolies Commission had also investigated the situation relating to the supply of standard metal windows and having approved the common price system also upheld the practice of resale price maintenance as being necessary to the successful operation of the common price scheme. It has been the Registrar's policy in the preparation of these cases, which take many days to hear, to bring out strongly the salient features of the case against an agreement rather than to test the Court's endurance by dragging in every argument that could be at all relevant. He seems to have been largely successful in this though, in so doing, issues which might have become important may not have been raised at all and it is arguable that the Registrar could have encouraged the Court to look more closely at the need for r.p.m. in these two industries.

In the absence of any submissions from the Registrar against r.p.m. the Court had little alternative but to accept the claim that it was solely an ancillary restriction necessary to the main price agreement. In the first of the two cases under review here - *Cement* - the Court seems to have given some small consideration as to whether r.p.m. is desirable or not and come down in favour of the practice on the grounds that it prevents price inflation in a sellers' market. In *Metal Windows* no separate consideration appears to have been given to r.p.m. at all.

The third case which concerns us here was that on the Net Book Agreement. This was in fact solely an agreement providing for resale price maintenance. The book trade has a number of special features. First, it is a highly speculative trade where it is, apparently, impossible to judge at all accurately the demand for a book before printing. Secondly, it is a trade where there is much impulse buying and as was stated in Court, 'books sell books'. So the problem for the publisher is to ensure a wide retail distribution of his publications. Thirdly, it is a decreasing cost industry; the economics of book publishing are such that the greater the size of the edition, the lower the average cost of publishing and therefore the lower the retail price. Similarly, the smaller the production run, the higher the unit cost and the higher the price. Fourthly, the demand for books tends to be inelastic. This is especially true in the case of textbooks and other books of limited appeal, though in the more popular fields such as novels and do-it-yourself books demand is more responsive to changes in price. Finally, it is a trade with an important export business - exporting 50% of books produced, which in 1961 earned £32 million out of a total publishers' turnover of £79 million.

Competition between publishers is very keen. There are about 400 publishers in this country of whom 360 are members of the Publishers Association. The remaining publishers are small, so the Association covers virtually the whole of the trade. It is estimated that some 12,000 establishments sell books of which 3,000 are members of the Booksellers Association, whilst 10% of all net books are bought by libraries. The stockholding booksellers, of whom it is estimated there are not more than 750 in Great Britain, are the real key to the book trade. They carry balanced and varied stocks and their pre-publication orders are important in helping the publisher to gauge the size of demand for a first edition. More than 21,000 new titles are now published each year with an average size of first edition of less than 5,000 copies, most of which are taken by stockholding booksellers. The Publishers Association argued their case before the Restrictive Practices Court mainly on the assumption that stockholding booksellers were vital to the industry and that if a substantial number were forced out of business, there would be no growth of new retail outlets to compensate.

Resale price maintenance was first introduced into the book trade at the end of the last century and the Net Book Agreement 1957 which the Court had to consider represents the continuation of a policy started some sixty years before. The Agreement had been revised following the Restrictive Trade Practices Act

1956 in order to exclude provision for a Stop List which had, however, rarely been used.

Ninety per cent of all new books are classified by the publishers as 'net books' and are sold under the terms of the agreement. These represent about 75% of the members' turnover. Those books which are not 'net books' are mainly educational books supplied in bulk to schools, the Book of Common Prayer and the Authorized and Revised Versions of the Bible.

The Agreement allows publishers complete freedom to decide whether or not to class their books as 'net books' and also as to the price they fix at which the book is to be resold. Certain standard conditions of sale are laid down –

(i) no net books are to be sold or offered for sale to the public at less than the net published prices;

except that a net book may be sold to the public at less than the published price if –

(ii) (a) it has been held in stock by the bookseller for more than twelve months from the date of the latest purchase by him of any copy of the book;

and (b) it has been offered to the publisher at cost price or the proposed reduced price, whichever is the lower and he has rejected the offer;[1]

(iii) a secondhand book may be sold below the published price if six months have elapsed since its publication;

(iv) discounts may be given on sales to libraries, quantity buyers, institutions, etc., subject to the approval of, and on the terms laid down by, the Council of the Publishers Association;[2]

(v) any consideration in cash or kind given by the bookseller in the sale of a book is treated as a reduction in the price of a net book.

All the signatories to the agreement appoint the Council of the Publishers Association to act as their agent in the collection of information on breaches of their conditions. The publishers also undertake and agree to enforce their contractual rights and

---

[1] These exceptions are not very important however, since most booksellers prefer to use the National Book Sale to clear stocks at reduced prices rather than make piecemeal reductions from time to time. The National Book Sale is not mentioned in the agreement.

[2] At present discounts of 10% are allowed to libraries.

their rights under the Restrictive Trade Practices Act 1956 if called upon to do so by the Council of the Publishers Association. If the publisher requires, the Publishers Association will indemnify the costs of any such action. For manufacturers formally to agree to enforce resale price maintenance is rather unusual, though not unique. However, the Association claimed, and the Registrar conceded, that although in theory there could still be r.p.m. without the agreement, in practice it would be impossible for publishers to enforce it and so the agreement was essential to the individual enforcement of resale price maintenance.

The Association based their case on two of the 'gateways' specified in section 21(1) of the Act. They claimed that the ending of the agreement would cause a denial of specific and substantial benefits and advantages to the public (s21(1)(b)) and a substantial reduction in the export earnings of the trade (s21(1)(f)). Their argument may be summarized as claiming that if the agreement were abrogated there would be no resale price maintenance (this was not disputed by the Registrar) and that the resulting retail price competition would cause a decline in the number of booksellers, sales would be at higher prices and fewer titles would be published. This tends to run rather contrary to the reasonings of normal economic theory which would expect that retail price competition would lead to lower prices and a higher volume of sales and led to the adoption by the Publishers Association of the now well-known claim that 'books are different'.

In support of their case the Association claimed a number of unusual circumstances existed in the book trade. Trade tends to be seasonal with 40% of sales being made at Christmas time and whilst demand is elastic between different retail outlets, the overall demand for books is inelastic; so a price cutting multiple store could take the lucrative trade in best sellers away from stockholding booksellers but would not cause any increase in overall sales. Further, it was argued that 'books sell books' and so the function of the stockholding bookseller in carrying a wide range of books is important in encouraging further impulse purchases. Best sellers are nowadays subjected to considerable publicity and would therefore be highly suitable for price cutting as loss leaders by supermarkets. In this trade action to stop price cutting without the agreement would be very difficult and it was argued that since the Restrictive Trade Practices Act had set the seal of approval on r.p.m. it would be wrong to deny the right to enforcement in this trade.

The first people to be hit by price cutting would be the stock-holding booksellers who, though few in number, handle a very large part of the total business. They would lose sales to two different types of trader. In the first place they would lose sales of popular books to the supermarkets. These carry the highest margin $33\frac{1}{3}\%$ and so provide a profitable field. The high margin is allowed here because although sales are fast, they are un-certain. The stockholding bookseller also needs high margins to compensate him for the extra services he provides in carrying wide stocks and in operating an ordering service for any titles he does not have in stock. Both these services are, as has already been noted, important to the trade. Thus it would not be true to claim that the high cost trader is necessarily inefficient – in the case of the stockholding bookseller it is because he provides more services. Price cutting would also cause him to lose his library sales to specialist library suppliers who, with smaller overheads, could afford to offer bigger discounts. Thus, competi-tion would cause a decline in the number of specialist booksellers and the extra trade taken by supermarkets would not be sufficient to offset the heavy decline in sales from the demise of these outlets.

The stockholding booksellers who did survive would react to protect themselves against price cutting by reducing their pre-publication orders and their buying for stock. They would be forced to take this action because at the time of publication they would not know which titles would be price cut by other traders. Evidence was accepted by the Court of the uncertainty which price cutting had caused to the bookselling trade in Canada. The assumption was that stockholders could not afford to cut prices to retaliate and still remain solvent. Since public taste in books is unpredictable the publisher would, in the face of lower pre-publication orders, reduce the size of his production runs and in this decreasing cost industry this would mean that higher retail prices would have to be charged. Because of the greater risk involved, booksellers would also press for larger discounts which would further raise the price of books. Again, since fewer books would be sold because of the decline of the specialist bookseller and as a result of the rise in prices (though granted that since demand is inelastic this is not such a serious problem), there would be fewer follow-up orders and therefore fewer reprints and hence higher publishing costs again.

The contraction in the bookselling trade would react to cause a further contraction in the publishing side of the business. Because of the changing structure of the trade, fewer titles would be published, only those likely to prove successful would find a publisher, since price cutters would only be interested in stocking fast selling lines. Those which would not be published would be slow selling titles with a limited popular appeal such as books connected with the arts and these often achieve great literary merit later on.

Thus it was claimed that the detriments to the consumer arising out of the ending of the agreement were that the breakdown of resale price maintenance in this trade would lead to a reduction in the number of stockholding booksellers and in the services they provide; that, because of the uncertainty that price cutting would cause, publishers' production runs would be reduced and prices would therefore be higher; and that as a result of the general contraction in the industry fewer titles would be published. All of these, it was argued, would cause a denial of specific and substantial benefits within the meaning of s.21(1)(b).

The fact that libraries and other large buyers might be able to obtain greater discounts with the ending of the agreement, was claimed by the Association not to be a detriment arising out of the operation of the agreement, since the higher prices consequent on the breakdown of r.p.m. would more than offset any saving in the form of larger discounts.

The Association's argument under the export 'gateway' was that the consequences of price cutting in England must cause a reduction in exports due to the resultant higher prices of books. This seems to assume that the export demand for books is more elastic in response to price changes than demand in the home market and indeed the Association's case does refer to competition from American publishers. To allow price cutting by home booksellers would also cause uncertainty on the part of foreign booksellers who would reduce their export orders for English books. In addition it was argued that exports of British books are important in helping to propagate British culture, ideas and influence and that, therefore, any reduction in exports of books would be undesirable. The closing words in the summing up of Counsel for the Publishers Association are interesting in their further attempt to convince the Court that books are different –

'This is the first case in which the court has been concerned with things of the mind. It would be a sad event and there would be a high price to pay if the result were that profit was to be the only criterion of service, popularity the only test of value and Philistinism the only virtue.'[1]

Having accepted that the agreement was essential to the continuance of r.p.m. on books, Counsel for the Registrar proceeded to a general condemnation of the practice in this trade. He claimed that the present system was unsatisfactory since it had failed to prevent a decline of good bookshops and that it resulted in chronic over-production. The method of protection was also costly. Since margins are fixed to cover the costs of those shops which give service, then those purchasers who do not receive service should not have to subsidize those who do. This is one of the basic arguments against r.p.m. – that it causes a standard margin to be fixed and enforced irrespective of the type of service given by each outlet.

The limitation of discounts to libraries was also attacked since they were not receiving the advantage which their size of purchase warranted. Further, by preventing specialist library suppliers offering better terms, which because of their lower overheads they were able to do, the supply of books to libraries was artificially diverted away from the most efficient channel of distribution.

The Registrar did not think the consequences of the ending of r.p.m. would be as serious as had been claimed. Stockholding booksellers would not go out of business since the mere fact that they carry stocks ensures to them a competitive advantage and, further, it would be possible for publishers to arrange to give them larger discounts to compensate for bearing a greater risk.

[1] L.R. 3 R.P. 297.

He claimed also that books were not suitable for use as loss leaders and any price cutting would not be prolonged or serious or on more than a few books; evidence given by supermarkets had suggested that they would only price-cut children's books.

In answer to the claim that the risk and uncertainty would cause a serious reduction in the number of titles published, the Registrar denied that there was evidence of greater risk here than in any other industry and that the present growth in importance of institutional buying of books, especially of those with limited appeal, would be an insurance to the publishers. Thus, books of limited appeal would continue to be published, irrespective of the agreement, at a suitable price and higher discounts and prices on less popular books would be a justifiable and economically desirable charge.

Turning to the effect which the ending of r.p.m. would have on prices, for the Registrar it was argued that any price reduction must increase sales and that the Association had failed to prove that on the ending of the agreement overall prices would be higher. Price cutting could lead to higher turnover and sales of books, therefore lower unit costs of production per copy and larger profits to publishers who could then afford to allow bigger discounts. The argument on the export 'gateway' was also challenged by the Registrar who did not agree that there would be a substantial reduction in the export business if the agreement were ended.

Should the Court accept the Publishers Association's arguments in favour of the agreement under either of the 'gateways' then it was claimed that there were five detriments arising from the agreement which outweighed any benefits it might give. These were (1) that the agreement reduces the incentive to lower costs; (2) it deprives booksellers of the freedom to dispose of stocks at their discretion and therefore tends to increase overheads, tie up capital and deprive the public of the benefit of being able to purchase cheaper books; (3) it causes higher prices to be paid for books in popular demand; (4) it stops libraries buying more books on their limited grants; (5) the public are forced to pay higher prices in general because the agreement protects the profit margins of all retail outlets.

In its judgment the Court emphasized the freedom left to

individual publishers by the agreement which ensured that the trade remained highly competitive and allowed innovation. It accepted that in this trade there could be no resale price maintenance without the agreement and saw that opinions as to the consequences of the ending of r.p.m. in this country could only be theoretical since no one had any experience of this. (Evidence had, however, been heard of what had happened in Canada and the U.S.A.) Thus the Court had to decide either in favour of the Association or in favour of the Registrar and, whilst accepting that others might disagree, found that, 'The evidence has certainly not satisfied us that on the balance of probabilities retail prices generally would fall' if the agreement were abrogated.[1]

The Court appears to have accepted completely the main points in the 'theory of uncertainty' on which the Publishers Association based their case.[2] It agreed that a wide range of books including popular fiction, standard series and reference books in popular demand could all be susceptible to price cutting and that by cutting prices on these the large retailer of other goods selling books as a side-line, would take away this profitable part of the bookselling business from stockholding booksellers. This would cause a number of stockholding booksellers to leave the trade, those remaining would carry less stocks and the special order business, which is already a nuisance and uneconomic, would increase. The greater risk created by the ending of r.p.m. would cause caution to be exercised over the holding of stocks and orders to publishers would be lower. This would lead, the Court found, to higher prices as the Association had claimed. The result would be that the 'marginal' books which often had most literary and scholastic merit would not be published. The Court did not expect the ending of the agreement to cause the development of any new pattern of trade which would eliminate the element of subsidization of one customer by another. Specialist library suppliers would take trade away from stockholding booksellers but would not purchase sufficient books themselves to offset the fall in publishers' sales to stockholders.

Uncertainty in the trade would also hit publishers, causing

---

[1] L.R. 3 R.P. 323.
[2] Only the claim that services given by booksellers would decline and that these services would be charged for was rejected by the Court under s21(1)(b).

them to exercise greater caution and to publish fewer copies of fewer titles at higher prices. This, the Court found, would prevent publication of works by authors in the higher reaches of literature and would therefore deny a specific benefit to the reading public. Prices were expected to rise, even the prices which libraries paid, notwithstanding the larger discounts they would obtain if library suppliers were freed from the restriction on maximum discounts. The Court decided that 'The upward thrust of the increased cost of production would be more urgent and effective than the reverse thrust of sales resistance' and therefore 'The public would pay higher prices for many and probably most books more readily than publishers would reduce their margins'.[1]

Thus the consequences of the ending of the agreement would, in the Court's opinion, be just as the Association had claimed – fewer and less-well-equipped bookshops would exist, books would be more expensive and fewer titles would be published.

'In our judgment, each of these heads is sufficiently explicit, definable and distinct in character to justify the description "specific" and the avoidance of any of these disadvantageous consequences can properly be termed a specific benefit or advantage. We are satisfied moreover that each of these consequences would arise in a sufficiently serious degree to make its avoidance a substantial advantage.'[2]

The detriments put forward by the Registrar as offsetting any advantages the Court allowed for the agreement were rejected and so the balancing provision was not required.

The Association's claim under the export 'gateway' was not upheld. The Court was neither satisfied that following the ending of r.p.m. on books in this country any significant amount of cut price competition between English and foreign booksellers would develop, nor that the higher prices prevailing after the ending of r.p.m. would seriously affect the ability of English books to sell overseas.

So the case for the Net Book Agreement was held by the Court to have been made out under s21(1)(b) but not under 21(1)(f). No detriment was to be taken into account in the 'tailpiece' or if

1 L.R. 3 R.P. 317-8.
2 L.R. 3 R.P. 323.

there was a detriment it was of insufficient weight to outweigh the advantages claimed and accepted for the Agreement.

Thus, after a hearing lasting twenty-four days, the Court decided that 'books are different' and resale price maintenance had survived its first major scrutiny in the Restrictive Practices Court. It had taken three years to prepare the case and cost nearly £50,000. These costs do not include any allowance for the time spent by members of the two associations in helping to prepare the case. Since costs are not recoverable in these cases they have had to be met by the trade, which presumably means that the book-buying public will have to pay eventually. The Registrar's costs, whilst not as high, must also have been fairly substantial, so it will be seen that the cost to the public of actions in the Restrictive Practices Court are, in monetary terms, considerable.

The Court's decision in this important case failed to achieve universal approval.[1] Indeed, whilst the Court has to decide on balance between two differing economic predictions about the future course of events should an agreement be abrogated, it is almost inevitable that their decisions will be open to objection from some quarter or another. Whilst the key to the Publishers Association's case was the importance of stockholding book-sellers and the anticipated consequences of the onset of price cutting on their future, the critics of the decision have pointed to the absence of any obvious empirical analysis by the Court of the likely consequences of the abrogation of the agreement. In his recent book with Professor Stevens on the Restrictive Practices Court, Professor Yamey has produced evidence from both the Canadian scene and the British book trade before r.p.m. was first imposed which suggests that the consequences the Court envisaged need not be those which would eventually ensue. Furthermore, he has doubted whether the sales of stockholding booksellers to libraries are of sufficient importance to justify the Court's view that the loss of this trade to specialist library

[1] See *e.g.* A. Sutherland 'Are Books Different?' *The Solicitor Quarterly* vol. 2 (1963) p. 323 and 'Whose Bad Books?' *The Solicitor Quarterly* vol. 3. (1964) p. 69 answered by P. W. S. Andrews 'In Mr. Sutherland's Bad Books' *The Solicitor Quarterly* vol. 3 (1964) p. 63 and 'Mr. Sutherland's Bad Books' *The Solicitor Quarterly* vol. 3 (1964) p. 260.
Also Stevens and Yamey *op. cit.* pp. 224-235.

suppliers would have serious consequences for the booksellers. Whilst the Court has to make economic predictions of the sort required in this case (and actions under the Resale Prices Act will require a similar approach) it is unlikely that their judgments will satisfy all commentators and room for genuine doubts will remain.

Thus, on the three occasions on which resale price maintenance has been challenged in the Restrictive Practices Court under the provisions of Part I of the Restrictive Trade Practices Act, it has been found not to be contrary to the public interest in the industries concerned, though it is true to say that in two of these r.p.m. was not the focal point of the case. In addition, one of the major arguments used to justify r.p.m. in general – that it saves buyers the need to 'shop around' – was also approved by the Court in the Black Bolt and Nut case.[1]

No exhaustive analysis of the Register of Restrictive Trading Agreements has yet been published and it is not, therefore, known exactly how many other agreements include provision for resale price maintenance. However, a recent inspection of a large number of agreements concerned with consumer goods has revealed that some do contain such a provision though often only as an incidental to other restrictions. Some of these agreements have already been adjudicated upon by the Court in undefended hearings, others have been voluntarily determined by the parties to them[2] and some are still live on the Register.

In February 1964 a second agreement involving the Publishers Association came before the Restrictive Practices Court.[3] This involved publishers who were signatories of the Net Book Agreement but not members of the Publishers Association. They were mainly publishers of books of a limited and special nature including, for example, a number of religious bodies. The agreement between them was the same as that between the members of the Publishers Association except that in this case, as they

[1] Re Black Bolt and Nut Association's Agreement (1960) L.R. 2 R.P. 50. This case concerned a common price agreement and the maintenance of resale prices as such was not an issue.
[2] Though the decision of the House of Lords in the Newspaper case means that all agreements, even those which have been voluntarily abandoned, will eventually have to be investigated by the Court – Associated Newspapers Ltd. v. Registrar of Restrictive Trading Agreements (1963) L.R. 4 R.P. 361.
[3] Re Net Book Agreement 1957 (No. 2) (1964) L.R. 4 R.P. 485.

were not members, there was no provision for the Association to indemnify them for any legal action taken to enforce their resale price conditions. In view of the similarity between the two agreements the Registrar of Restrictive Trading Agreements had agreed with the Association that in the event of the Court finding in their favour on the first occasion he would not state a case against the agreement on the second hearing. After receiving evidence on affidavit from the Secretary of the Publishers Association that the agreement was the same in substance as the first Net Book Agreement, the Court declared the agreement to be not contrary to the public interest. This is the only case which has been decided in this way and it had the great merit of avoiding a further expense of time and money in the case of an agreement on which the Court had already passed judgment not long before.

A number of agreements have been referred by the Registrar to the Court for hearings to commence and have then been voluntarily abandoned by the parties rather than go to the expense of defending them. In each of these instances the Court has therefore declared the restrictions contrary to the public interest. Some of these undefended agreements have contained references to r.p.m.

In The General Trading Code of the Electric Light Fittings Association the members of the Association agreed with each other not to supply industrial, commercial or decorative fittings except on or subject to terms or conditions including the following wording:

'Goods are sold on condition that on a resale purchasers charge not less than our current List Price, subject to any discount authorized by us on such resale and impose a like condition on any sub-purchaser: the acceptance of such goods by purchasers will constitute an acceptance of this condition.'

The agreement was referred to the Court and just over a month before proceedings were due to commence in 1960 the Association passed a resolution determining all agreements that were within the scope of the Act. So the Court declared the restrictions contrary to the public interest and received an undertaking from the Association through Counsel that the parties would not try to enforce the agreement or enter into any other similar agreement.

The 'four firm' agreement between Cadbury, Fry, Rowntree and Terry, regulating trading conditions for the supply of confectionery contained the following clause –

'*Re-sale Prices* – Each signatory will stipulate as a condition of supply, that its goods must not be sold by retail at prices other than the consumer prices shown on the label or price ticket accompanying the goods.'

When referred to the Court in 1962 the manufacturers concerned did not defend the agreement and it was declared contrary to the public interest. The manufacturers undertook not to enforce the agreement or make any similar agreement without the leave of the Court.

In the motor cycle trade a series of trading agreements existed between the British Cycle and Motor Cycle Industries Association and the individual manufacturers which included provision for the enforcement of resale price maintenance, though these were later voluntarily abandoned. Some other parts of the agreements were not withdrawn and when referred to the Court all the restrictions contained in the original agreements (including, therefore, those relating to r.p.m.) were declared contrary to the public interest in an undefended hearing. The Objects of the National Federation of Ironmongers contained, at the time of the passing of the Act, a reference to the taking of 'such steps as may be deemed expedient to prevent price cutting, price deflation or price inflation', and their bye-laws required members to observe the stipulated prices on maintained goods. These had to be registered but were quickly withdrawn.

Some agreements containing references to r.p.m. still remain live on the Register. Thus the Booksellers Association requires all members, other than personal members, to sign the Net Book Agreement; and the Camping Trade Association of Great Britain requires members to impose a fixed resale price condition of sale on their products. A further agreement of interest which is still 'live' on the Register involves the maintenance of prices in one of the important voluntary groups in the grocery trade. The wholesaler members of the Spar group have an agreement with the parent company Spar (Britain) Ltd. not to supply Spar

M

branded goods to retailers except at the wholesale price fixed by
Spar (Britain) Ltd. and on terms requiring their resale at prices
fixed by Spar (Britain) Ltd. There is, perhaps, a slight touch of
irony that one of the important voluntary groups who owe their
success in the grocery trade largely to the breakdown of r.p.m.
should find it convenient to impose a fixed resale price on their
goods. It is understood, however, that the terms of this restriction have never been enforced by Spar and there is no intention
of defending it when it is referred to the Restrictive Practices
Court.[1]

Whilst the number of agreements registered actually requiring the imposition or enforcement of fixed resale prices may not
be large, other restrictions which appear more frequently on the
Register also work in favour of the maintenance of resale prices.
The most important are those restrictions which provide for a
limitation in the size of discounts allowed to traders since the
giving of large discounts acts as a strong inducement to cut
prices. The preparation of lists of approved dealers which manufacturers adhere to in deciding whom to supply also provides a
possible means of keeping out traders who might cut prices.[2]

The Registration department of the Office of the Registrar of
Restrictive Trading Agreements has been active in 'chasing up'
unregistered agreements. It is estimated that their activities have
been responsible for the registration of more than 10% of the
agreements on the Register. Trade associations have had to be
particularly careful that they do not make recommendations to
their members which are registrable. This has especially hit
local associations of retailers in the grocery trade who have
traditionally made recommendations to their members about
prices to be charged for non-branded or non-price-maintained
lines.

Following the passing of the Act many small grocers' associations continued to issue recommended price lists, ignorant of the

[1] The rules of membership of Wavy Line Grocers Ltd., another voluntary
group, also contained provision for a form of r.p.m. since they required all
retailers in the group to adhere to a specified selling price for the duration of
any special selling campaign. This was abandoned in August 1961.
[2] The tyre trade register maintained a list of approved dealers and it may be
argued that the Court's findings that this was contrary to the public interest
contributed to the breakdown of r.p.m. on tyres – *Re Tyre Trade Register
Agreement* (1959) L.R. 3 R.P. 404.

fact that these were registrable under Part I of the Act. On hearing of them, the Registration Department would offer the association concerned the alternative of registering or withdrawing the recommendation. Always the choice was to withdraw, though when the breakdown of r.p.m. in the grocery trade was gaining momentum in 1958, it is understood that some associations did consider registering an agreement in the hope that a favourable Court decision would halt the trend. The Wholesale Grocers' Federation also became involved with the Registration Department over an attempt in 1960 to recommend a price for sugar. They intervened in an effort to stabilize the trade because wide fluctuations in the price of sugar had caused some wholesalers to refuse to handle it at all. Faced with the alternative of registering or withdrawing the recommendation they, too, chose to withdraw as they did not have the financial resources necessary to allow them to fight a case before the Restrictive Practices Court.

Thus, in the grocery trade the first part of the Act contributed, though in a small way, to the collapse of r.p.m. The reluctance of local grocers' associations to become involved with the Restrictive Practices Court meant that the recommendations they had traditionally made to their members would not now be made and so any possibility of a unified resistance on the part of small grocers to the breakdown of r.p.m. disappeared. In most other trades the registration and adjudication by the Court of restrictive agreements appears not to have weakened the practice. In defended cases before the Court resale price maintenance has been upheld on the three occasions on which it appeared as a restriction. Where it has been one of a group of restrictions declared by the Court in undefended cases to be contrary to the public interest this has not caused the individual suppliers concerned to weaken in their insistence on the observance of fixed resale prices on their products.[1] On balance, therefore, we find that, as with Part II of the Act, Part I failed to cause a major weakening in resale price maintenance outside the grocery trade. Individual manufacturers have continued to prescribe the same conditions of sale even where their collective agreements to do

---

[1] Though the cycle and motor cycle manufacturers have not sought permission under the Resale Prices Act to continue to enforce r.p.m. on their products.

so have been prohibited and the favourable Court decisions especially in the widely publicized case on the Net Book Agreement must have provided, at least temporarily, a serious setback to the opponents of r.p.m.

CHAPTER XIII

THE MONOPOLIES COMMISSION
AND R.P.M.

Since it was first established as a result of the Monopolies and Restrictive Practices (Inquiry and Control) Act 1948, the views of the Monopolies Commission have undergone a radical change where resale price maintenance is concerned. In order to see how this change has come about, we will need to look briefly at those reports which were prepared before 1956 and then to consider in a little more detail three important recent reports concerned with monopolies of scale which have been carried out by the Commission under its powers as revised by Part III of the Restrictive Trade Practices Act.

In a number of early investigations the Commission discovered the existence of schemes for the collective enforcement of resale price maintenance. In its first report, on the Supply of Dental Goods, the Commission objected strongly to this practice on the grounds that enforcement was by means of collective boycott and exclusive dealing, and because they found that the practice –

'has been developed into a complete system for the restriction of competition between dealer members of the Association of Dental Manufacturers and Traders and for the protection of their gross margins and profits. It has also afforded a general protection for the level of manufacturers' prices'.[1]

The majority of the Commission recommended that the use of the collective boycott and exclusive dealing should be made illegal though a minority of two thought that it was unfair to single out this one trade when it was well known that a similar situation existed in others. The majority recommendation was accepted by the 'competent authorities' the Ministry of Health and the Secretary of State for Scotland and with the approval of both Houses of Parliament the Monopolies and Restrictive

[1] *Report on the Supply of Dental Goods* 1950 para. 229.

Practices (Dental Goods) Order 1951[1] was made. This prohibited the use of exclusive dealing and the collective boycott in that trade in so far as they were likely to restrict entry into the trade or to be used to enforce resale prices.

In the report on electric lamps,[2] collective enforcement was again encountered and although fines and the Stop List were used in moderation, the practice was opposed. The Commission was particularly anxious that it should not continue here since it had approved the existence of a scheme to fix common manufacturer prices. It is interesting to note that even in these early reports, the Commission had already developed the idea that the abolition of r.p.m. would reflect competition back on manufacturers and so help keep their prices and profits reasonable. Despite changed opinions on a number of matters during the course of its existence, the Commission seems to have retained this view.

In the report on copper-semis[3] the Commission found an agreement between manufacturers to enforce r.p.m. though there were not the usual means in existence here for collective enforcement such as private court or Stop List. However, the fact that there was an agreement over resale price maintenance caused the Commission's opposition to the practice. A similar situation was found in the reports on hard fibre cordage[4] and electrical machinery,[5] where there was no machinery for collective enforcement, only a collective agreement to enforce r.p.m. Again, the Commission decided that the practice did not serve the public interest in these industries.

The report on tyres[6] disclosed that r.p.m. on tyres was enforced through probably the most effective collective enforcing body in the country – the British Motor Trade Association (the Cycle Trade Union being responsible for protection of prices of cycle tyres). Whilst accepting that the collective boycott was the most efficient means of enforcing resale prices and that r.p.m. helped

[1] S.I. 1951 No. 1200.
[2] *Report on the Supply of Electric Lamps 1951.*
[3] *Report on the Supply and Export of Certain Semi-Manufactures of Copper and Copper Based Alloys 1955.*
[4] *Report on the Supply of Hard Fibre Cordage 1955.*
[5] *Report on the Supply and Export of Electrical and Allied Machinery and Plant 1956.*
[6] *Report on the Supply and Export of Pneumatic Tyres 1955.*

preserve the necessary large number of small and medium sized replacement outlets for tyres, the Commission still found that collective enforcement of r.p.m. was contrary to the public interest.

The terms of reference for the Commission's inquiry into the Supply of Electronic Valves and Cathode Ray Tubes[1] were subsequently varied to call for a factual report only after the passing of the Restrictive Trade Practices Act. Here, too, a collective enforcement scheme existed, but during the investigation, the British Radio Valve Manufacturers' Association dropped all reference to collective enforcement from their Constitution.

Thus it will be seen that the Commission had always strongly opposed collective enforcement of resale price maintenance and in each case, except where the factual report alone had been required, had recommended that it should no longer be allowed to continue. Although the dental goods case is the only one in which a Statutory Order was used to put the Commission's recommendations into effect, so far as collective enforcement of r.p.m. is concerned, in every other instance the recommendations were accepted by the Government and the industry concerned voluntarily agreed to abandon the practice. The decision in 1956 to prohibit all collective enforcement schemes was taken largely on the strength of the conclusions of the Commission in these reports and their report on Collective Discrimination.[2]

The attitude of the Commission towards individual enforcement of r.p.m. in its pre-Restrictive Trade Practices Act reports tended to vary, though in the cases where r.p.m. really counted it was usually approved. In the report on copper-semis the Commission emphasized that the objection to r.p.m. was only against the fact that a number of manufacturers agreed to enforce – a judgment on individual enforcement was deliberately avoided –

'We express no opinion about the policy which individual manufacturers might find it expedient to pursue independently.[3]

The report on dental goods made it clear that the objection was to collective enforcement, there was no objection to the

---

[1] *Report on the Supply of Electronic Valves and Cathode Ray Tubes* 1956.
[2] The Collective Discrimination Report has been discussed in ch. i above.
[3] *Op. cit.* para. 311.

enforcement of resale price conditions by an individual manufacturer. This approbation of individual enforcement was continued in the rubber footwear report,[1] where not all manufacturers adopted a fixed price policy and in view of the small margins allowed on price maintained lines price cutting was not considered likely. Individual enforcement by manufacturers was again approved by the Commission in the case of standard metal windows.[2] The Commission saw that, in this case, as merchants and manufacturers sold in competition with each other, resale price maintenance was a necessary adjunct to the common price system of which it also approved. This conclusion anticipated by five years a similar decision by the Restrictive Practices Court.

In three investigations the Commission took an unfavourable view of individual enforcement. In two of these the conclusions were unsubstantiated by any argument to justify the findings and anyway are not important since r.p.m. was inconsequential in these trades. The first of these was the report on linoleum.[3] Here there was no r.p.m. as such, though there was, in practice, no price competition at the wholesale level where manufacturers and wholesalers sold in competition with each other. For some reason, which is not apparent in the Report itself, the Commission recommended that there should continue to be no fixing of retailers' prices by the manufacturers - i.e. no enforcement of r.p.m. Similarly, the report on electrical and allied machinery and plant found r.p.m. to be of little consequence in the industry - there was a collective agreement to enforce but no collective enforcement mechanism. Having condemned the agreement because it supported a common price scheme to which it also objected, the Commission went on to find that if r.p.m. existed without the common price scheme it would still operate against the public interest because it would create undesirable rigidity in the industry. In both these instances no attempt is made to explain or justify the condemnation of individual enforcement of r.p.m. and therefore hardly contributes to any general discussion of the merits or demerits of this practice. It is perhaps

[1] *Report on the Supply of Rubber Footwear* 1956.
[2] *Report on the Supply of Standard Metal Windows* 1956.
[3] *Report on the Supply of Linoleum* 1956.

significant to observe that both reports were prepared at a time when the Commission was allowed to work in groups rather than as a whole and that the same members were responsible for each report.

The third report in which individual enforcement of r.p.m. was condemned was that on tyres. As we have already seen, collective enforcement was found to be against the public interest, but a majority of the Commission felt that in their desire to introduce a measure of competition between manufacturers, the ending of price discussions and of the collective enforcement of r.p.m. would not be sufficient. Their reason for advocating prohibition of the individual enforcement of r.p.m. also was that in the special circumstances of this industry the strength of the leading manufacturers would mean that they would not miss the prohibition of collective enforcement, but it would hit the small manufacturer whose competition the Commission wanted to promote. Further, if all forms of retail price fixing were stopped, large traders would have the opportunity of bargaining over terms with manufacturers whilst manufacturers would have less incentive to fix identical prices because they would not know what the final retail selling price of their products would be. The Commission's argument was not, therefore, against the individual enforcement of r.p.m. as such, but that in this particular industry, because of the strength of the leading manufacturers and the price leadership regularly practised, it would be in the public interest to encourage price competition at the retail level.

Four members[1] signed a note of dissent to the recommendation that individual enforcement be prohibited. They argued that the Commission's other recommendations – the ending of discussion on price levels in the Tyre Manufacturers' Conference and the abolition of collective enforcement – would prove sufficient to establish competition between manufacturers. Drawing attention to the approval which the Greene and Lloyd-Jacob Committees had given to individual enforcement of resale price maintenance, they did not accept that the practice was detrimental to the public interest in this trade. To deny the individual manufacturer the right to enforce his conditions of sale would

[1] Mr J. Archdale, Sir T. Barnes, Mr W. G. Cullen and Professor A. L. Goodhart.

not cause the introduction of any novel marketing scheme but would merely adversely disorganize distribution leading to a decline in the standards of service and prejudicing distribution in small towns. Overcharging could also arise. Further, to disallow the right to individually enforce resale price conditions would deprive some manufacturers of their proprietary rights as patent holders to take action to deal with price cutting. The Dissentients did not agree that exceptional circumstances existed in this trade which would justify such action being taken. So strongly were the dissentient arguments put that the Government took no action to secure the abandonment of individual enforcement of r.p.m. in this trade.

Thus, in its investigations until the passing of the Restrictive Trade Practices Act, we find that without exception collective enforcement was opposed by the Commission and individual enforcement was often upheld. Of the three cases where the Commission objected to individual enforcement of r.p.m., two can be dismissed as being unsupported by any explanation in the report. In the case of tyres special justification was claimed due to the lack of competition in the industry and even then the recommendation received the support of only a narrow majority of the members of the Commission making the report.

The Commission objected so strongly to collective enforcement wherever they found it to exist because it provided too easy a support to other measures to restrict competition between manufacturers and the methods used - boycott and Stop List - were particularly undesirable. The approval which the Commission normally gave to individual enforcement seems due to several reasons. The Lloyd-Jacob Committee had just reported favourably on the practice and one member of the Commission - Sir Richard Yeabsley - had also been a member of that Committee. Other members of the Commission are known to have felt that r.p.m. as such was a desirable practice when individually enforced and this opinion had not been changed by their findings in the two industries investigated up to that point - rubber footwear and metal windows - where individual enforcement did exist. It was this general philosophy of disapproval of collective enforcement (which the Collective Discrimination Report had further developed) and acceptance of individual enforcement, which became embodied in the sections dealing with resale price maintenance in the Restrictive Trade Practices Act.

Strictly speaking, the Report on the Supply of Tea should have been included in our discussion of investigations carried out before the passing of the 1956 Act. However, although much of the work for this Report was completed before the Act was passed, it was not signed until September 1956, and in its discussion of resale price maintenance, the Commission referred to the changed situation brought about as a result of the Act. (The Report on Standard Metal Windows was also signed in September 1956, but does not refer to any changed situation.)

In this inquiry the Commission found that four small tea blenders were members of the G.P.A.C., the collective enforcing body in the grocery trade, and noted that as a result of the Act, collective enforcement would no longer exist so did not consider this further. The three largest tea blenders – Brooke Bond Ltd., J. Lyons & Co. Ltd., and Ty-Phoo Tea Ltd., who between them were responsible for about one-half the tea sold in the United Kingdom, individually enforced conditions as to resale price on their distributors. Enforcement action was rare because price cutting was rare, only Ty-Phoo having withheld supplies and that on only five occasions. The Commission's conclusion (in a generally favourable report) was that –

'We have found no special circumstances or practices in the tea trade which would distinguish it from other trades in this respect. We therefore find that, in the tea trade, individual resale price maintenance does not operate, nor may it be expected to operate, against the public interest.'[1]

This was the last time that the Commission unanimously approved resale price maintenance in any trade. The first sentence quoted is interesting since it indicates how the Commission initially saw its duties in relation to resale price maintenance in the light of the Act. Clearly it was recognized that individual enforcement was accepted as being generally above reproach and that only in exceptional circumstances should the Commission condemn the practice.

The post-1956 activities of the Commission have been rather

[1] *Report on the Supply of Tea* 1956 para. 171.

limited. Besides the follow-up report on timber[1] it has only completed reports on the supply of fertilizers,[2] cigarettes and tobacco,[3] electrical equipment for mechanically propelled land vehicles,[4] wallpaper,[5] and now petrol.[6] Each of these were investigations into industries where a firm (or firms) held a 'monopoly' position. Six reports in ten years can hardly be considered fast work and it is valid to ask why there should have been such slow progress.

Rather than see, however, the electrical equipment report as having taken six years to complete, it is more exact to say that each report took on average a year and a half since a number were in progress at the same time. The fact that the Commission was no longer allowed to divide into sub-groups was a major factor contributing to the slow progress, it was back to the pre-1953 situation again which had been criticized by the Select Committee on Estimates and which the Monopolies and Restrictive Practices Commission Act 1953[7] had rectified. Some industries were particularly complex and it took the Commission a long time to really get to grips with the problems under investigation, whilst in some cases it was difficult to obtain full co-operation from the industries involved especially as regards answers to Commission questions and to fix dates for hearings. In addition there was the problem that the Commission was not a full-time body, only four days per month were set aside for meetings and during two months in the summer it did not meet at all. Some of the pre-arranged meetings were not held because the Secretariat had not prepared the necessary work. Thse drawbacks were certainly not conducive to enabling the Commission to work speedily. It is clear that if the Commission is to continue to play a worthwhile part in the investigation and control of industry it needs to meet more frequently if this is at all possible

[1] *Imported Timber : Report on whether and to what extent the Recommendation of the Commission has been complied with* 1958.
[2] *Report on the Supply of Chemical Fertilizers* 1960.
[3] *Report on the Supply of Cigarettes and Tobacco and of Cigarette and Tobacco Making Machinery* 1961.
[4] *Report on the Supply of Electrical Equipment for Mechanically Propelled Vehicles* 1963.
[5] *Report on the Supply of Wallpaper* 1963.
[6] *A Report on the Supply of Petrol to Retailers in the United Kingdom* 1965.
[7] 1 & 2 Eliz. 2, c. 51.

and the size of the Secretariat should be enlarged. Better co-operation from certain sections of industry would also be looked for. Whilst the new proposals for the Commission[1] will probably make it a more effective body, it seems that these particular problems will still remain.

Three of the reports begun and completed since 1956 concern us, since they dealt with resale price maintenance and have been of great importance in helping to re-shape current public and parliamentary opinion on this problem. The reports concerned are those on cigarettes, electrical equipment for motor vehicles, and wallpaper.

The supply of cigarettes and tobacco was referred to the Commission in November 1956. It reported in January 1961. The dominant supplier, Imperial Tobacco Ltd., held a powerful monopoly position having been responsible for 75·4% of United Kingdom supplies of cigarettes and tobacco in 1954 and 63·4% in 1959. Thus they were clearly 'monopolistic' suppliers as defined in the legislation. Their declining share of the market in the later 1950s was due to the growth in importance of Gallaher Ltd. who had increased their share of the market from 11·2% to 29·3%.

Resale price maintenance was an important feature of this trade, being enforced at both wholesale and retail levels. It had been enforced collectively between 1926 and 1956 (though Imperial did not enter the scheme until 1934), and since 1956 by individual enforcement methods under section 25 of the Restrictive Trade Practices Act. Little direct use has been made of the powers under this section since the firm line taken by all manufacturers and the dominant market position of Imperial, without whose products no tobacconist could continue in business, ensured that little price cutting existed in the trade. An increasing proportion of sales, 65% in 1960 as opposed to 50% in 1955, went direct from manufacturer to retailer, thus making it easier to discipline the trade without resorting to legal action.

The Commission found few grounds on which to criticize the activities of Imperial. It found merely that Imperial's holding in Gallaher was contrary to the public interest (though this was

[1] Monopolies and Mergers Act 1965 c. 50, foreshadowed in the White Paper *Monopolies, Mergers and Restrictive Practices* 1964 Cmnd. 2299.

a passive holding and had not been used to affect Gallaher's trading policy) and that the giving by Imperial of bonuses to retailers dependent on Imperial receiving preferential advertising or display facilities, was also contrary to the public interest. It recommended that both these practices should cease.

Individual enforcement of resale price maintenance was, for the first time, a matter of major practical importance in the Commission's investigations and the discussion of this problem shows a clear understanding of the issues involved. Imperial argued that r.p.m. was in the public interest for a number of reasons. Consumers benefited because it prevented overcharging in hotels and various other types of outlet where higher costs would encourage price inflation; if cutting became widespread, there would be a reduction in the number of outlets selling cigarettes and this would cause inconvenience to buyers. Distributors benefited from r.p.m. since it avoided the possibility of cigarettes being used as loss leaders by non-specialist retailers and so upsetting the trade for tobacconists. The manufacturer favoured r.p.m. since it preserved the largest number of outlets thereby giving him the widest possible range of distribution. The onset of price cutting would also raise the problem of an increase in bad debts. This would cause the manufacturer to restrict the period of credit which he allowed, and so distributors would have to finance their own stocks and the cost of doing this would lead them to require a higher margin of profit which would therefore raise the retail price of the product.

The case against r.p.m. was that a fixed price ignored the possibility of variations in distributors' costs and therefore prevented competition between distributors and an effort to reduce costs. Further, there was the possibility that if resale price maintenance ended, competition between distributors might reflect itself back to create increased price competition between manufacturers.

To balance these arguments, the Commission saw a number of reasons why r.p.m. was desirable in this industry. These were, of course, mainly those which Imperial had put forward. With low margins and a small unit cost for a packet of cigarettes, the size of any price reduction would be small, unless cigarettes were to be used as loss leaders when larger price reductions might be made. If loss leading did become prevalent, this would only benefit Imperial and possibly Gallaher and so strengthen their market dominance still further. This is because only brand leaders are attractive to retailers for use as loss leaders and this would therefore distort demand patterns and concentrate consumer demand on the cut-price brands. A reduction in the number of outlets selling cigarettes and tobacco would not be in the interests of either consumers or manufacturers whilst the cost of retailers financing their own credit would be higher than the cost of Imperial doing this for them.

The Commission saw that the general effects of r.p.m. and the dominance of Imperial in this trade were that Imperial was able to impose uniformity and rigidity in trading methods to the detriment of experiment and innovation in distribution. However, having weighed up the case the Commission, with one exception, found that 'in this trade ... and so long as competition between manufacturers continues on the present scale, r.p.m. does not, either as a practice of Imperial or generally, operate against the public interest nor may it be expected to do so'.[1]

The dissentient to this conclusion was Professor G. C. Allen who held that the weight of evidence and argument showed that resale price maintenance in the tobacco industry was against the public interest and thought therefore that the practice should be abolished. In a reconsideration of the main arguments over r.p.m. discussed in the report he rejected the idea that consumers would suffer if a number of outlets went out of business because they would only be forced to close if insufficient consumers were prepared to pay the relatively higher prices in such high cost shops. Even a moderate smoker might be able to achieve fairly considerable savings on the ending of r.p.m. Further, it might be possible to encourage consumers to buy larger sized packets if lower prices were offered and this would be desirable since it would allow economies of distribution.

Loss leader selling would, he thought, be unlikely to arise since normal retail prices would not be known. Even if price cutting did become widespread and severe, he doubted whether

[1] Op. cit. para. 568. The report continued: 'We wish to emphasize that this conclusion relates only to the cigarette and tobacco industry and must not be taken to imply any judgment on the desirability of the practice as applied in other industries.'

Imperial would necessarily gain most – Gallaher might benefit even more. The argument that competition at the retail level would reflect back to cause competition between manufacturers was also re-introduced in the Note of Dissent, Professor Allen deciding that manufacturers might, in such a situation, be forced to compete with each other on price rather than through competitive advertising as at present. The fear of increased bad debts was also rejected as unreasonable on the grounds that this would only be a problem in the transitional stage while the marginal, inefficient, retailers who had been kept in business by r.p.m. closed down.

Thus Professor Allen concluded that r.p.m. on cigarettes was against the public interest and, suggesting that it ought to be abolished, claimed that 'If improvements in the ordering of economic affairs were to be successfully resisted whenever it could be shown that their first impact would have disagreeable consequences for a minority of high-cost traders, then little material progress would be possible.[1]

Following the publication of the report, a fellow London Professor, B. S. Yamey, came to the support of Professor Allen.[2] Professor Yamey drew attention to the similarity between the cigarette industry and the tyre industry. Both were oligopolistic and in such a situation direct price competition between manufacturers was unlikely to arise naturally. Since in their report on tyres a majority of the Commission thought that for this reason individual enforcement of r.p.m. should be prohibited, so, Professor Yamey argued, he would expect to find a similar recommendation in this report, too. The national press also rallied to the side of Professor Allen and supported his condemnation of r.p.m. in this trade. However, shortly after publication of the report further evidence was made public showing a positive relationship between the smoking of cigarettes and the incidence of lung cancer. This brought the argument for or against r.p.m. on cigarettes on to a moral plain with many people feeling that to discourage smoking, prices ought to be raised not lowered.

[1] *Ibid.* para. 618.
[2] 'The Monopolies Commission Report on Cigarettes and Tobacco' *Modern Law Review* vol. 24 (1961) pp. 747-56.

This report contained the first consideration by the Commission of the problem of resale price maintenance since the Restrictive Trade Practices Act had been functioning. It served to highlight the controversy which had broken out the previous year, between Yamey on the one hand and Messrs Andrews and Friday on the other, on the merits of resale price maintenance. Publication of the report came within a year of the Board of Trade's fact-finding inquiry into r.p.m.[1] Thus interest was keenly centred on the Commission's views. So much so in fact that when one M.P., anxious to point to the general approval given to r.p.m. in the report, asked the President of the Board of Trade whether he would take account of the Commission's findings on r.p.m. in his departmental inquiry, the President drew attention to both the majority and the minority view.[2]

Whatever the reader's opinion of the Commission's view on the desirability of resale price maintenance on cigarettes, and the present writer feels that the arguments of Professor Allen are more cogent than those of the rest of the Commission, at least it is quite clear that both sides of the argument were carefully considered. It suggests also that rather than take a highly dogmatic position on one side or other of the r.p.m. fence it is necessary to consider the case for or against resale price maintenance in relation to each particular trade. With conditions differing so widely in each trade it becomes extremely tenuous to adopt a general approval or condemnation of r.p.m. on broad theoretical grounds.

Except where there are clearly evils arising from the maintenance of resale prices on a product, a decision whether r.p.m. is in the public interest or not becomes largely a subjective opinion based on ideas about the probable consequences of the ending of the practice since empirical evidence is hard, if not impossible, to obtain. Except for confectionery, no trade which at present enforces r.p.m. has really experienced the consequences of price cutting in this country for more than sixty years. The use of evidence from other countries in an effort to evaluate the likely consequences of the abolition of r.p.m. here is generally unreliable because of differing retail trading structures and

[1] See below chap. xiv.
[2] *Hansard* vol. 645 (Commons) col. 588-9.

N

differing consumer habits and reactions. In view, therefore, of the difficulty of reaching a fair decision on the desirability of r.p.m. and with the growing concern of public opinion in the early 1960s over r.p.m., it is unfortunate that in two later reports the Monopolies Commission has placed what seems to be undue emphasis on the benefits to be derived from the abolition of r.p.m. in the particular industries under investigation.

The Report on the Supply of Electrical Equipment for Mechanically Propelled Land Vehicles (which we will refer to as the report on motor accessories) was completed in February 1963, having been referred to the Commission in April 1957. It was published in December 1963. Eight categories of good were covered by the report, each of which had a monopoly supplier as defined in the legislation. In some classes replacement sales were important, in others they were not. The basic data relating to the supply situation may be tabulated as follows:

TABLE 25

Classification of Motor Accessories investigated by the Monopolies Commission

Class	Description	Monopoly supplier	Monopoly supplier's share of total sales in class in 1960 %	Importance of Replacement Sales
(i)	Batteries	Chloride	41·5	Very important
(ii)	Ignition coils, magnetos, distributors, suppressors	Lucas	78·9	Fairly important
(iii)	Dynamos, current-voltage control units, starter motors	Lucas	94·9	Fairly important
(iv)	Windscreen wiper motors	Lucas	79·1	Fairly important
(v)	Air moving devices for heating or ventilating equipment	Smiths	76·1	Not important
(vi)	Clocks, ammeters, indicating equipment	Smiths	65·1	Not important
(vii)	Lamps, horns, trafficators	Lucas	85·1	Fairly important
(viii)	Plugs	Champion	71·2	Very important

In the construction of an ordinary private car of up to 1½ litres, the total cost to the vehicle manufacturer of these reference goods would be about £20 - a small proportion of the total manufacturing costs of a motor car. At the time of the report all manufacturers imposed a condition of sale as to the price at which their goods were to be resold and all the leading manufacturers took active steps to enforce this. As will be seen from the above table, resale price maintenance was really only of significance in classes (i) and (viii), where replacement sales were particularly important. At the other extreme, on goods in classes (v) and (vi) replacement sales only amounted to about 10% total sales of that good and even then some replacements were sold to the vehicle manufacturer acting as a factor.

Having established that monopoly conditions did apply in respect of each of the reference goods, the Commission then had to investigate the 'things done' by the various manufacturers concerned either for the purpose of establishing or maintaining their positions or as a result of their positions as monopoly suppliers. The first problem was that of price differentiation between the initial equipment and replacement markets.

The initial equipment market was dominated by the leading vehicle manufacturers who were in an oligopsonistic position. It could also happen that in some years either Ford or B.M.C. were in the position of monopsonists – buying one-third or more of the output of a particular reference good, but since this did not happen regularly the Commission found it was unnecessary to consider this situation. The effect of the existence of powerful buyers was that prices in the initial equipment market were kept at a particularly low level by the vehicle manufacturers' exercise of countervailing power. They could threaten either to buy from other suppliers or to create their own sources of supply. Whilst most manufacturers reckoned to sell initial equipment just above cost price, Champion sold plugs to the vehicle manufacturers at a loss of between 7½d and 8d per plug. They regarded these unprofitable sales as a promotional expenditure to ensure sales for the replacement trade which takes 75% of all sales of plugs, the natural tendency being for users to replace their initial equipment with equipment of the same make.

Whilst accepting that certain economies were effected by selling large quantities of accessories to the vehicle manufacturers, the Commission found that prices on such sales were below an economic level. It found that price differentiation had been used by the accessory manufacturers to establish and keep positions of dominance in the trade, and that this position of dominance was used to secure an excessive rate of profit overall and so the Commission concluded that the practice was contrary to the public interest.

Inextricably connected then, with the question of price differentiation was that of the level of profits earned. The Commission calculated rates of profit earned over a period of seven or eight years (though only four years for class (vi) goods) on an historical cost basis. Two alternative figures were calculated, profit on sales and profit on capital, the capital figure being calculated on the assumption that for each supplier the ratio of costs to capital was the same for both the initial equipment and replacement business.

TABLE 26

Average Annual Profits of Monopoly Suppliers

		Profits on		Total
Manufacturer		*Initial equipment*	*Replacements*	*Profits*
Lucas Profit on Sales		6·1%	13·0%	7·4%
Profit on Capital		18·2%	42·1%	22·6%
Chloride Profit on Sales		2·6%	15·6%	10·0%
Profit on Capital		5·3%	34·1%	21·2%
Champion Profit on Sales		−124·6%	36·9%	23·6%
Profit on Capital		−102·2%	107·7%	57·0%
Smiths class (v) Profit on Sales		6·6%	13·4%	7·2%
Profit on Capital		11·2%	24·5%	12·2%
Smiths class (vi) Profit on Sales		1·3%	22·1%	4·7%
Profit on Capital		2·1%	47·8%	8·3%

Source – Op. cit. from table at para. 705.

On the basis of this information, the Commission decided that Champion's profits were so high as to be contrary to the public interest even allowing for the extra risks involved in their case which would justify somewhat higher profits than normal. Smiths' profits were found to be moderate and warranted no criticism. The overall profits of Lucas and Chloride were found to be high, but not so high as to be contrary to the public interest. In the case of automative batteries, although Lucas was not a monopoly supplier, it was a member of a scheme for restricting competition through the British Starter Battery Association, it was the price leader and was earning profits which were so high as to be contrary to the public interest (the rate of profit on sales in this case being 9·2%).

Table 26 shows clearly the much higher profits earned by all manufacturers on replacement sales than on initial equipment sales. Champion relied entirely on replacement sales for their profits whilst Lucas, Chloride and Smiths all earned much higher rates of profit on replacements than on initial equipment. So the Commission found that it had to deal

'with a replacement trade which because of the differential policies pursued by the dominant manufacturers concerned is extremely profitable to them in itself and is one of the principal contributory factors in providing them with high and in some cases with unreasonably high overall rates of profit'.[1]

Attention was then drawn to the fact that despite these high profits to manufacturers the distributor's share of the retail price amounts to about one half. The Commission therefore suggested that,

'in these circumstances it seems to us very pertinent to consider whether the advantage of bringing competitive pressure to bear upon retail prices might not outweigh any possible disadvantages of abolishing resale price maintenance'.

The whole of the industry - manufacturers and traders - argued strongly for the retention of r.p.m. Abolition would cause distributors to lose confidence in the trade and to carry fewer stocks thereby making them ill-equipped to deal with repairs on the spot. Reduced margins would cause the standard of service to decline and this could affect safety on the roads. Any reduction in the number of small distributors would lead to the establishment of monopolies in distribution. Margins were not excessive and by fixing prices overcharging was avoided. Any competition might reflect back on the manufacturers and cause a debasement of the quality of reference goods. So as a result of any or all of these possibilities the public interest would be harmed if r.p.m. were ended. Further, Champion argued that to force them to drop resale price maintenance would be a denial of their patent rights which they claimed should only be removed under

---

[1] *Op. cit.* para. 1,023. Smiths were excluded from this as they had few replacement sales. We shall argue that Lucas ought also to have been omitted from this condemnation.

special circumstances, which were, they suggested, non-existent in this case.

The Commission rejected the industry's arguments in favour of r.p.m., pointing out that the margin allowed of about 50% was excessive and not related to the service provided. An increasing number of motorists were competent to identify and fit their own components, so it was not right that they should have to pay for a service they did not require. The possibility of overcharging was dismissed as being no more likely than it was at that time – with a regular dealer it would not arise, whilst overcharging for emergency services probably already took place. The plight of the small trader also failed to evoke much sympathy – those giving an efficient service could expect to survive.

Certain advantages would be expected if r.p.m. were to end in this trade. Prices would for the first time be tested by competition and whilst large buyers such as fleet owners would probably benefit immediately, the general public would, in the long run, gain from the ending of r.p.m. through being able to buy at lower prices. Price competition at the retail level would reflect back in pressure on manufacturers to lower their selling prices on replacement goods and this would therefore help reduce the extent of price differentiation between initial equipment and replacement sales.

So, impressed by the strength of its own arguments, the Commission concluded that resale price maintenance operated against the public interest and recommended that it should be prohibited on the goods under investigation. By abolishing r.p.m., it argued, the buyer in the replacement market would be strengthened and this would go some way towards providing countervailing power which would help achieve a better balance between the initial equipment and replacement markets and would therefore 'prove at any rate a partial remedy for what we regard as the principal existing abuse on the part of the monopoly suppliers'[1] – namely the high profits taken by manufacturers.

The Commission also reacted unfavourably towards the situation on batteries where common prices had been fixed by agreement until 1957, discounts had been fixed by agreement

[1] *Ibid.* para. 1,059.

until 1960 and where, at the time of the investigation, provision existed for the exchange of information which, according to the Commission, helped the maintenance of uniform manufacturers' prices. This was also held to be contrary to the public interest since it kept prices high and limited the effects of competition from cheaper batteries. Slow standardization of batteries was also commented upon but the Commission expected that 'in the light of our findings on resale price maintenance . . . the pressure of competition may be expected to compel Chloride to seek the highest possible means of economy in its organization'.[1] Lucas's failure to disclose its ownership of Robert Guthrie, a distributor, Rists, manufacturers of coils, and KX Lamps, manufacturers of lamp bulbs, were also found to be against the public interest.

So far as the actual quality of the products was concerned the Commission was well satisfied. Apart from the lack of standardization on batteries, the various monopoly suppliers were functioning satisfactorily. It was therefore only in relation to sales policy that the Commission had strong criticism to make.

To summarize the conclusions: the Commission found price differentiation between initial equipment and replacement sales to be contrary to the public interest, the pricing policies of Champion in class (viii) and Lucas in class (i) were contrary to the public interest because excessive rates of profit were achieved, whilst the profits of Lucas in the other classes of goods it manufactured and of Chloride in class (i) tended to be on the high side though not so high as to be against the public interest. Distributive margins were high and 'might with advantage be subjected to the test of competition'[2] and resale price maintenance on all eight classes of goods was held to be contrary to the public interest. The agreement between members of the B.S.B.A. (1960) to exchange information on prices and terms for batteries was against the public interest. So, too, was the failure of Lucas to disclose its ownership of certain subsidiaries. The Commission also had some reservations regarding differentiation in prices on sales to wholesalers and on the slow progress achieved by Chloride in rationalizing and simplifying the production of automotive batteries.

The recommendations to cure these ills are interesting. All

Ibid. para. 1,031.   [2] *Ibid*. para. 1,055.

suppliers of reference goods should cease to enforce r.p.m. and manufacturers and importers should publish prices and terms including quantity terms, for all sales of replacement goods. The regulation of the British Starter Battery Association (1960) providing for exchange of information on members' terms, prices, guarantees, etc., should be terminated and not replaced by any agreement or arrangement having similar effect. Lucas's interests in other companies were to be made known in the report.

Thus the main problems the Commission thought should be dealt with were the high profits of some manufacturers and the price differentiation between the two markets arising largely from the absence of countervailing power in the replacement goods market. The method suggested to deal with these – the abolition of resale price maintenance on all goods. Whether this was the right policy to suggest is open to serious doubt. Certainly in earlier Commission reports such a recommendation would not have been made. To deal with high prices and profits, some form of direct governmental price control would probably have been suggested, whilst to provide the necessary countervailing power in the replacement market if price control were not to be adopted, some sort of central buying agency might have been advocated. Why was there this change in the nature of the recommendations? Maybe the Commission was becoming disheartened at having its most constructive and far-reaching suggestions ignored by the Government. Perhaps also the members of the Commission were influenced by the change in public opinion over r.p.m. and remembering their bad press after supporting the practice in the cigarette report were determined to make amends this time. It has also been suggested that the abolition of r.p.m. was recommended in this case because no other alternative recommendation could be thought of. This may well be true especially if the members were convinced the Government would not agree to a drastic intervention within the industry itself, but it still does not make the recommendation a good one.

We must first of all ask whether the ending of r.p.m. could help to reduce those manufacturer profits which the Commission considered too high. The following table, which indicates the contribution to total profits of initial equipment and replacement sales, is interesting in this respect.

TABLE 27
Contribution of Initial Equipment and Replacement Sales to Total Profits *

Manufacturer	Init. equip. £m.	Contribution %	Replace. sales £m.	Contribution %	Total profit £m.	Contribution %
Lucas class (i)	0·27	67·5	0·13	32·5	0·40	100
Lucas classes (ii) (iii) (iv) (vii)	1·21	65·4	0·64	34·6	1·85	100
Lucas all classes	1·48	65·8	0·77	34·2	2·25	100
Chloride class (i)	0·08	11·6	0·61	88·4	0·69	100
Champion class (viii)	−0·15	−45·1	0·48	145·1	0·33	100
Smiths class (v)	0·05	83·3	0·01	16·7	0·06	100
Smiths class (vi)	0·01	14·3	0·06	85·7	0·07	100
Smiths all classes	0·06	46·2	0·07	53·8	0·13	100

* *Source* – calculations based on table at para. 705.

The two places where profits were found to be so high as to be contrary to the public interest were on Lucas sales of class (i) goods and Champion sales of class (viii) goods. Now as regards Champion sales of plugs, it is quite clear that replacement sales made the sole contribution to profits and so if the ending of r.p.m. was able to affect manufacturer profits on replacement sales then here it could be an important contribution to lowering total profits to a reasonable level. The situation as regards Lucas's profits on class (i) goods is rather different. The Commission found that a rate of profit of 9·2% on sales was so high as to be contrary to the public interest in this case, and again thought that to abolish r.p.m. would bring manufacturer profits down to a reasonable level. However, as the above table shows, rather more than two-thirds of Lucas's profits on sales of class (i) goods came from initial equipment sales where countervailing power already existed and where the abolition of r.p.m. would have no effect. Thus it would seem that here the wrong remedy has been suggested.

Similarly with those goods on which the Commission found profits to be 'on the high side' - Chloride in class (i) and Lucas on its other reference goods: Chloride earned most of their profits from the replacement market and so the abolition of r.p.m. might help to lower these. Again, however, it is to be observed that nearly two-thirds of Lucas's profits derived from initial equipment sales where resale price maintenance was not a factor. So to suggest that Lucas's high profits stemmed from an exploitation of the replacement market is not correct, as a simple calculation such as that made in the previous table would have shown the Commission. Therefore it would seem quite clear that to think that Lucas's overall profits would be lowered by preventing resale price maintenance on sales of replacement goods is based on the wrong reasoning. To control Lucas's profits (and we might further doubt whether an overall rate of 7·4% on all sales and 9·2% on sales of batteries alone is too high) it would be necessary to introduce further countervailing power in the initial equipment market.[1]

Clearly, the major contribution to Champion's and Chloride's profits came from their replacement sales where retail price competition might help by reflecting back on manufacturers and squeezing their profits. Whether this would in fact happen is very much a matter of opinion which would be difficult to justify *ex ante*. However, assuming that the ending of r.p.m. would lower manufacturer profits in the way the Commission hoped and help to achieve a closer relationship between prices in the initial equipment and replacement markets, what would be the consequences? The Commission seemed to envisage a lower overall rate of profit being achieved as a result of two actions - a substantial lowering of prices and profits in the replacement market and a (smaller) rise in prices and profits in the initial equipment market. This would, however, be a contradiction of evidence which the component manufacturers put to the Commission. They argued that any rise in initial equipment prices would cause them to lose this business altogether either to

[1] It should be emphasized that this discussion takes issue with the Commission's recommendation to deal with the high *total* profits earned by Lucas taking initial equipment and replacement sales together. Had the Commission chosen merely to argue that Lucas were making too high a level of profit on replacement sales alone this would have been an entirely different matter since their percentage profits on replacements were much higher than on initial equipment. Though it is, perhaps, worth pointing out that, as Table 26 shows, profit on replacements earned by Smiths expressed as a percentage of sales turnover was higher than that earned by Lucas, and the Commission had no adverse comments to make about Smiths's profits.

foreign component manufacturers who would still be prepared to sell at about cost price or to the vehicle manufacturers themselves who could produce at about the same costs as the manufacturers concerned in this investigation. Since the Commission did not attempt to refute or reject this, we must assume it accepted the argument.

The loss of the initial equipment market would severely hit the accessory manufacturers who have tended to rely on initial equipment sales as a form of advertising since it is usual to replace a battery or plug with the same make again. Thus, not only would initial equipment sales be lost, but also, consequently, a large part of the replacement market, too, thereby causing production to be restricted and production economies lost, and thereby necessitating even higher prices on those replacement sales they did retain. Thus it would appear that whilst some reduction in profits on replacement sales in the case of Chloride and Champion might in theory be achieved by the ending of r.p.m., any attempt to reduce the amount of price differentiation by raising at the same time prices on initial equipment would not succeed.

The merits of the discussion of the value or desirability of the continuance of resale price maintenance in this industry have tended to be lost because the Commission insisted on seeing the abolition of resale price maintenance as a panacea for all ills. To suggest that the ending of r.p.m. would cause Chloride to further standardize the batteries they produce is taking what is at best a tenuous argument (that retail price competition directly reflects back on manufacturers) well beyond the bounds of what is feasible. So we must conclude that in this report, whilst the case against resale price maintenance on motor accessories may have been strong, it was wrong to treat its abolition as the major cure for the more serious ills which were to be found at the manufacturing end of the motor accessories industry.

The supply of wallpaper was referred to the Commission for investigation in September 1961, the report being signed in December 1963 and published the following month. All in all, a very speedy piece of work compared with some of their other reports! The Commission's terms of reference were rather more limited than has normally been the case. Whereas for most inquiries the Commission has been asked to investigate and report on –

1. Whether the conditions to which the Act of 1948 as amended by the 1956 legislation applies, prevail;

2. the things which are done by the parties concerned as a result of, or for the purpose of preserving those conditions;

3. whether the conditions in question or all or any of the 'things done' operate or may be expected to operate against the public interest.

The Commission was asked to investigate in the case of wallpaper whether the conditions to which the Act applies prevailed and if so whether certain things were done by the parties concerned as a result of, or for the purpose of preserving, those conditions. Instead of being allowed to investigate any 'things done' the Commission had to restrict its investigation to:

(a) the acquiring of interests in other undertakings engaged in the manufacture or supply of wallpaper;

(b) the imposition or acceptance of agreements or arrangements as respects restrictions on the supply or acquisition of wallpaper;

(c) the acquisition or use or permission for use of premises for the purpose of carrying on the business of supplying wallpaper;

(d) the taking or threatening of action which is calculated or likely to have the effect of –

(i) restricting or preventing the supply of wallpaper to or its acquisition by, any person carrying on the business of supplying wallpaper;

(ii) preventing or restricting such supply or acquisition at normal trade prices or on normal trade terms;

(iii) otherwise penalizing any such person in the carrying on of such business;

and if so whether or not any or all of those things operate or may be expected to operate against the public interest.

Whilst the terms of reference seem to be quite wide, unless the Board of Trade was absolutely certain that the reference covered all the practices which were pursued, which need not necessarily have been known, such limitation of the extent of an inquiry can hardly be in the public interest. Neither was the

Commission asked to decide whether the monopoly position of the largest firm, which gave rise to the inquiry in the first place, was in the public interest or not. It is to be hoped that in future inquiries the Commission's scope will not be limited since it is very difficult to ensure that in specifying the practices to be investigated, other more serious ones are left untouched.

The largest manufacturer was the Wall Paper Manufacturers Ltd. (W.P.M.), which included amongst its subsidiaries Arthur Sanderson and Son Ltd. and Shand Kydd Ltd. W.P.M. was responsible for 79% of the total supply of wallpaper in this country, and also owned both merchants and retailers, these retailers handled some 12% of W.P.M.'s output. In the distribution of wallpaper, merchants handled, as wholesalers, the greater bulk of supplies, though some retailers and mail order businesses were supplied direct. Decorators, who supplied and hung wallpaper, normally charged the customer the retail price for the wallpaper and were responsible for about 30% of sales. With the growth of 'do-it-yourself' decorating, the share of total sales handled by retail outlets was increasing and the share of decorators decreasing.

W.P.M. distinguished two broad categories of wallpaper – pattern book ways and starred ways. Pattern book ways were intended primarily for the decorators' trade (though this distinction was becoming blurred, by 1963 one-third of pattern book ways were sold by retailers (equal to about 20% retailers' sales)). Pattern book ways were issued every two years and their availability was guaranteed. Resale price maintenance at all stages of distribution was a condition of sale on these papers, but formal action to enforce the conditions had never been needed. Starred ways were issued annually and their availability was not guaranteed. They were intended essentially for sale in retail outlets and were cheaper and of lower quality than pattern book ways. Pattern book ways were responsible for 45% of W.P.M.'s sales by volume but 50% by value. No other manufacturers distinguished between pattern book ways and starred ways since their production was too small to allow them to do this.

Apart from the enforcement of resale price maintenance to which we shall return later, the Commission found that within the terms of reference there were two other 'things done'. These were the acquisition of manufacturers and distributors by W.P.M. and the use of exclusive dealing arrangements. The acquisition of manufacturing concerns was found to limit competition in the manufacture of wallpaper and was a 'thing done' to protect W.P.M.'s monopoly position. Even allowing for the fact that the twelve mills in the W.P.M. Group competed on design, service, etc., and the existence of the Group did allow some advantages through bulk buying of materials and economies of scale in production, these did not, in the Commission's view, outweigh the fact that price was centrally controlled and competition suppressed. The disadvantages thus outweighed any advantages. Here we are led to the conclusion that if the Commission was so strongly opposed to central price fixing as it seems to have been, had it been given a free hand to investigate whether the monopoly itself was against the public interest, consideration might have been given to whether W.P.M. should divest itself of some of its subsidiaries in order to break up the monopoly. If there are serious detriments in the present structure of this industry, this would have been a far-reaching recommendation but more valuable than any which the Commission was in a position to make as a result of its terms of reference.

The acquisition by W.P.M. of interests in the distribution of wallpaper was found by the Commission not to be contrary to the public interest. Their holdings here represented only a small proportion of the total trade in wallpaper and there were sufficient other distributors to handle the products of the independent manufacturers.

Until 1961, to qualify for a discount a distributor had to trade exclusively with W.P.M. This was dropped late that year and failed to find favour with the Commission who concluded that it was a practice which was intended to help preserve the Group's monopoly position. Its effect was that independent manufacturers had to look for new distributors in order to establish outlets for their products, thereby creating a condition of excess capacity in the distributive trade with the resultant need for higher margins, and competition between manufacturers was therefore limited. So the Commission found exclusive dealing to be contrary to the public interest and recommended that should

W.P.M. ever revive it whilst they had a dominant share of the market, it would be expected to operate again against the public interest.

W.P.M. argued that their policy of enforcing resale price maintenance on pattern book ways was not for the purpose of preserving their monopoly position. Without r.p.m., they claimed, pattern book way merchants would be unable to meet the heavy cost of producing pattern books and maintaining stocks over the two year guarantee period. Further, they would have difficulty in resisting the demands of decorators for higher margins. This could well lead to higher prices on all wallpapers and possibly even a collapse of the pattern book system of distribution. As evidence of what might happen if r.p.m. were abolished, they drew attention to the situation prevailing in the U.S.A. where a mark up of between 500% and 700% on factory prices was customary, whereas to merchants in this country it was only 100% and discounts to decorators had recently been reduced. Since there was growing competition in retail outlets between pattern book ways and starred ways, the pegging of prices by means of r.p.m. on pattern book ways also helped to keep prices on starred ways down. Merchants also gave evidence to the Commission in favour of resale price maintenance on the grounds of the high cost of providing pattern books and servicing them and on the loss which had to be accepted on papers left at the end of the two year period.

The Commission found that resale price maintenance was a 'thing done' by W.P.M. to help preserve their near-monopoly on sales through decorators. The fact that their pattern book ways were subject to r.p.m. provided an incentive to merchants to stock W.P.M. lines in preference to those of other manufacturers. The smaller manufacturers were not able to enforce r.p.m. on their products to compete with W.P.M., since they did not distinguish between pattern book and starred ways and whilst W.P.M. did not enforce a resale price on starred ways the smaller manufacturers were not able to prescribe r.p.m. as a condition of sale at all.

The Group's arguments for r.p.m. were rejected by the Commission. Evidence on margins in the U.S.A. was considered inappropriate because a different situation was held to prevail there. An increase in the size of margins was not to be expected on the abolition of r.p.m. neither was there likely to be any decline in the provision of better class wallpapers. The main concern of the Commission was with the high distributive margins which were being protected by resale price maintenance, the total distributive margin amounted to about 60% of the retail price excluding purchase tax. Because they were so high – notwithstanding the services which merchants had to provide out of their share, the Commission felt that any action to reduce the pressure of competition on retail prices was *prima facie* undesirable, so for r.p.m. to be in the public interest a substantial advantage would have to be lost if r.p.m. were abolished. The abolition of r.p.m. would mean that merchants and retailers would be encouraged to increase efficiency and reduce costs by the knowledge that other traders might undercut their prices and this might eventually lead to lower retail prices not only on pattern books but on all wallpaper.

The Commission's conclusion was:

'Our judgment as to the effect of resale price maintenance in the wallpaper trade is considerably influenced by the fact that it is practised by the monopoly supplier and by no other supplier, that it is applied to only one-half of the monopoly supplier's products with a view to supporting a particular method of trading, and that some of the goods to which it is applied are nevertheless supplied through other channels where they exercise an influence on the price structure.'[1]

So resale price maintenance was held to be contrary to the public interest.

Three recommendations were made by the Commission. W.P.M. should not acquire interests in other manufacturers without the consent of the Board of Trade. They should not reintroduce exclusive dealing without the Board's consent. The Group should terminate their existing arrangements for the enforcement of r.p.m. and should not enter into such arrangements in the future whilst it continued to be responsible for at least one-third of the total home supply of wallpaper.

Of these recommendations, one related to a practice (exclusive dealing) which W.P.M. said they had no intention of

[1] *Op. cit.* para. 180.

recommencing, and it was hardly likely that any further take-overs by W.P.M. would be allowed without strong public opposition. This meant that again the abolition of r.p.m. was the Commission's main recommendation.[1] Now, r.p.m. covered only about 40% by value of wallpaper sales and the trading conditions for which it was set up - sales via merchants and decorators - were declining in importance. Where the decorator hung the wallpaper for a member of the public he could always cut prices if he wanted to by not adding on the full cost of the labour provided in hanging the paper. Further, distribution of pattern book and starred ways was no longer through entirely separate channels, since decorators were tending to hang starred ways and the general public to buy pattern book ways in retail outlets. There had been no need for W.P.M. to take formal action to enforce their conditions of sale on pattern book ways and there was little or no cutting of the non-maintained prices on starred ways. These all make it clear that resale price maintenance was of little practical importance here and suggest that the Commission's recommendation was accorded a significance out of all proportion to its influence in this trade.

In this chapter we have seen that until the report on cigarettes, the findings of the Commission, so far as resale price maintenance was concerned, were generally consistent and satisfactory. The cigarette report proved the turning point, for the Commission's approval of r.p.m. on cigarettes received a certain amount of adverse publicity from commentators, who tended to support the dissentient - Professor G. C. Allen. The later reports on motor accessories and wallpaper mark a complete change of view in relation to r.p.m. and whilst their condemnation of the practice will have received wide support in many quarters, the emphasis put upon this recommendation as a cure for the ills of the industries concerned (especially is this true of motor accessories) seems to have been entirely misplaced.

The Monopolies Commission has, in the years of its existence, had an important influence on public opinion and, as we have observed, contributed significantly to the basic philosophy (both

[1] Although it is fair to recall that in this report the Commission did not find the same number of problems as in their inquiry into motor accessories - they would not even state categorically that prices and margins on wallpaper were too high.

O

on restrictive trading agreements and r.p.m.) underlying the Restrictive Trade Practices Act. The recommendations regarding r.p.m. on motor accessories and wallpaper also received wide publicity, but it is difficult to avoid the feeling that here the tendency was to follow rather than lead public opinion. Certainly, the findings in these two reports do not appear to constitute sufficient justification for the new legislative action to deal with r.p.m. which was introduced shortly after the reports were signed.

CHAPTER XIV

R.P.M. AND THE RESTRICTIVE TRADE PRACTICES ACT

We have now come to the stage where our findings can be summarized. Some doubt must remain as to the real intentions of the Government where resale price maintenance was concerned in the Restrictive Trade Practices Act. In fact, in many trades the practice continued to thrive after 1956, with trade associations finding ways and means of participating in the enforcement of r.p.m. and manufacturers finding injunctions easy to obtain. The number of instances where legal action has ultimately been taken are greatly outweighed by the occasions when the threat of such action has proved sufficient to compel a price cutting trader to adhere to the manufacturer's conditions of sale.

Challenges to resale price maintenance in defended hearings in the Restrictive Practices Court have so far been unsuccessful and the voluntary abandonment of some agreements providing for the adoption and enforcement of resale price conditions has not caused the individual manufacturers concerned to alter their traditional trading practices. Two recent reports of the Monopolies Commission have condemned resale price maintenance but too much weight should not be attached to their findings since, especially in the report on motor accessories, they placed undue emphasis on the abolition of r.p.m. as a cure for more serious ills in the industry with which r.p.m. has, at best, only a tenuous connection.

The breakdown of resale price maintenance in the grocery trade is at least partly attributable to the Act in that it caused manufacturers, some of whom were already weakening, to rethink their attitude towards r.p.m. In the absence of collective pressure brought to bear by distributors and other manufacturers the practice was generally abandoned by grocery manufacturers in 1957 and 1958 and substantial savings are now available to consumers as a result of price cutting on branded groceries. It is largely due to the growth of the self service movement that price cutting has become so prevalent and the practice of supermarkets especially of handling other household goods has caused the breakdown of r.p.m. here, too. It is doubtful whether the collapse of r.p.m. on these products would have come as quickly as it did without the impetus provided by the Act.

The continued strength of r.p.m. in many trades is due to a number of factors. Between 1956 and 1964, consumer demand remained generally buoyant and so there was no incentive to traders to cut prices in order to clear stocks. The weakening of r.p.m. in the electrical appliance field in 1960-61 is the exception that proves this rule. The structure of the non-food retail trades has also been of importance. Whilst in any main shopping centre a number of food shops are to be found competing for custom with each other, the same does not normally hold true in many non-food trades where only one or two specialist retailers selling a particular product are to be found. Far from there being competition between non-food retailers it is argued that many hold a spatial monopoly in which the desire to cut prices to gain a competitive advantage is non-existent. In some trades this monopoly position is further enhanced by the policy of manufacturers appointing one retailer in an area to an exclusive dealership.

The failure of discount stores, anxious to sell consumer durables at cut prices, to establish themselves in this country has also contributed to the strength of r.p.m. The problem here is one of 'the chicken and the egg'. A concerted outbreak of price cutting would probably have broken r.p.m. - witness the experience of G.E.C. in the United States who, between 1953 and 1958, are said to have spent five million dollars in filing 3,000 petitions for injunctions against price cutters. Ultimately though, as price cutting became widespread, they were forced to capitulate.[1] Had there been a large number of price-cutting non-food retailers in this country, r.p.m. might have disappeared in more

[1] Ralph Harris and Arthur Seldon *'Advertising in a Free Society'* (London) 1959 p. 200.

trades due to the physical impossibility of controlling the situation, but since they have to be able to cut prices to succeed, the existence of r.p.m. has itself prevented the growth of the discount stores who alone could have broken down the system on consumer durables.

Once the initial difficulties were overcome of ensuring that adequate notice, etc., was given, the ease with which manufacturers have been able to obtain injunctions has discouraged traders from price cutting. Though in some cases where legal action has been taken, manufacturers have found it expensive not only in terms of the legal costs involved and the man-hours spent in preparing a case but also because of the resultant adverse publicity and unpleasantness with the trader concerned. One surprising feature is the number of manufacturers who were mis-informed about their rights under section 25. Thus at one stage Nestlé stated publicly that as a result of section 25 it was no longer legally possible to stop supplies to price cutters.[1] Other manufacturers, too, who had also been anxious to prevent price cutting, were uncertain of their exact powers, and recently a number of manufacturers have experienced similar doubts about their right to prevent the giving of trading stamps.

Opinion is divided as to the relative effectiveness of individual and collective methods of enforcement of r.p.m. Individual enforcement under section 25 seems to have three main potential advantages. The manufacturer is able to act independently and does not need to rely on support from other manufacturers, interim injunctions are quickly obtainable and action under section 25 has proved a more effective way of stopping price cutting when wholesalers are important in the distributive system. Under collective enforcement schemes there was a danger that a price cutter who had been stop listed could still obtain supplies from one wholesaler or another either because the wholesaler was prepared to deliberately flout the Stop List or, due to the possibility of human error, the wholesaler would not remember that a particular trader had been stop listed and so his orders would still be met. Where trade associations have continued to participate in collecting information on price cutting, making the necessary test purchases and even assisting

1 See *The Grocer* March 1, 1958 p. 36.

with legal costs, action under section 25 has involved the individual manufacturer in little inconvenience. The sales manager of a leading toiletry concern summed the situation up succinctly –

'Since the Restrictive Trade Practices Act the problem [of enforcing r.p.m.] has been simplified. It is not now necessary to adopt the laborious and sometimes only partly successful attempt to stop up all possible avenues of supply and to solicit the co-operation of all manufacturer members to withhold supplies. Conditions as to resale prices can now be enforced and the possibility of such action is in itself often sufficient to act as a deterrent . . . With the knowledge that the [P.A.T.A.] is prepared to take charge of enforcement proceedings and defray legal costs, any reluctance on the part of manufacturers to embark on such proceedings should be dispelled.'[1]

A number of manufacturers have found the opposite to be the case. They refer to the cost of time and money in complying with the conditions of the section and in obtaining the necessary evidence of price cutting. In the opinion of one manufacturer, 'It is a rather ponderous procedure to deal with one small trader.' Then there is the problem of adverse publicity which enforcing manufacturers have to face. One of the advantages of collective enforcement was that the action was taken by the trade association rather than by any individual manufacturer. This meant that the aggrieved retailer had no opportunity of singling out an indivdual supplier and refusing to stock his brands. This would, of course, adversely affect the small manufacturer rather than a dominant supplier without whose products no retailer can afford to be. There is, however, no evidence so far in this country that brands of small manufacturers have been singled out for severe price cutting. Price cutting has tended to be concentrated on brand leaders. But this is not to deny that such a situation could arise in the future.

Collective action also tended to be completed sooner. In trades such as chemists' goods and tobacco, if a trader persisted in price cutting after being warned, he would immediately be stop listed. In the motor trade, the use of a private court meant that more time was required but even here a trader would be stop listed in

[1] *Quarterly Record* October 1957 p. 14.

less time than it has taken to have an injunction made final, although, of course, an interim injunction can be obtained very rapidly.

Thus there are potential advantages in both systems of enforcement. Preference for one rather than the other depends on a number of factors such as the system of enforcement which existed before 1956, the frequency with which cutting has occurred and the amount of assistance given since 1956 by trade associations. The facts indicate that since 1956, in the majority of trades, section 25 has proved perfectly adequate in dealing with the price cutting that there has been. This form of individual action would, however, prove unsatisfactory if price cutting by a large number of distributors occurred. This would make it financially and physically impossible for the manufacturer to take the necessary action and would clearly therefore weaken manufacturer insistence on r.p.m. Here the advantages of collective enforcement would be large.

In the trades where resale price maintenance has proved to be of greatest practical importance since 1956, the potential effects of section 24 have been outweighed by section 25. Section 25 has proved of considerable value in dealing with price cutters, especially where they do not obtain goods direct from the manufacturer. In trades which had not previously had a system of collective enforcement the new conditions were important since they improved the reliefs available to a manufacturer. To trades which had relied previously on collective enforcement, the section provided an alternative that was at least viable whilst there was no strong impetus to a large-scale outbreak of price cutting.

The Act brought the whole question of resale price maintenance to a head. It ensured that manufacturers would make their own decisions whether or not to enforce r.p.m. It also indicated official approval for individual enforcement which was an encouragement to manufacturers who wanted to retain the system. At the same time, however, it provided a focal point for retailers who were anxious to ensure that manufacturers did take the appropriate action against price cutters. It has been suggested that this proved an embarrassment to manufacturers who would gladly have dropped the practice. The evidence collected by this writer is, however, that in only one trade might this be true. It would be right to say that in other instances the retailer trade associations may have proved a little too anxious in encouraging manufacturers to act, and as we have already observed, there is evidence that r.p.m.-enforcing manufacturers have not received the support from traditional retailers that they were entitled to expect.

In some trades such as clothing, toys, photographic and sports goods, the Act has had little direct influence simply because there has been very little need for enforcement action, and where instances of price cutting have arisen, it has normally proved possible to settle them privately.

Wholesalers have also benefited from the Act. Prior to 1956 they were responsible for enforcing the manufacturers' conditions of sale on the retailers - a responsibility which could prove burdensome. Now the right given to the manufacturer to take this simple effective action against third parties relieved the wholesaler of this function and left him free to concentrate on his basic job of providing an adequate distributive system between manufacturers and retailers.

It was not long after the passing of the Act that people began trying to assess its effects and, having sampled the apparent benefits of the collapse of r.p.m. in the grocery trade began to agitate for a more general prohibition of the practice. Thus at the end of 1957 Lord Lucas of Chilworth held section 25 responsible for a 3% rise in retail prices in the previous year whilst wholesale prices had fallen by 6%.[1] In 1959 Sir Lyn Ungoed-Thomas told the then President of the Board of Trade that the effect of section 25 had been to 'keep prices up, cut down competition and keep up the cost of living'.[2]

The attack on r.p.m. then became insistent. In their second report the Cohen Committee claimed that by putting legal sanctions at the disposal of the manufacturer, the Act had strengthened r.p.m. and suggested that section 25 should be repealed.[3] The national press took up the attack and by January 1960 the Government were reported to have been thinking of

[1] *Hansard* vol. 206 (Lords) col. 1,026.
[2] *Hansard* vol. 603 (Commons) col. 789.
[3] *Council on Prices, Productivity and Incomes Second Report* 1958 para. 118.

withdrawing the individual manufacturer's right of enforcement. In June 1960 the Board of Trade instituted a departmental inquiry into r.p.m. The basis on which this was conducted was strongly criticized by the late Frank Friday.[1] As is customary with departmental inquiries of this nature the report has not been published but the general belief is that it recommended that r.p.m. should be prohibited perhaps with provision for exemptions in certain cases. It was a long time before any action was taken on the report. Numerous M.P.s asked successive Presidents of the Board of Trade when they would make a statement about r.p.m., but every time were met with non-committal replies. According to the *Financial Times* the report was brought to the Cabinet three times – 'a little airily' by Mr Maudling, 'doggedly' by Mr Erroll and 'successfully' by Mr Heath.[2] It would seem that whilst the economists in the Board of Trade wanted the abolition of r.p.m. the politicians did not consider such action expedient.

Meanwhile, the attacks continued. The Moloney Committee entered the fray, although r.p.m. was outside its terms of reference. Their report contained the following:

'A few of our number considered that the existing law in favour of r.p.m. was *prima facie* inimical to the interest of the consumer and welcomed the signs that this fetter on free competition and restraint on a natural price level was loosening in some trades in which it operated.'[3]

The Monopolies Commission's reports on motor accessories and wallpaper also condemned r.p.m. and their findings, especially in the former report, received wide publicity. In December 1963 the Government-sponsored Consumer Council also recommended that r.p.m. be made illegal,[4] though it is understood this was agreed only by a narrow majority. In 1964 the National Economic Development Council also noted with obvious approval the recently published Bill to deal with r.p.m.[5]

---

[1] Frank A. Friday – *'Shops and Prices: Inquiry into Resale Price Maintenance'* (London) 1961.
[2] *Financial Times* January 16, 1964.
[3] *Final Report of the Committee on Consumer Protection* 1962 Cmnd. 1781 para 7.
[4] *The Times* December 20, 1963.
[5] *The Growth of the Economy* (H.M.S.O.) 1964 paras. 487-9.

Although the body of opinion thus brought to bear against r.p.m. is extremely weighty there is much that is unsatisfactory about their conclusions. Many of the remarks contain little evidence of objectivity, the approach of the Board of Trade's own inquiry is open to criticism, so, too, is the basis on which the Monopolies Commission recommended that r.p.m. be prohibited on motor accessories.

There are, however, grounds for thinking that the Government still did not intend to act against r.p.m., at least until after the 1964 General Election. But two parliamentary events ultimately forced their hand. In the ballot for private members' Bills in the House of Commons, Mr John Stonehouse came first and Mr John Osborn second. Stonehouse (a Labour M.P.) introduced a Bill to abolish resale price maintenance.[1] Osborn (a Conservative M.P.) introduced a Bill, which ultimately received the Royal Assent, on trading stamps.[2] This sought, amongst other things, to require that each trading stamp bore a cash value and to make all stamps redeemable for cash when their value exceeded five shillings. Publication of this Bill followed closely upon the controversy between Cadbury and various supermarket companies over Cadbury's insistence that the giving of trading stamps constituted a breach of their resale price conditions and so re-opened this whole question.

Faced with these developments, the Government were forced to take action and in January 1964 announced that they were to introduce legislation to abolish resale price maintenance.[3] Five weeks later their Bill was published and after a difficult passage through Parliament in which an amendment to exclude chemists' goods from the working of the Act was only defeated by a Government majority of one vote,[4] became law on July 16, 1964.[5]

Some commentators have suggested that the Restrictive Trade Practices Act did not cause any weakening in the practice of

[1] Abolition of Resale Price Maintenance Bill published December 11, 1963.

[2] Trading Stamps Act 1964 Eliz. 2 c. 71.

[3] That this was a hurried decision is suggested by the failure of the Government to publish a White Paper foreshadowing the new Bill. In view of the strong public concern felt over r.p.m. it is suggested that this omission was a serious error on the part of the Government.

[4] *Hansard* vol. 692 (Commons) col 400.

[5] Resale Prices Act 1964 Eliz. 2 c. 58.

resale price maintenance. Thus, in his Hobart Paper, Professor Yamey says:

'The changes of 1956 do not seem to have brought about either a reduction in the scope of r.p.m. in our economy or any material weakening in its enforcement.'[1]

Whilst the Rt. Hon. Edward Heath, during the debate on the Second Reading of the Resale Prices Bill, stated:

'Experience of the operation of the 1956 Act showed very soon that the move from collective to individual enforcement made comparatively little difference to the economic effects of the resale price maintenance system and that those who said that by the removal of collective enforcement it would wither away were shown not to have been justified in their expectations.'[2]

In fact it is the argument of this study that as a result of the existence of section 24 and the increased competition between manufacturers arising from Part I of the Act, the Restrictive Trade Practices Act has contributed to a material weakening in r.p.m. on certain products. Certainly this is true of the situation on tyres and groceries and through groceries on certain other household consumable items. Similarly it has also weakened r.p.m. on some capital goods which are outside our field of investigation.

Elsewhere, r.p.m. has remained strong and undoubtedly the powers given in the Act to individual manufacturers to deal with price cutting have been important here. Though it should be observed that the great majority of the injunctions obtained have been sought by manufacturers of only four classes of goods – motor vehicles and accessories, chemists' goods, hardware and electrical appliances. In other trades section 25 may be held to have given a moral backing to resale price maintenance but its actual practical significance has been minimal since there has been little attempt to cut prices. Whatever conclusions the Restrictive Practices Court reaches as to the desirability of the continuance of r.p.m. in the various trades whose cases it will have to consider, it is the structure of the retail trade and the attitude of both manufacturers and distributors that will deter-

[1] B. S. Yamey *op. cit.* p. 41.
[2] *Hansard* vol. 691 (Commons) col. 260.

mine whether consumers are to benefit from lower prices. The new legislation can only create one of the conditions necessary for price cutting to take place.

CHAPTER XV

PROGRESS WITH THE RESALE
PRICES ACT, 1964

The Resale Prices Act falls into two main parts. Sections 1-4 constitute a general ban on activities to enforce a fixed resale price other than a maximum price, and sections 5-8 provide for the granting of exemptions from this ban where the Restrictive Practices Court finds that the public interest is best served by the retention of r.p.m.

The first four sections came into force on April 30, 1965. Except where exemption has been granted, either temporarily or permanently, actions to prescribe or enforce a minimum resale price are no longer permitted.[1] Contracts and agreements between a supplier and dealer providing for the maintenance of a minimum resale price are void and attempts by suppliers to require agreement to such a condition of sale are unlawful. Prices are not to be prescribed unless they are clearly understood to be recommended or maximum prices only.

Other measures intended to maintain resale prices are also prohibited.[2] It is unlawful for a supplier to withhold supplies from a dealer on the grounds that that dealer has been or is likely to be cutting the prices of the suppliers' products or that the dealer has sold or is likely to sell such goods to a third party who had sold or would be likely to sell them below the resale price. In addition to actual refusal to supply, a supplier is treated as withholding supplies of goods if he refuses or fails to supply those goods to the order of the dealer or if he discriminates against a trader by supplying him on significantly less favourable terms as regards prices, credit, discounts, method or time of delivery than to other dealers carrying on business in similar circumstances.[3] Where these provisions are contravened a civil

---

[1] Resale Prices Act 1964 c. 58 Section 1. [2] Section 2 [3] Section 2(3).

proceeding on behalf of the Crown for an injunction or other appropriate relief is the prescribed remedy (though individuals may also bring civil proceedings).[1]

A supplier may, however, lawfully withhold supplies from a dealer if he has reasonable cause to believe that within the previous twelve months the dealer or any other dealer supplied by that dealer had been using as loss leaders any goods of the same or similar description, whether obtained from that supplier or not.[2] Loss leading is defined in the Act as the resale of goods.

'not for the purpose of making a profit on the sale of those goods but for the purpose of attracting to the establishment at which those goods are sold customers likely to purchase other goods or otherwise for the purpose of advertising the business of the dealer'.[3]

Sections 5-8 make it possible for suppliers to obtain exemption for their goods from this ban. Applications for exemption had to be registered with the Registrar of Restrictive Trading Agreements by suppliers between August 16 and November 15, 1964. It is the responsibility of the Registrar to maintain a list of goods which have been registered and to refer them to the Restrictive Practices Court for adjudication. Where a class of goods has been registered they are exempt from the ban on the enforcement of resale price maintenance and remain so until the Court has decided whether the public interest is best served by the continuance of r.p.m. on the goods in question.

The Court may make an order exempting a class of goods from the ban if it is satisfied that in the absence of r.p.m. one or more of five specified detriments (the 'gateways') would ensue and that such detriment would, on balance, be disadvantageous to the public as consumers or users of the goods (the 'tailpiece'). The 'gateways' and 'tailpiece' are:

That in the event of the abolition of r.p.m. on particular goods:

'(a) the quality of the goods available for sale, or the

---

[1] Section 4(3).   [2] Section 3.

[3] Section 3(2). This definition was introduced during the passage of the Bill through Parliament. The original definition of loss leading contained in the Bill was the sale of goods by a dealer 'at or below the price paid by him for those goods'.

varieties of the goods so available, would be substantially reduced to the detriment of the public as consumers or users of those goods; or

(b) the number of establishments in which the goods are sold by retail would be substantially reduced to the detriment of the public as such consumers or users; or

(c) the prices at which the goods are sold by retail would in general and in the long run be increased to the detriment of the public as such consumers or users; or

(d) the goods would be sold by retail under conditions likely to cause danger to health in consequence of their misuse by the public as such consumers or users; or

(e) any necessary services actually provided in connection with or after the sale of the goods by retail would cease to be so provided or would be substantially reduced to the detriment of the public as such consumers or users,

and in any such case that the resulting detriment to the public as consumers or users of the goods in question would outweigh any detriment to them as such consumers or users (whether by the restriction of competition or otherwise) resulting from the maintenance of minimum resale prices in respect of the goods.'[1]

Once one supplier of a class of goods has registered an application for exemption all suppliers of that class are entitled to continue to enforce r.p.m. until the Court has made an order on their application. Thus the exemption relates to a class of goods rather than to a supplier. Despite this provision the Registrar received a large number of overlapping applications,[2] including over 100 relating to wines and spirits and over ninety for toiletries and cosmetics. In addition many applications contained a number of separate items. On average there are nearly eight items specified per application but three applicants have each specified over 100 items.

In all, in the three months during which applications for registration were made to the Registrar, about 700 applications were received, 70% of which were made in the last two weeks

[1] Section 5(2).
[2] In some trades the trade association registered on behalf of its manufacturer members and those same suppliers also registered independently.

and over 90% of which relate to consumer goods and less than 10% to producer or capital goods.

In order to be allowed to register, the supplier was required to specify in his notice to the Registrar claiming exemption particulars of the arrangements used for maintaining resale prices and documentary evidence in support of this.[1] Some suppliers found difficulty in complying with this requirement. In a fairly large number of instances the required documentary evidence was not available because it had never been necessary to give formal notice to traders that it was a condition of sale that the manufacturer's resale prices be observed. The Registrar has been helpful to suppliers in this matter. If the supplier could not point to an invoice, etc., making r.p.m. a legally enforceable condition of sale, a copy of a letter written to a price cutter or evidence of an office minute agreeing on verbal action was usually accepted.

Altogether it is estimated that out of a total of 654 applications which have finally been registered, in about ninety of these, from the documentary evidence provided to the Registrar, legal action to prevent price cutting under section 25 of the Restrictive Trade Practices Act would be impossible because the required notice of a condition as to the resale price at which the goods could be resold did not exist. The details given to the Registrar of arrangements for the enforcement of r.p.m. included the following – 'understanding, lapses taken up and rectified', 'custom of trade', 'refusal to supply'. More than twenty-five suppliers stated that they had appointed dealers who were expected to adhere to the manufacturer's price structure. In a further twenty-three instances it was only during October and November 1964 that suppliers made the maintenance of resale prices a legally enforceable condition of sale. Almost all of these are to be found amongst suppliers in trades where price cutting has never been a serious problem but just because formal enforcement action has not been necessary it does not mean that r.p.m. does not exist.[2]

Despite the latitude allowed by the Registrar in the evidence

[1] S.I. 1964 No. 1115 The Resale Prices (Registration of Goods) Regulations.
[2] These findings support the argument in chapter iii above that r.p.m. exists in a number of cases where it does not take a legally enforceable form. The existence of r.p.m. is to be judged by the action that is, or would be, taken rather than by the existence of a form of words.

that he accepted that r.p.m. is enforced, of the 700 or so applications received for registration only 654 were ultimately placed on the Register. That nearly fifty were not registered was mainly due to the inability of the suppliers concerned to provide satisfactory evidence. In the majority of these cases there were already other similar applications on the Register so the supplier is still covered by the exemption granted to his class of goods and he may still appear before the Court as an unregistered supplier.[1] It is also understood that some suppliers who initially applied for registration changed their minds before the register closed on November 15, 1964, and they have therefore not been included on the Register.

Four lists of classes of goods for which applications for exemption had been duly registered were published by the Registrar between February and June 1965 using the classification employed in the Brussels Nomenclature. Any supplier whose goods are not included on the Register may now only apply for exemption by leave of the Restrictive Practices Court and this leave will not be granted unless *prima facie* evidence can be provided of facts on which an order exempting the goods from the ban on r.p.m. could be made.[2]

Neither the number of registered applications for exemption nor the classification of registered goods according to the Brussels Nomenclature provide a clear guide to the extent of r.p.m. in this country at the present time. So we must work backwards from our knowledge of the goods which until the passing of the Resale Prices Act were subject to r.p.m. and identify those for which an application for exemption has not been registered. There are six main categories of product which until 1964 were subject to r.p.m. for which exemption has not been sought. These are motor cars and accessories, sports goods, newspapers, razor blades, bicycles and motor cycles and wallpaper and paint.[3] In addition, a number of individual manufacturers have stated that they would not continue to enforce r.p.m. although they were covered by a general exemption obtained for their classes of goods by other suppliers. Such manufacturers are Distillers,

[1] S.I. 1965 No. 236 The Restrictive Practices Court (Resale Prices) Rules. Rule 9.
[2] Resale Prices Act Section 7(4)(a).
[3] Though a few products within these categories have been registered e.g. safety belts and table tennis balls.

P

Acmé, Meredew, Hoover, James A. Jobling and Black and Decker. Several of these announced that they were abandoning r.p.m. because they had been advised that they had little or no chance of success in their application for exemption to the Restrictive Practices Court. Following Distillers' decision in February 1964, the Wine and Spirits Trade Association announced that they had reluctantly agreed also to drop r.p.m. These developments mean that some 5% consumer expenditure has been freed from r.p.m. as a direct consequence of the passing of the Resale Prices Act and leaves 23% consumer expenditure on goods and services (29% on goods alone) still subject to r.p.m.

The immediate consequences of this action have varied from product to product. Razor blades are increasingly sold through supermarkets and price cutting is therefore extensive. It is common now for a 3s 6d packet of razor blades to be sold for 2s 11d. Jobling, the manufacturers of Pyrex, seem also to have benefited from cut-price promotions of their products in the supermarkets. Victor Value, a leading supermarket company, have publicly claimed that their sales of Pyrex goods have increased ten times as a result of price cutting.

Price cutting has also broken out on spirits. Again, this was started by supermarket companies with reductions of up to 7s a bottle of whisky being offered, though Distillers threatened to stop supplies to traders offering such a large reduction on the grounds that they were loss-leading. A 4s price cut can now be obtained. Although supermarkets own only a small proportion of the off-licences in existence, their activities have caused traditional off-licence traders to take defensive action – by cutting prices or selling own-brand goods. Towards the end of November 1965 it was reported that some public houses were selling bottles of whisky and gin across the bar at cut prices. This was the first time the brewers had actively entered the cut-price war. As to the consequences of this price cutting on wines and spirits, it is interesting to find that at March 16, 1965, the index for the wines and spirits section of the Retail Price Index was 111·3 (January 16, 1962 = 100) compared with 111·8 at February 16, 1965. Since r.p.m. was abandoned on these goods at the beginning of March 1965 it would seem that this is a tangible benefit from the breakdown of r.p.m. But the compilers of the Retail Price Index do not commit themselves on this point, they merely state that 'there were falls in the average levels of prices of wines and spirits'![1]

Little price cutting seems to have arisen on most of the other goods on which r.p.m. has recently been abandoned. In the motor trade high trade-in allowances have always provided a way round r.p.m. but open cutting of new car prices hardly exists at the time of writing. The same is true of motor cycles except for the well-publicized action of the Oxford retailer who, at the end of July 1965, made price reductions of 5%-8% to reverse falling sales.

Hoover's decision to drop r.p.m. was greeted by a limited amount of price cutting, some of which was at the hands of large department stores such as Debenham and Selfridge. But these remain fairly isolated instances especially whilst the Area Electricity Boards do not cut prices.[2] Hoover have claimed that their decision was well received and has 'cushioned the company to an encouraging degree against the general decline in home sales of washing machines'.[3] It is suggested, however, that had their abandoning of r.p.m. encouraged more retailers to begin to cut prices and thereby impinged on the trade of other electrical appliance manufacturers they, too, would by now have also dropped r.p.m. In view of the falling level of sales of electrical appliances it is surprising that other manufacturers have stayed firm in their insistence on r.p.m.

As we have seen, where goods are no longer exempt from the ban on r.p.m. the Resale Prices Act attempts to ensure that suppliers do not continue to maintain resale prices or to treat unfairly actual or potential price cutters. Whether these provisions will be contravened remains to be seen. Certainly the evidence from Sweden which in 1954 adopted a similar policy to deal with r.p.m. suggests that violations will occur. In Sweden, according to Mr Bernitz,[4] between 1957 and 1963 there were

[1] *Ministry of Labour Gazette* (1965) p. 187.
[2] A recent National Board for Prices and Incomes Report, No. 7 *Electricity and Gas Tariffs* (1965) Cmnd. 2862 para. 37 has challenged the policy of Area Boards in charging recommended prices on appliances which are no longer subject to r.p.m. on the grounds that this lowers their competitive standing.
[3] *Financial Times* August 19, 1965.
[4] Ulf Bernitz – *Swedish Anti-Trust Law and Resale Price Maintenance* (Stockholm) 1964 p. 39.

fifty-seven violations of the ban on r.p.m. out of which two entrepreneurs were prosecuted and 447 cases of complaints over refusal to deal were investigated.

The responsibility for providing an adequate enforcement mechanism rests with the Board of Trade. But no positive steps have so far been taken in this direction. To what extent active enforcement of the ban on r.p.m. will be necessary is difficult to determine at present but should the need arise it must be strictly enforced. It could well be argued that such enforcement as is necessary should not be the responsibility of the Board of Trade. In view of their close co-operation with industry on other matters, an active rôle in the control of any form of restrictive practice could prove invidious.

The Registrar has power to group together applications for exemption in referring them to the Restrictive Practices Court.[1] It is open to the applicants to object to the grouping when the Court hears the preliminary application for directions. Already the Court has amended the reference for two classes of goods to exclude products which the applicants claimed should be treated separately. Thus, on an application by The Scholl Manufacturing Co. Ltd., foot exercise sandals have been removed from the footwear reference[2] and domestic and office furniture now form two separate references to the Court rather than the one which the Registrar proposed.[3] Whilst it is right that one product should not be grouped with others with which the supplier feels there is no affinity and where different considerations regarding the desirability of r.p.m. apply, there is much to be said in favour of a few broad references being made rather than a larger number of small groupings. In the first place it will mean that the costs of an action will fall less heavily on each individual supplier and their attentions will not be diverted to several cases. (Counsel for Scholls pointed out that the thirteen products they had registered have been placed in eleven different references.) Secondly, it will probably mean that the Court will deal with the applications sooner and this will reduce the uncertainty hanging over the heads of manufacturers and distributors. Although composite cases might mean that the Court would have to consider

---

[1] Section 6(6).   [2] *Re Footwear Reference* L.R. 5 R.P. 351.
[3] *The Times* July 21, 1965.

more evidence (and the Court has recently protested about the mass of evidence that was given in the case on the Locked Coil, Mining Rope and Wire Rope agreements under the Restrictive Trade Practices Act[1]) this problem may be obviated by the special provision which allows the Court to give directions as to the formulation by the parties to proceedings under the Resale Prices Act of the issues of fact and law which fall to be determined in a particular case.[2] This is a new innovation in English court procedure but may prove an important aid to the speeding up of the Court proceedings.

Some doubts which suppliers must have felt about allowing themselves to be involved in composite cases have been dissolved as a result of the remarks by Megaw J. during the application for directions on the footwear reference in which he stated that the Court had power to exempt a sub-class of goods from a general ban. For example, in the case of footwear it would be open to the Court to exempt, say, men's footwear whilst declaring r.p.m. on all other forms of footwear included in the reference to be against the public interest. This means, therefore, that a supplier who feels that there are grounds on which the Court might approve r.p.m. on his products which other suppliers included in the same reference could not claim, will not be forced to seek a separate reference for his own goods with its additional costs but will be able to make a special plea during the course of the hearing of the composite reference.

Already notices of reference have been issued for fifty classes of goods covering, it is estimated, 70% of the applications for exemption that have been registered. These references include many important products – confectionery, radio and television receivers, electric cooking and heating appliances, toiletries and cosmetics, and cigarettes. But there are also some goods where r.p.m. is important which have not yet been referred including books, pharmaceuticals and records, where some of the hardest cases may be expected.

Because of the time required for the legal formalities it is not expected that the Court will hear the first applications for

[1] *Re Locked Coil Ropemakers' Association's Agreement, Re Mining Rope Association's Agreement, Re Wire Rope Manufacturers' Association's Agreement* L.R. 5 R.P. 147.
[2] S.I. 1965 No. 236 The Restrictive Practices Court (Resale Prices) Rules. Rule 19.

exemption until the autumn of 1966. Confectionery, footwear and baby carriages are likely to be the first cases heard. Already, however, some suppliers have decided not to proceed with their applications for exemption and on November 30, 1965, the Restrictive Practices Court made declarations refusing to exempt seeds and compound fertilizers, glassware and related classes of goods and vacuum flasks from the ban on r.p.m.[1] Although it is open to unregistered suppliers, retailers of goods involved and trade associations representing employees in the distributive trades to be represented in proceedings before the Court, little interest has been shown in this provision and it appears that the usual procedure will be for the large manufacturers (in some cases supported by their own trade associations) to carry the burden of the case.

The procedure adopted in the Resale Prices Act is the pragmatic one of registration and case by case investigation by the Restrictive Practices Court which is also used in proceedings arising out of the Restrictive Trade Practices Act. Whether such judicial procedure is appropriate is a matter for personal opinion.[2]

Detailed considerations of the legal points arising out of the Act are now to be found in a number of works.[3] But the ultimate effects of the Act depend on a range of factors, such as the attitude of the Restrictive Practices Court, the effectiveness of the enforcement of the ban on r.p.m. on non-exempt goods, the attitudes of manufacturers and distributors and the prevailing economic climate, which are not easily predictable in advance.

As Stevens and Yamey point out,[4] by emphasizing the interests of consumers only and avoiding a general 'gateway' such as that which has been extensively employed in actions arising under the Restrictive Trade Practices Act, the Resale Prices Act has helped make the issues with which the Court will be concerned

---

[1] *The Times* December 1, 1965.

[2] The issues involved have been discussed in Stevens and Yamey *op. cit*, ch. iii and R. B. Stevens – 'Justiciability: The Restrictive Practices Court Re-examined' *Public Law* 1964 pp. 221-55.

[3] V. L. Korah 'The Resale Prices Act, 1964' *Journal of Business Law* (1965) pp. 6-14 and 123-9; 'The Resale Prices Act' *Modern Law Review* (1965) pp. 193-7. Jeremy Lever 'The Law of Restrictive Practices and Resale Price Maintenance' (London) 1964; I. A. MacDonald 'Resale Price Maintenance' (London) 1964; Lord Meston 'Shaw's Guide to the Resale Prices Act' (London) 1964.

[4] Stevens and Yamey *op. cit.* p. 44 and p. 86.

more readily justiciable. Whether the Act has gone far enough in this direction is open to debate. Certainly by requiring the Court to choose between alternative economic hypotheses as to the likely consequences of the abolition of r.p.m. in a trade, the Act will undoubtedly cause many of the Court's findings to be attacked from one side or another. However, this writer is of the opinion that the judicial approach to such problems is, on balance, preferable to the alternative of a dogmatic ban on r.p.m. in all trades or a process of investigation by an administrative body such as the Monopolies Commission whose findings are only made effective at the discretion of Parliament.

It has already been suggested that the present provisions for the enforcement of the prohibition of r.p.m. on non-exempt goods may prove to be inadequate, while Mrs Korah has argued[1] that these sections should be strengthened by making their violation a criminal offence. It may be, however, that enforcement action will prove unnecessary since experience so far shows that once r.p.m. has been abandoned on a product the manufacturer is glad of the promotional interest which appropriate cut price traders are prepared to show in his products.

One possible danger to manufacturers which might arise is the likelihood of 'switch-selling'. In many trades, e.g. electrical goods, clothing, sports goods, motor cars and cycles, etc., the consumer usually buys only one item per visit to the retail outlet. Thus it becomes possible for the unscrupulous dealer to offer one brand (A) at a cut price in the hope of attracting to his shop customers wishing to purchase that brand. Once the customer has been won in this way, it then becomes possible for the retailer to try to sell a different brand (B) on which there is no cut price offer, arguing that B is superior to A or that stocks of A are no longer available, etc. Such actions, which are at present not unknown, could occur with greater frequency and are clearly damaging to the interests of the manufacturer of A, who should therefore be empowered to discipline such a trader by refusing to supply him. Whether he would be entitled to take this action under the loss leader provisions of the Act seems uncertain but certainly ought to be permitted.

[1] V. L. Korah *Journal of Business Law* (1965) at p. 14 and *Modern Law Review* (1965) at p. 197.

It seems likely that the Court will be hearing applications for permission to continue to enforce r.p.m. until the early 1970s. This does, of course, depend on the speed with which cases can be prepared and heard and on the number of applications which are actually proceeded with. At varying stages between the serving of the notice of reference and the commencement of the final Court hearing a number of applications will be dropped. The stronger the line taken against r.p.m. by the Court the fewer the applications that will be argued out before it.

Where the Court finds the public interest is not served by the continuance of r.p.m. some price reduction will inevitably follow. Price cutting is most likely to be found on goods which can conveniently be sold in supermarkets. The successful expansion of the discount store would make lower prices available on a wider range of goods, so, too, would any general entry into the field of cut-price merchandising by department stores. The information that two large department stores in London have recently been cutting the price of Hoover products is interesting in this respect since Professor Yamey has shown that departmental stores played a leading part in the price cutting that was rife at the end of the last century.[1]

But, as experience with some goods on which r.p.m. has recently been abandoned shows, an immediate overall reduction in price levels is not to be looked for. Many prices are unlikely to be reduced and indeed the abolition of r.p.m. heightens the possibility of consumers being overcharged especially on goods which they purchase infrequently and where there is only a limited degree of competition in a given shopping centre between retailers selling a particular product. The public interest requires that suppliers should continue to enforce a maximum price as they are, of course, allowed to do by the Act. If it appears that maximum prices are not being enforced, information on the actual retail prices charged for a wide range of consumer goods throughout the country should be made available to consumers at frequent intervals. Only then will it be possible for the consumer to take advantage with confidence of such benefits as the working of the Resale Prices Act may offer.

---

[1] B. S. Yamey – *The Economics of Resale Price Maintenance* p. 134.

INDEX

GEORGE ALLEN & UNWIN LTD

London: 40 Museum Street, W.C.1

Auckland: P.O. Box 36013, Northcote Central, Auckland, N.4
Bombay: 15 Graham Road, Ballard Estate, Bombay 1
Barbados: P.O. Box 222, Bridgetown
Buenos Aires: Escritorio 454-459, Florida 165
Calcutta: 17 Chittaranjan Avenue, Calcutta 13
Cape Town: 68 Shortmarket Street
Hong Kong: 105 Wing On Mansion, 26 Hancow Road, Kowloon
Ibadan: P.O. Box 62
Karachi: Karachi Chambers, McLeod Road
Madras: Mohan Mansions, 38c Mount Road, Madras 6
Mexico: Villalongin 32-10, Piso, Mexico 5, D.F.
Nairobi: P.O. Box 4536
New Delhi: 13-14 Asaf Ali Road, New Delhi 1
Ontario: 81 Curlew Drive, Don Mills
Rio de Janeiro: Caixa Postal 2537-Zc-00
Sao Paulo: Caixa Postal 8675
Singapore: 36c Prinsep Street, Singapore 7
Sydney, N.S.W.: Bradbury House, 55 York Street
Tokyo: P.O. Box 26, Kamata

TEN GREAT ECONOMISTS

JOSEPH A. SCHUMPETER

In this collection of essays, one who ranked amongst the greatest economists of our day has given us brilliant evaluations of the men most influential in shaping economic thought during the past century. The essays are biographical in character but with a penetrating critical approach that makes them classics in their field.

The 'ten great economists' are, in chronological order, Karl Marx, Marie Esprit Léon Walras, Carl Menger, Alfred Marshall, Vilfredo Pareto, Eugen von Böhm-Bawerk, Frank William Taussig, Irving Fisher, Wesley Clair Mitchell, and John Maynard Keynes. An Appendix includes George Frederic Knapp, Friedrich von Wieser, and Ladislaus von Bortkiewicz. Each of the essays, with the exception of the one on Marx, was written for an economic journal, either to celebrate an anniversary or on the occasion of the death of an economist. The essay on Karl Marx gives a comprehensive treatment of Marx as prophet, sociologist, economist and teacher.

A particular warmth and interest is given to these biographical essays by the author's having known, with the exception of Marx, each of the subjects personally. Professor Schumpeter's awareness of the contributions of these men, not only to economics but also to the main current of thought in our century, makes this book important to economists and to everyone seeking to understand our times. *U.U. Book 21s. net*

THE STATIONARY ECONOMY

J. E. MEADE

'It is a long time since anyone attempted to write a treatise; as distinct from a textbook, on economic analysis in general. Professor Meade has taken the plunge however, and here is the first volume of "Principles of Political Economy" . . . This is a splendid and bold idea. Professor Meade is a master of lucid and rigorous theoretical exposition . . . ' *The Economist.*

'It is outstandingly lucid. And, by bringing the basic notions of activity analysis and linear programming together with traditional price theory, it performs a much needed piece of synthesis at an elementary level.' *New Society.* *U.U. Book 18s. net*

ECONOMIC SURVEY 1919-1939

W. ARTHUR LEWIS

'Any history or analysis of the economic events of the inter-war years is likely to be either ponderously unreadable or inaccurately sketchy. Professor Lewis has contrived with great skill to provide something which is neither; which, without pretending to be more than a "starting point" ... gives the reader both a perspective against which to set special knowledge or to verify speculations, and a guide to further learning, and which introduces and relates to one another facts and theories, hitherto only available in specialist publications, in a style which any intelligent lay reader can appreciate.' *The Economist.*

'A little masterpiece of succinct analysis.' *New Statesman.*

'Useful and stimulating. . . . A provocative study in that it links recent history with the larger march of events, seeing these inter-war years not as an isolated and depressing period of time.' *The Scotsman.*

'Penetrating in analysis and closely packed in thought.' *Financial Times.* *U.U. Book 15s. net*

THEORIES OF ECONOMIC DEVELOPMENT AND GROWTH

Y. S. BRENNER

This work summarises the theories of economic growth, ancient as well as modern, and presents them in a form particularly suitable for university students both in the developing countries and elsewhere. The author's object is to enable students to assess the major factors making for economic development and to encourage them to *think* about ways of applying their knowledge to the particular problems of their own countries. He deals in turn with the theories of the Mercantilists and Physiocrats, of the classical economists and the neoclassical and historical schools, with Marxist theories of growth, and with the writings of the Keynesian school on the growth problems of modern developed states.

In addition, there is a special survey of growth and of limiting factors in the economies of underdeveloped countries, with an important analysis of the economic results of planning in the U.S.S.R. While dealing fully with the theoretical answers to growth problems, the author does not neglect the importance of the human factor, nor the need to provide adequate incentives if a steady rate of development is to be promoted. *Minerva Series 21s. net paper, 35s. net cloth*

DEVELOPMENT PLANNING
W. ARTHUR LEWIS

Since the end of the Second World War nearly all the countries of Asia, Africa and Latin America have produced 'Development Plans', varying greatly in structure and usefulness. Yet very little has been written about how a Development Plan is made, what the chief snags are and what distinguishes good planning from bad. The ordinary citizen's life is affected by these plans and he needs a short and simple explanation of them.

Professor Arthur Lewis is exceedingly well qualified to write on this subject. He has taken part in much development planning; his *Theory of Economic Growth* is one of the most widely read and authoritative statements of the philosophy of the subject; his keen eye and unshakeable commonsense distinguish the feasible from the self-deluding, the human, political and administrative points of friction, and the sort of results which can be reasonably expected in different circumstances.

'In making a Plan, technique is subsidiary to policy. Hence, although the basic techniques are displayed, the emphasis is throughout on policy. The Economics of Development is not very complicated; the secret of successful planning lies more in sensible politics and good public administration.'

This book will be most widely read and, on account of the simple lucidity and humour of its style, most widely enjoyed.

U.U. Book 18s. net

THEORY OF ECONOMIC DYNAMICS
M. KALECKI

This is the first paperback edition of a classic book by probably the most widely-known Polish economist of today, a book now in its fourth printing in its present form, one which was originally presented as two shorter essays and which has become part of the corpus of modern economic literature. As the reviewer in *Economica* put it: 'Mr. Kalecki's contributions have been of the greatest importance in the development of dynamic theories and methods of analysis.' Since this was written the importance of dynamic analysis has been more fully recognised. *U.U. Book 15s. net*

GEORGE ALLEN & UNWIN LTD

DATE DUE

7/3			
GAYLORD			PRINTED IN U.S.A.